by David A. Crowder

BICENTENNIAL
1807
WILEY
2007
BICENTENNIAL

Wiley Publishing, Inc.

Google® Earth For Dummies®

Published by
Wiley Publishing, Inc.
111 River Street
Hoboken, NJ 07030-5774

www.wiley.com

Copyright © 2007 by Wiley Publishing, Inc., Indianapolis, Indiana

Published by Wiley Publishing, Inc., Indianapolis, Indiana

Published simultaneously in Canada

For general information on our other products and services, please contact our Customer Care Department within the U.S. at 800-762-2974, outside the U.S. at 317-572-3993, or fax 317-572-4002.

For technical support, please visit www.wiley.com/techsupport.

Wiley also publishes its books in a variety of electronic formats. Some content that appears in print may not be available in electronic books.

Library of Congress Control Number: 2006936825

ISBN: 978-0-470-09528-7

Manufactured in the United States of America

10 9 8 7 6 5 4 3 2 1

WILEY

About the Author

David A. Crowder has authored or coauthored more than 25 books, including the bestsellers *Building a Web Site For Dummies* and *Cliffs Notes Getting on the Internet*. His two most recent books were both listed as essential for all library collections by the magazine *Library Journal*.

Professor Crowder is equally at home with high technology or with working his way through the backcountry on horseback or in a dugout canoe. When he is not writing, he spends his time with his wife Angela, wandering through villages in the Andes or frolicking in the Caribbean surf.

Dedication

This one's for Angie, *la luz de mi vida*.

Author's Acknowledgments

No book makes it into a bookstore solely by the efforts of its author. So many other people are involved in the process — from the first contact with the Acquisitions Editor to the time when a bookstore employee cuts open the box and stocks the shelves with your freshly printed title — that it would probably take a whole other book just to list their names.

I would like to particularly thank my literary agent, Bob Diforio, without whose tireless devotion this book might never have seen the light of day. My editors at Wiley are among the best I have ever worked with. From the first day, their input has made this book better than I could have done it without their help. My acquisitions editor Steve Hayes, project editor Chris Morris, copy editor Teresa Artman, and technical editor Paul Wolfe all deserve hearty thanks for their invaluable assistance in getting this book from the basic idea through print and onto the shelves.

Publisher's Acknowledgments

We're proud of this book; please send us your comments through our online registration form located at www.dummies.com/register/.

Some of the people who helped bring this book to market include the following:

Acquisitions, Editorial, and Media Development

Senior Project Editor: Christopher Morris

Senior Acquisitions Editor: Steven H. Hayes

Senior Copy Editor: Teresa Artman

Technical Editor: Paul Wolfe

Editorial Manager: Kevin Kirschner

Media Development Manager: Laura VanWinkle

Editorial Assistant: Amanda Foxworth

Sr. Editorial Assistant: Cherie Case

Cartoons: Rich Tennant (www.the5thwave.com)

Composition Services

Project Coordinator: Erin Smith

Layout and Graphics: Carl Byers, Stephanie D. Jumper, Barbara Moore, Barry Offringa, Laura Pence

Proofreaders: Lisa Stiers

Indexer: Techbooks

Anniversary Logo Design: Richard Pacifico

Publishing and Editorial for Technology Dummies

Richard Swadley, Vice President and Executive Group Publisher

Andy Cummings, Vice President and Publisher

Mary Bednarek, Executive Acquisitions Director

Mary C. Corder, Editorial Director

Publishing for Consumer Dummies

Diane Graves Steele, Vice President and Publisher

Joyce Pepple, Acquisitions Director

Composition Services

Gerry Fahey, Vice President of Production Services

Debbie Stailey, Director of Composition Services

Contents at a Glance

Table of Contents

Introduction

● ●

Want to stroll down the Champs Elysees in Paris? Feel like taking a personal look at the Great Wall of China? Or perhaps you'd like to explore the island of Tahiti on your lunch break? Thanks to Google Earth, you can.

With Google Earth, you can forget the Frequent Flyer miles. All you have to do is plop down in front of your monitor to see the world up close the easy way. No lousy airline food, no baggage claim, no customs line — just plain fun!

And I'm not just talking about some plain old maps here. Google has gone to the trouble to bring you the latest in high-tech GIS (Geographical Information Systems) — and has done it right. Although the program can easily compete with most of the high-end GIS software around today, Google Earth isn't just for the *cognoscenti:* It's for the masses.

About This Book

Yes, there is such a thing as love at first sight. I fell in love with Google Earth about 30 seconds after I installed it. I found but one thing lacking. As several other Google Earth users once lamented, there was no such thing as *Google Earth For Dummies.*

Well, now there is. This is the book that I wish I had had on my desk during my early explorations with this fabulous program. It's designed from the ground up to provide you with all that you need to know to get the most from Google Earth from the very start.

In this book, you'll see not just how to spin a digital globe on your screen but also how to dig into all the wonderful features that Google Earth has to offer. That means that you can find — in a single resource — everything from how to search for pizza parlors to understanding how latitude and longitude work.

How to Use This Book

Put it on top of your desk. Keep it there. That'll save you a bunch of walking to the bookshelf. Trust me — after you start playing (or working) with Google Earth, you'll want to do more. And more. And more.

If you use this book the way a typical reader does, you'll want to hit the Table of Contents and the index to find whatever it is you want to know about. But this isn't just a reference book. It's designed to show you how to get the most enjoyment and practical use out of the program, and it's chock-full of examples that (trust me) will enhance your Google Earth experience, so feel free to just flip from place to place and see what you find.

Foolish Assumptions

I assume that you have at least some vague idea that the world is composed of a lot of oceans and a bunch of land masses. Other than this simple beginning, you need no special geographic knowledge — Google Earth will take care of the rest for you.

Beyond that, this book assumes that you know at least the basics of how to operate your computer. For example, if I tell you that you need to make a menu selection, I assume that you know that a menu is that list of words at the top of the screen, like File, Edit, and so forth, and that you know how to move your mouse pointer over those words and click them to reveal further options. If not, you might first want to check out a copy of *Windows XP Just the Steps For Dummies* or *Windows Vista Just the Steps For Dummies* (Wiley), both by Nancy Muir. If you don't have Google Earth loaded yet, not to worry: See how in Chapter 1.

Conventions Used in This Book

A lot of folks have labored for many years to make the *For Dummies* series as user-friendly as possible, and we're all as thankful as can be that they've done that. (I've authored several *For Dummies* books, but I don't just write them — I rely on them, too, just like you do.)

When you find a listing that says to choose something like File➪Save from the menu, that means to first click the word File on the menu and then choose

Save from the resultant drop-down menu. (If you're running Windows Vista, File has been replaced by the Office Button, at the top left of the window.)

Code listings, which you'll find in the chapter on KML (the native language of Google Earth's files), look like this:

```
<Placemark>
    <name>
    ...
    </name>
    <description>
    ...
    </description>
</Placemark>
```

The ellipsis (. . .) shows that further information needs to be supplied.

When I need to show how to do that, I use an italic placeholder, like in this example:

```
<name>
Name goes here.
</name>
```

When you see those words in italics (and they should always be obvious in any event), simply replace the placeholder with your own text, perhaps something like this:

```
<name>
Grandpa's farm
</name>
```

Whenever you see the URL for one of the top sites you can use to enhance your Google Earth experience, it appears in a special typeface within the paragraph, like this: www.dummies.com. Or it might appear on a separate line, like this:

```
www.dummies.com
```

How This Book Is Organized

This book is divided into six parts, each of which has various chapters in it. Each of the chapters is further subdivided into logical segments that cover various activities that you will probably want to pursue to increase your knowledge of Google Earth. Here's an overview.

Part I: Getting to Know Google Earth

Part I introduces you to how the Google Earth program works and how you can use its search and location features to find just about anything in the world. It then goes on to explore the program's basic visual features as well as its most exciting tools, like Tilt and Zoom.

Part II: Personalizing Google Earth

This part covers how to modify Google Earth's options and modify the program's screen display to suit you. This part also digs into how to use the built-in *layers,* which show where everything from school districts to hospitals is located. Then it goes on to deal with *placemarks,* which are the Google Earth geographical equivalent to Web browser bookmarks.

Part III: Becoming a Cybertourist

Part III shows how to jump into the world of satellite tourism, looking at routes from one place to another from a bird's-eye viewpoint. It then goes on to show you how to participate in the Google Earth Community, which is the huge group of fellow users who are there to share and help.

Part IV: Advanced Features

Well, you knew it couldn't all be simple. Google Earth does have some more complex features, and this part explains how they work and how you can tap into them for your own uses.

These four chapters delve into how you can import external data — ranging from image overlays to the output from your GPS device — into Google Earth. You can also read here how to use the companion program Google SketchUp to add custom 3-D models to your world. Finally, see how to get under the hood and understand the basics of *KML* — the markup language that is at the heart of Google Earth.

Part V: The Part of Tens

Part V tosses in 30 extra little items that will make your Google Earth experience into all that it can be. From sources for external map images to Web sites that can give you all the location info you could ever want to a few other programs you'll want to install, this is the icing on the cake.

Part VI: Appendixes

Part VI includes a glossary of the technical terms that you might need to look up, along with details on just what is included in the Layers pane and a guide to a bunch of interesting places you'll want to visit.

Icons Used in This Book

You'll find several special graphics (icons) in the margins of various chapters. Each of these is there for a reason, so you need to keep watch for them.

Hey, just between you and me, here's the best way to handle this situation.

Watch your step, or things could get very ugly.

Just in case anybody reading this wants the egghead's view, here it is.

These note something special to keep in mind.

Where to Go from Here

I advise you to dive in and explore! That's the operative word for Google Earth, of course, but it's also the best way to take this book. Dig into everything, flip through the chapters, stop at some random location, and then just do whatever you find there. You'll be glad you did, as every part of the book introduces you to some new and wonderful feature of Google Earth.

Part I
Getting to Know Google Earth

The 5th Wave   By Rich Tennant

"Go back to Google Earth and hit the Back button."

In this part . . .

Chapter 1 gives you a general overview of the program and its uses, and Chapter 2 shows you how to quickly and easily get a look at any location on Earth. Chapter 3 then explores Google Earth's basic visual features and its most exciting tools, like Tilt and Zoom.

Chapter 1

The Earth According to Google

Google Earth is not just another map program or some kind of digitized globe inside your computer, but rather, a social phenomenon. Although it can stand on its own with other Geographic Information System (GIS) software, its focus is on giving the public a unique experience.

With everything from *National Geographic* articles to live Webcams to local commentaries built into it, the program doesn't just display maps and photos but launches the era of satellite tourism. Calling it *a 3-D interface to the planet,* the folks at Google are backing it to the hilt with both their incredible wealth and their enviable marketing savvy, and it seems destined to grow into one of the largest of all the online communities.

With Google Earth, you have wings. You can fly high above the planet or zoom right down to the ground. In seconds, you can zip from the deserts of the American West to the tropic isle Tahiti. No tickets to buy, no bags to pack, no long lines or customs or anything else. Just go!

The View from Google Earth

Because Google relies upon many outside providers for its satellite and aerial imagery, the quality of images in different locations varies somewhat. Figure 1-1 shows the program's clean interface design as well as the kind of detail it can achieve. This close shot of New York's Yankee Stadium is typical of the world's major metropolitan areas.

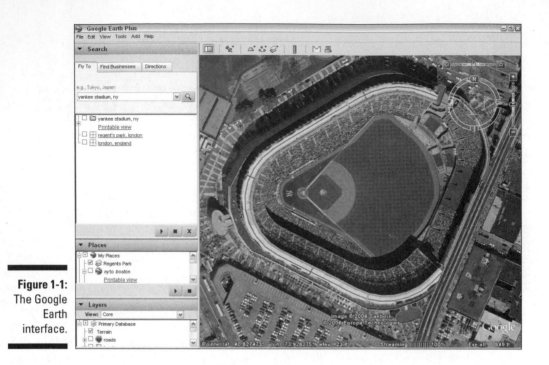

Figure 1-1:
The Google
Earth
interface.

The same level of detail is not, of course, generally available in rural areas, which have not been as extensively photographed from space. This is not a limitation of Google Earth but rather of the current state of available data, and this constraint applies to all GIS programs. The simple rule is that the more expensive the real estate, the more likely it is to have been the subject of detailed — and costly — satellite analysis.

Although it relies upon imagery from satellite photos taken anytime in the past three years, Google Earth isn't merely a static collection of warmed-over satellite images from dusty sources. Rather, it's continuously kept current through a vigorous program of updates. Such attention to detail and timeliness is one of the reasons why people ranging from casual users to real estate professionals have come to rely upon the Google Earth service.

Google Earth also makes it a point to respond quickly to breaking news. As an example, when a deadly earthquake struck Pakistan, Google Earth had updated, higher-quality satellite imagery of the quake area available online in less than a week, freely available to everybody from news junkies to international rescue workers. The first time such on-the-fly updating was used was during the Hurricane Katrina response. Google Earth, working with the National Oceanographic and Atmospheric Administration (NOAA), had very detailed imagery of the entire affected region online within five days after the event.

Exploring the Earth Online

The images in Google Earth are composed of zillions of separate photographs. Most were taken from orbit by satellites or the Space Shuttle, but there are also much more detailed close shots taken from airplanes.

Each of these images is a *tile,* and these tiles are laid together side by side to form a mosaic of the entire planet. In most cases, the tiles are seamless, but in some places, the structure is a bit more obvious because the tiles come from different sources and have varying appearances. Figure 1-2 shows an example of one of these areas with varying tiles.

It's nice to just buzz around the planet, seeing whatever there is to see. Sometimes, though, you need to get really specific, and the Search portion of Google Earth provides you with a tremendous helping hand.

You can enter an address and go right to it, or you can specify a particular set of longitude/latitude coordinates. You can find monuments, famous locations, cities, and just about anything else you can think of by just typing in the appropriate name. Want a look at the Eiffel Tower of Paris, France? Just tell Google Earth, as I did in Figure 1-3, and it'll take you right there. Even the names of major buildings are in the Google Earth location database.

Life isn't all about geography and satellite tourism, though. Sometimes you've just got to do simple, practical things — and once again, Google Earth comes through for you. You can do everything from hunting down the nearest Computer City to mapping out the locations of the seafood restaurants in your town. In Figure 1-4, you can see the results of my hunting for seafood restaurants in Honolulu.

You can even give Google Earth two locations and have it plan the best way for you to drive between them.

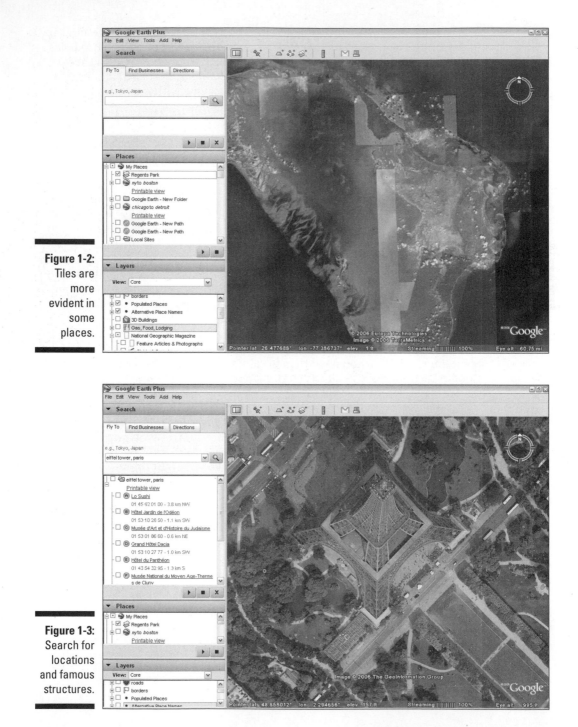

Figure 1-2:
Tiles are more evident in some places.

Figure 1-3:
Search for locations and famous structures.

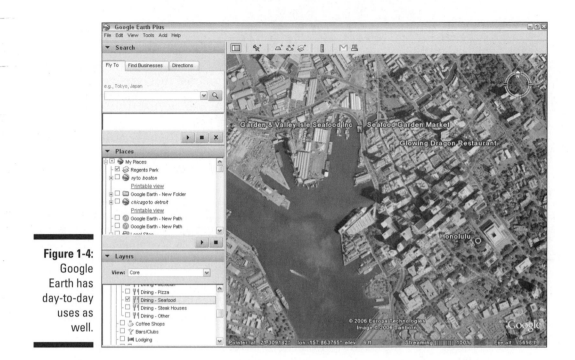

Google Earth Gives You Options

For the most part, sophisticated GIS software has always been out of reach of the public. It's generally very costly, and it isn't easy to use. In fact, you generally needed a Masters Degree in GIS to begin to comprehend how to work with it. Until Google Earth, that is.

However, Google Earth isn't a toy, either. It has three levels, each a bit more powerful than the last. The free version is simply called Google Earth; the mid-level one is Google Earth Plus; and the high-end, professional level is, of course, Google Earth Pro.

The cost of Google Earth Plus is a measly $20 a year, and Google Earth Pro goes for $495 a year.

If you're going to use the program for commercial purposes, the license agreement requires you to pop for the Pro version.

Starting with what's free

You get an astonishingly powerful piece of software for free with Google Earth. It's not some pathetic little wimp of a program that doesn't do much of anything; it's actually everything that the average person could need — and then some.

Not only do you get the program itself for zero bucks, but you get the *data* for free, too. This is perhaps the most incredible deal you will ever see because the cost of the satellite and aerial imagery alone would bankrupt the average citizen.

And you can spend all the time you want checking out every square inch of the Earth without ever buying one photo. You never have to learn what SRTM means or deal with the technicalities of geocoding or anything like that. Just fire up Google Earth, and you're ready to rock and roll.

The slick and intuitive interface lets you easily view whatever you want in various combinations of angles and altitudes. Zoom in and out and spin things around all you want; it's amazing what you can discover when you do that.

The Layers feature of Google Earth is one of its most impressive features. *Layers* are extra bits of information above and beyond the mere pictures — things like the locations of public parks or the incidence of earthquakes in an area. Other layers give you crime and population information for various locales or even let you step out of Google Earth and see through live Webcams, like the one in Figure 1-5.

Figure 1-5:
National Geographic Live WildCams add a nice touch.

NATIONAL GEOGRAPHIC MAGAZINE   Online@NGM.COM

WildCam Africa
Photograph by Roger de la Harpe

See animals in the wild at an African watering hole 24/7. Meet lions, elephants, leopards, giraffes, baboons, zebras—more than 40 species frequent Pete's Pond in Botswana.
View the live WildCam...

From "WildCam Africa,"
National Geographic, September 2005

Check out an interactive animal photo/video gallery and download wallpaper to decorate your desktop.

© 2006 National Geographic Society. All rights reserved.

As if all this weren't enough, another freebie — the companion program, Google SketchUp (see Figure 1-6) — lets you make your own 3-D models and add them to Google Earth. Go ahead and design your dream house; then drop it right onto your vacant lot in the real world. You can read more about SketchUp in Chapters 11 and 12.

Looking at Plus and Pro versions

You can stick with the free version to do most things you'd like. However, upgrading has some advantages. With the Plus version, you get a few extras, like the Hurricane Katrina databases from ImageAmerica and NOAA, as shown in Figure 1-7.

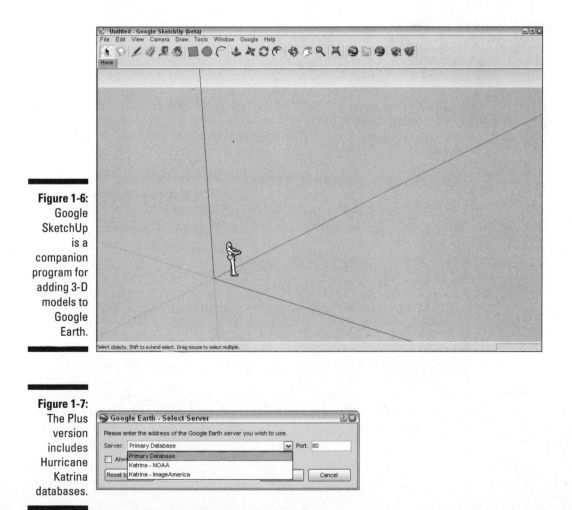

Figure 1-6:
Google
SketchUp
is a
companion
program for
adding 3-D
models to
Google
Earth.

Figure 1-7:
The Plus
version
includes
Hurricane
Katrina
databases.

You also get the ability to import several extra kinds of data (see Chapter 9) including image files and the output from your GPS (Global Positioning System) device. However, in my opinion, the best reason to go for Google Earth Plus is its greater speed and higher printing resolution. It's important to note here that this isn't a higher *screen* resolution — all versions of Google Earth share the same main database — but it can make a difference if you need to make hard copies.

The Pro version, as you might expect, is even faster and adds the ability to perform more sophisticated measurements such as area calculations. A few add-on modules at this level enable you to do things, such as print extremely high-resolution images or add traffic count information. You also get personalized tech support with Google Earth Pro.

So What Can I Really Do with Google Earth?

Google Earth is a tool and, just as with any other tool, you can use it for lots of things. Whether you're just playing around for the sheer fun of it or you desperately need it to perform your professional tasks, it'll take the challenge.

Of course, right off the bat, it's one of the best pieces of educational software out there, and it will doubtless quickly become a trusted part of every teacher's toolset, but it has so much more to offer as well.

Plenty of personal uses

I don't think I've seen too many homes that didn't have an atlas and a globe, and it's getting hard to imagine one that doesn't have Google Earth. The program has everything the old style approach does and adds so much more to boot.

The next time you're thinking of moving, fire up Google Earth and check out the boundaries of school districts, the location of fire stations, and all the other things that might help you choose your new neighborhood (see Figure 1-8). While you're at it, have Google Earth figure out the best route to your job from there.

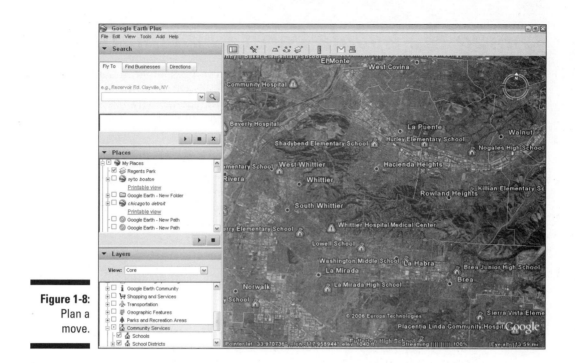

Figure 1-8:
Plan a
move.

Tired of watching the news and having only a vague idea of where something is happening? Now you can see for yourself. You can fly from China to Antarctica to Africa and back in seconds.

And businesses might want to . . .

Businesses of almost every kind can benefit from Google Earth, whether they're already using GIS technology or not. These are just a few of the uses to which it's already being put:

- ✔ Law firms can use it to investigate any location involved in a criminal or civil action.
- ✔ Civil planners can research traffic patterns.
- ✔ Real estate agents have a powerful sales and marketing tool in Google Earth, enabling them to pitch the virtues of any location.
- ✔ TV stations now have their own instant source of satellite images to supplement their newscasters' reports.

Don't forget, either, that the learning curve for Google Earth is a lot less steep than other GIS software. This means less time lost when training employees.

Joining the Google Earth Community

Professional GIS users, such as real estate developers, environmental engineers, law firms, and the like, aren't the only folks who find this program a wonderful tool, nor is it just a great new way to teach geography and history. Google Earth draws its users from a broad segment of the general population as well.

Many of the users of the program participate in an official community that keeps in close touch with one another, sharing both technical tips and interesting finds. The quest for unusual items is one of the high points of using Google Earth (see Figure 1-9). Hundreds of thousands of people are in the Google Earth Community's membership, which is growing fast, with thousands more signing up every week.

Of course, you don't have to register and participate in the official forums. There's also an ever-growing number of other user-supported sites that offer help and information as well as companionship.

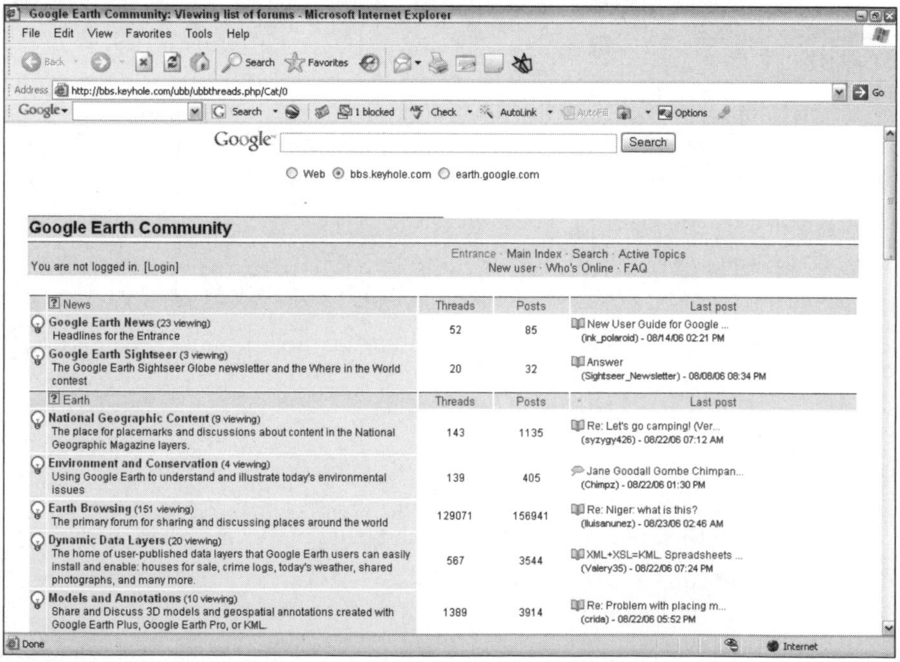

Figure 1-9: The Google Earth Community is growing fast.

Getting Geekier with GPS, KML, and Overlays

If you want to get into some of the more advanced things about Google Earth, no problem. It can interface with a *GPS device,* which is a global positioning system that uses signals from satellites in orbit to determine your latitude, longitude, and (depending on how sophisticated it is) altitude (see Figure 1-10).

Figure 1-10:
A GPS
device.

As long as I'm going alphabetical, allow me to throw in KML. It's the language that Google Earth uses, and it's a lot like HTML. If you have any kind of experience creating even simple Web pages, you can go under the hood of Google Earth and really make it sing by controlling every little detail of its display.

And maybe you want to dress things up a bit with some outside data. Go ahead and pop in an *overlay,* which is an image that you add on top of the basic data in Google Earth. Figure 1-11 shows an 1827 map of Regent's Park in London on top of the satellite shot of the modern city.

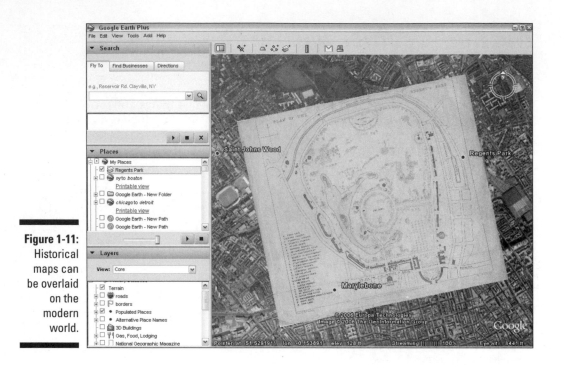

Figure 1-11:
Historical
maps can
be overlaid
on the
modern
world.

Downloading the Program

Before you can experience any of these wonderful things, you have to get your hands on Google Earth, of course. Fortunately, Google makes this an easy and painless task:

1. **Open your Web browser and go to http://earth.google.com (see Figure 1-12).**

2. **Click the Get Google Earth link on the upper-right side.**

3. **On the resulting Web page, as shown in Figure 1-13, select the check box if you want to subscribe to the Google Earth newsletter.**

4. **Select the appropriate radio button for the version of Google Earth for your operating system (Windows, Mac, or Linux).**

5. **Click the Download Google Earth button.**

   This takes you to the Web page shown in Figure 1-14, and the download should start automatically. If you are using Windows, the download might fail to start. Either click the yellow information bar at the top of the Web page and select Download File from the options, or just click the Click Here to Start It link.

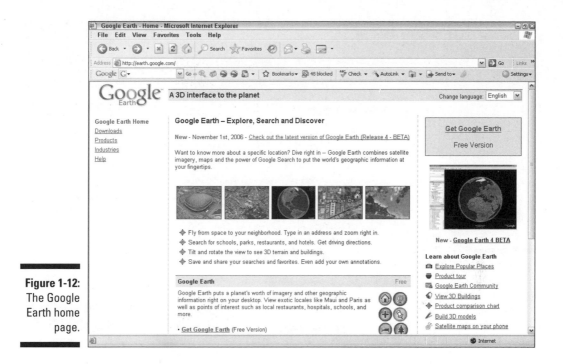

Figure 1-12:
The Google
Earth home
page.

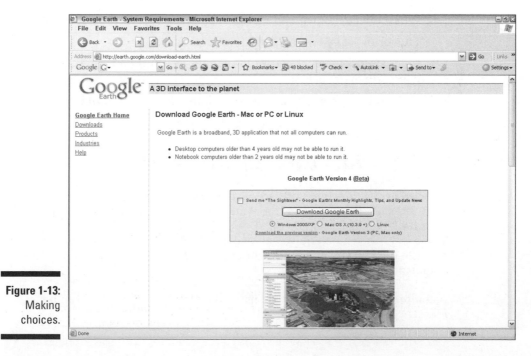

Figure 1-13:
Making
choices.

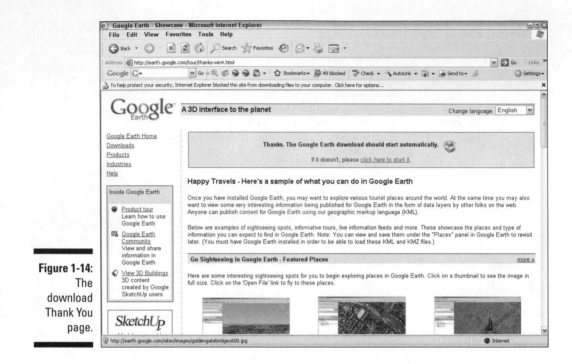

Figure 1-14:
The
download
Thank You
page.

6. **When the File Download dialog box appears, click the Save button.**

   This brings up your computer's Save As dialog box.

7. **Navigate to where you want to save the file and then click Save to complete the process.**

8. **To install Google Earth, double-click the downloaded file.**

A Note for Mac and Linux Users

Google Earth's three versions are as close as a very skilled group of programmers can make them. In fact, the Windows commands are the same as the ones for Linux. For example, Alt+F opens the File menu in both systems. There is, however, no equivalent Mac key combination. For key combinations that use the Ctrl key in Windows or Linux, just use the corresponding Mac command (⌘) key instead.

A comprehensive and up-to-date list of the platform differences can be found at

```
http://earth.google.com/userguide/v4/ug_keyboard.html
```

Chapter 2

Finding Businesses, Places, and Things

In This Chapter

- Locating things in Google Earth
- Getting directions
- Using the Overview Map
- Surfing with the Integrated Web Browser

The world's a very big place, of course, and you don't always know where everything is. When you've got the whole planet tucked inside your computer, though, Google Earth is there to lend a hand, helping you find whatever you're looking for.

Make that three hands, actually. You can use the Fly To tab to zip from place to place in many ways — by address, latitude and longitude, city names, or ZIP codes, to name a few. The Find Businesses tab (as shown in Figure 2-1) allows you to quickly track down various kinds of establishments like stores or restaurants. Finally, the Directions tab helps you map a route from one place to another.

The best way to quickly familiarize yourself with the various ways Google Earth has of finding things is to play with them. Click the three tabs in the Search pane — Fly To, Find Businesses, and Directions — and note the examples shown. Now, do it again. And again. Each time, you see a different possibility (until the built-in samples start to repeat, of course — there are limits to this sort of thing).

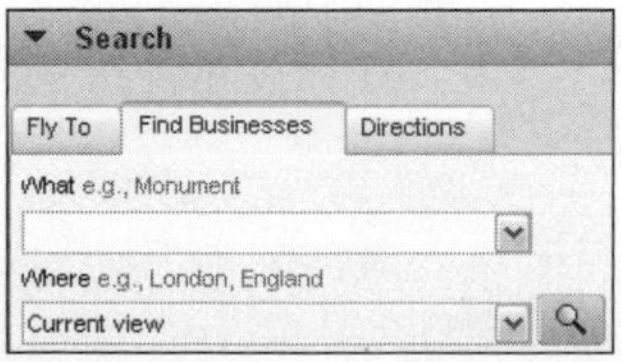

Figure 2-1: Check out the example searches first.

Flying Down to Rio (Or Anywhere Else)

The Fly To tab has the greatest variety of possible ways to enter your search terms. Say you want to get a look at Tokyo; just type in the name of the city. Of course, sometimes you'll find more than one place with the same name. For example, if you type **Washington,** you'll end up looking at the northwestern United States state and not the capital city, so be as specific as you can. You might, for instance, add a ZIP code. Of course, if you have an exact address, so much the better. Examples are shown in Table 2-1.

Table 2-1	Fly To Search Entry Examples
Example	*Type*
37 25' 19.1"N, 122 05' 06"W	Latitude/Longitude - Degrees, minutes, seconds
37.407229, −122.107162	Latitude/Longitude - Decimal
1600 Pennsylvania Avenue, 20006	Address with ZIP code
Reservoir Rd. Clayville, NY	Street with city and state
94043	ZIP code
San Francisco	City name
Tokyo, Japan	City with country
New York, NY	City with state
Hotels near JFK	Type of business near location

Now that you know what you can enter, here's how to do it:

1. **Enter the search term in the text box (see Figure 2-2).**

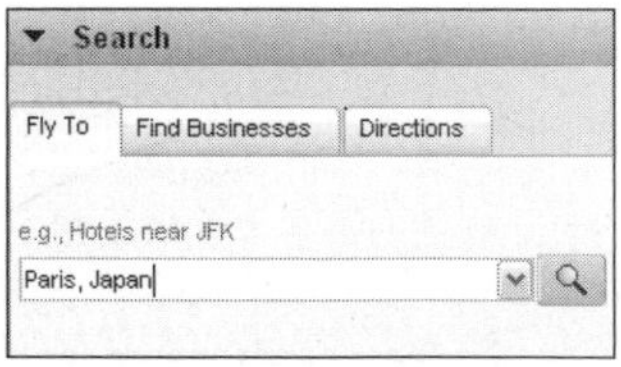

Figure 2-2:
Searching
for a
location.

2. **Press Enter or click the Begin Search button.**

   Google Earth flies you to the location.

3. **If the search term isn't recognizable by Google Earth, you get a pop-up error message (see Figure 2-3). Click OK and try another one.**

Figure 2-3:
Sometimes
you can't
find what
you're
looking for.

> **Google Search Error** ☒
>
> ⚠ Your search returned no results
>
> [OK   ]

4. **To redo an earlier search, click the down arrow at the right of the text box to access a drop-down list, as shown in Figure 2-4. If necessary, scroll down to find the one you want, and then click it.**

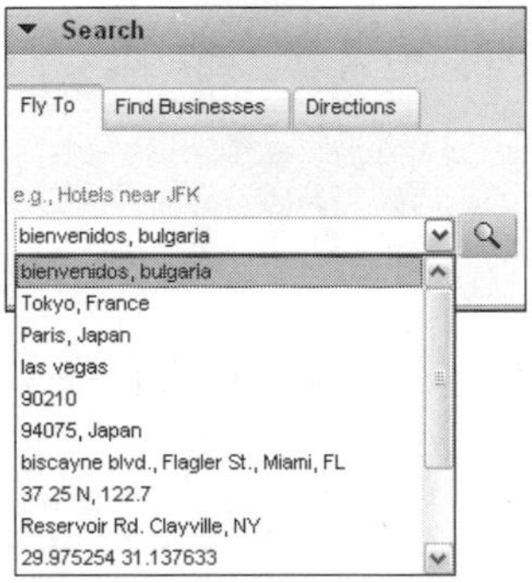

Figure 2-4:
Repeating a
previous
search.

> ▼ **Search**
>
> | Fly To | Find Businesses | Directions |
>
> e.g., Hotels near JFK
>
> bienvenidos, bulgaria ▼ 🔍
>
> bienvenidos, bulgaria
> Tokyo, France
> Paris, Japan
> las vegas
> 90210
> 94075, Japan
> biscayne blvd., Flagler St., Miami, FL
> 37 25 N, 122.7
> Reservoir Rd. Clayville, NY
> 29.975254 31.137633

Right on the dot: Understanding latitude and longitude

Latitude and longitude enable you to pinpoint the location of any place on Earth. As shown in Figure 2-5, lines of *latitude* show how far north or south you are from the equator, and lines of *longitude* show how far east or west you are from the *prime meridian* (an arbitrary north-south line drawn through Greenwich, England). Thus, latitudes to the north are larger and larger positive numbers, whereas the ones to the south are progressively larger negative numbers. When you see a positive latitude, you automatically know that it is north of the equator (and, conversely) that a negative latitude is south of it. The higher the number, the farther away from the equator the location is.

The same system also holds true with longitudes except that the negative numbers are to the west (left) of the prime meridian and the positive numbers are to the east (right) of it. No land is found where the two meet: The equator and the prime meridian cross in the Atlantic Ocean off the coast of Africa.

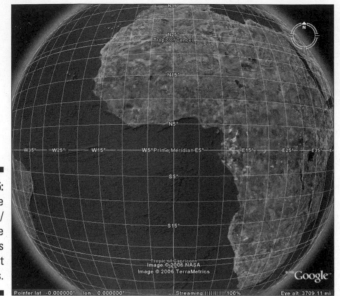

Figure 2-5:
The
Latitude/
Longitude
Grid shows
exact
coordinates.

The two commonly used ways to specify latitude and longitude are

✔ **Sexagesimal degrees:** This older system, still in use today, is also one that you will often find in historical records. It uses three measures: degrees, minutes, and seconds.

✔ **Decimal degrees:** This modern system makes the minutes and seconds into a decimal fraction of a degree.

Okay, take a deep breath and bear with me. Look at a spot in Tahiti, located at latitude 17°31'25.00"S. This is 17 degrees, 31 minutes, and 25 seconds south of the equator. The same spot is expressed more neatly in decimal degrees as –17.523611°. The sexagesimal version uses S at the end to specify south of the equator, and the decimal version uses a minus sign at the beginning.

To turn the Latitude/Longitude Grid on and off, use either the menu option View⇨Grid or the keyboard shortcut Ctrl+L.

When you zoom in on a location (see Chapter 3), the lines of latitude and longitude become more precise, as shown in Figure 2-6.

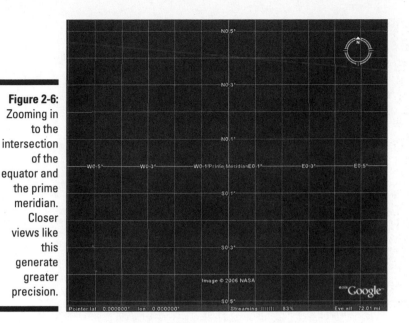

Figure 2-6:
Zooming in
to the
intersection
of the
equator and
the prime
meridian.
Closer
views like
this
generate
greater
precision.

To set how latitude and longitude are displayed, follow these steps:

1. **Choose Tools⇨Options from the menu.**

2. **Click the 3D View tab.**

3. **The Show Lat/Long panel has three radio buttons, as shown in Figure 2-7. Select the first one to use the Degrees, Minutes, Seconds method. Select the second one to select decimal Degrees instead, or the third to choose Universal Transverse Mercator.**

   The Universal Transverse Mercator (UTM) coordinate system is not actually a method of specifying latitude and longitude but one which specifies a predetermined zone of the Earth's surface.

4. **Click OK to finish.**

   This changes both the display in the status bar at the bottom of the screen and the figures on the grid.

Regardless of which way you have the display set, you can still enter either type of latitude/longitude figures in the Search pane. However, you cannot mix and match. If the latitude is in decimal format, the longitude has to be the same.

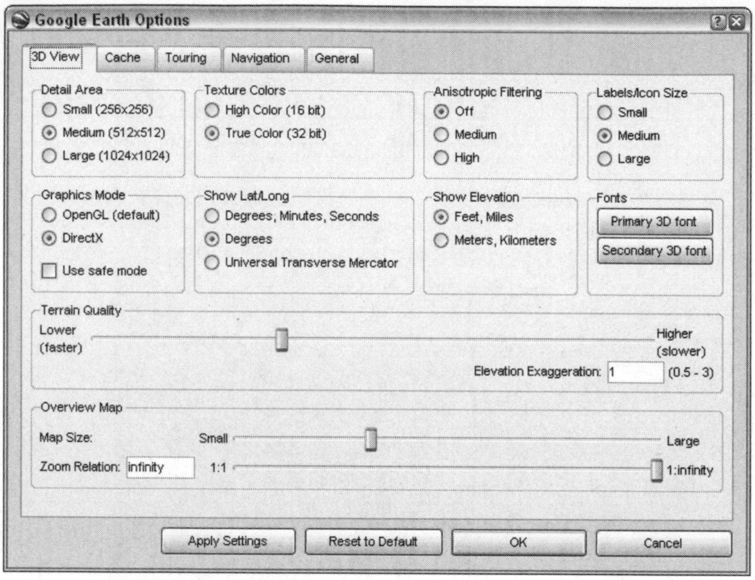

Figure 2-7:
Set the
latitude/
longitude
display
method.

Deciphering geocoding

Geocoding is a fancy word for matching latitude and longitude with a spot on a computerized map. (See the earlier section, "Right on the dot: Understanding latitude and longitude.") When you enter a location (either by address/intersection or exact latitude and longitude), Google Earth has to look up those coordinates to find out what image to show on your computer screen.

Latitude and longitude have been fairly well determined for most places in the civilized parts of the world. Even within cities, however, there's an extra wrinkle involved with using street addresses. You see, people don't build houses, office buildings, hospitals, and so forth according to a worldwide grid. Instead, they're largely built wherever nature left enough flat space to put them or where TNT and bulldozers can make a large enough flat area.

Nonetheless, most larger towns and cities are built according to some sort of plan today, even if they started out as a freeform cluster of farms way back when and just sort of grew into a municipality. How closely the "on-paper" version of city planning matches the reality you find when you walk or drive around the land varies widely from place to place, however.

On top of this, a standard lot size doesn't exist. Two homes side by side can take up very different amounts of space on the map. If one is on a ten-acre lot and the other is on a half-acre lot, they just aren't the same. Computer maps, however, know nothing of this kind of detail. Instead of knowing for sure where an address is, they make an educated guess.

The method used is *interpolation,* which is a fancy word meaning that you estimate an unknown value that falls between two known values. Say, for example, that you know something is more than a yard long but less than two yards long. You know that its length has to be around four or five feet.

It's the same with addresses in Google Earth. Say you have an ideally designed city, well laid out with a standardized address system. Each street is numbered sequentially from 1 to 100, north to south, and each avenue is numbered in the same manner from west to east. Thus, a building with an address of 100 Fifth Avenue would be on the corner of 1st Street and 5th Avenue, and one with an address of 200 Fifth Avenue would be at the intersection of 2nd Street and 5th Avenue. It logically follows that 150 Fifth Avenue would be right smack in the middle of that block.

However, it might not be there in reality. For example, take three structures along the shore of Lake Erie in Cleveland, Ohio. The Rock and Roll Hall of Fame's address is 751 Erieside Avenue. To its west, at 601 Erieside Avenue, is the Great Lakes Science Center. One more block west, and you're at Cleveland Browns Stadium, located around the corner at 1085 W. 3rd Street.

As you can see in Figure 2-8, the official locations in Google Earth are a mixed bag. As you might expect with address interpolation, only two of the three street addresses (marked by gray squares) fall on the exact spot. Of the built-in placemarks, only the Rock and Roll Hall of Fame is perfectly accurate.

Figure 2-8:
The Rock
and Roll Hall
of Fame in
Cleveland,
Ohio.

Gray squares

Thus, although Google Earth shows the stadium's and the Great Lakes Science Center's addresses correctly, the Science Center's location is shown where the stadium actually lies, and the stadium's placemark (as opposed to its address) is found to the south of the actual structure.

This sort of thing isn't the fault of Google Earth — the same thing happens in any similar program because of the current state of geographic data.

This means that you sometimes have to do a bit of looking around after you get to where you're supposed to be. If necessary, zoom out and scroll around a bit. If you know the area, look for identifiable landmarks, major intersections, and the like in order to get your bearings. If you don't, you might need to compare a map with the satellite image in order to figure out exactly what's where.

Searching for a Tailor in Tulsa: The Find Businesses Tab

Strictly speaking, the Find Businesses tab isn't really about just businesses. You can use it to find anything from museums and colleges to libraries and hospitals. This tab uses a very straightforward approach. Here's how to get the most out of it:

1. Enter the type of business in the What text box (see Figure 2-9).

Figure 2-9: Choose the kind of business to search for.

2. Enter the location in the Where text box.

If you don't enter a location here, Google Earth defaults to Current View. It assumes, in this case, that you're already looking at the area you want to search in.

3. Press Enter or click the Begin Search button.

Like with the Fly To search, Google Earth displays the location. This time, though, it includes icons marking the location of each business of the specified type. The Search pane also generates a linked list, as you can see in Figure 2-10.

4. **Click the icons in the viewing area or the links in the Search pane to generate a pop-up window with more information, such as the address and telephone number (see Figure 2-10).**

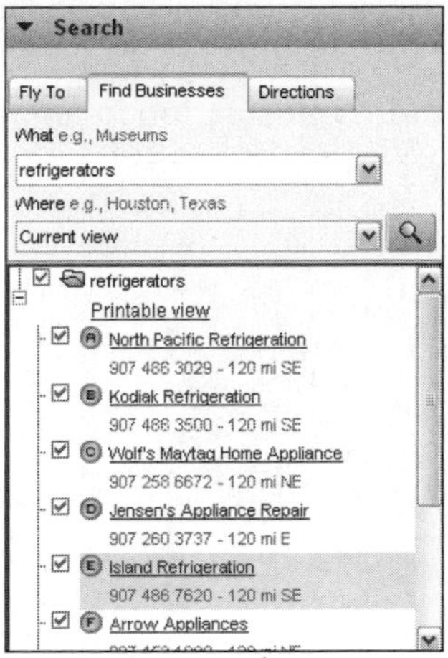

Figure 2-10:
Get more
info.

Getting Directions

When you need to figure out how to get from point A to point B, it's time to do that thing that wives always complain that their husbands never do — ask for directions.

Guys, nobody but you will know you did it.

To find out how to get from here to there, click the Directions tab and then do the following:

1. **Enter the starting point in the From text box (see Figure 2-11).**

    This can be anything from a street address to a city name.

Figure 2-11:
Finding
directions.

2. **Enter the end point in the To text box.**

3. **Press Enter or click the Begin Search button.**

Google Earth displays the area between the two points along with a series of icons marking each turn you need to take along the way. The waypoints are also shown as links in the Search pane.

A *waypoint* is a marking of a specific location on a map. Typically, these are specified by citing the latitude and longitude — and, in most cases, altitude as well.

4. **Click the icons or the links to get more information in a pop-up balloon (see Figure 2-12).**

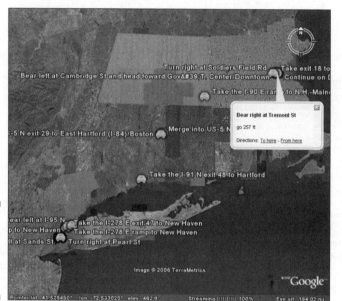

Figure 2-12: Get more info from pop-up balloons.

Whenever you see a pop-up info balloon in Google Earth, it has two links for Directions. If you click the To Here link, that location is automatically entered into the To text box in the Search pane; if you click the From Here link instead, that info goes right into the From text box.

Going Global: The Overview Map

Unless you're a geography teacher or an explorer, you'll probably get confused as to exactly where you are from time to time in Google Earth. To solve this little problem, the program includes an Overview Map feature that keeps you up to date on how your current location relates to the rest of the world (see Figure 2-13).

Overview Map

Figure 2-13:
The
Overview
Map.

You turn it on and off by choosing View⇨Overview Map from the menu or using the Ctrl+M keyboard combination.

TIP

In addition to showing you where you are, the Overview Map also gives you another quick way to move about. Just double-click within it, and you're flying to the point you chose.

You can change both the screen size of the Overview Map and the amount of detail it shows. Here's how:

1. **Choose Tools⇨Options from the menu.**

2. **Click the 3D View tab.**

3. **To change the amount of space the Overview Map takes up onscreen, move the Map Size slider (see Figure 2-14).**

   Moving it to the right enlarges it; moving it to the left shrinks it.

4. **To change the level of detail, move the Zoom Relation slider.**

   Taking it all the way to the left means that the Overview Map shows the same view as the viewing area does (1:1). Taking it all the way to the right (1:Infinity) means that the whole world is shown in the Overview Map regardless of how much you zoom into the viewing area. Figure 2-15 illustrates the two extremes.

5. **To finish up, click OK.**

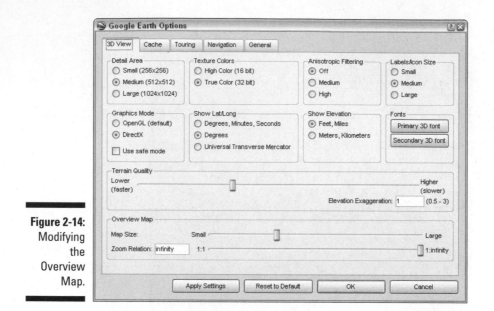

Figure 2-14:
Modifying
the
Overview
Map.

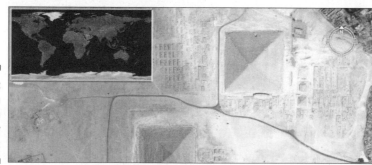

Figure 2-15:
Going from
1:1 zoom
to 1:Infinity
zoom.

You can also manually enter a zoom factor in the text box to the left of the slider.

When you have the Zoom Relation slider toward the left, the land in the view-ing area is shown as a red box. If you set the zoom to more than 52, the box symbol changes to a cross that marks the center of the viewing area.

Surfing with the Integrated Web Browser

The built-in Web browser comes in mighty handy when you need to check something out. For example, you might want to go to some of the places listed in Chapter 15 to copy some latitude and longitude figures so that you can paste them into the Search pane without having to switch back and forth between Google Earth and your external browser.

The home page in the integrated browser is (you guessed it) the Google search page, so you can be off and running right away. To display it, choose Tools⇨Web from the menu. If you want to turn it off later, use the same menu option. By default, it shows up at the bottom, as shown in Figure 2-16, but it can also be moved to the side if you prefer (see Figure 2-17) by clicking its title bar and dragging it.

Figure 2-16:
The internal
Web
browser.

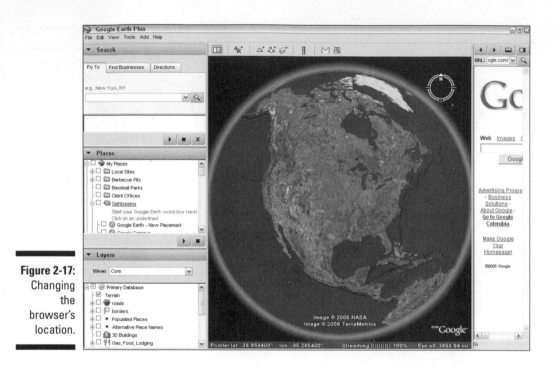

Figure 2-17:
Changing
the
browser's
location.

If you're going to dock the Web browser on the side, you might want to turn off the sidebar so that the Viewing pane isn't too crowded. To do so, click the Hide Sidebar button on the Google Earth toolbar, press Ctrl+Alt+B, or choose Tools➪Sidebar from the menu.

The browser is easy to use; its toolbar contains the few controls you need to operate it. Table 2-2 tells how to use them, starting from left to right.

Table 2-2	Web Browser Controls
Control	**Description**
Go Back	Display a previously viewed Web page.
Go Forward	Return from a previous page to the current page.
URL	Enter the Web address here.
Search the Web	Click this to go to the URL.
Dock Web window on the bottom	Keep the Web browser in its default location.
Dock Web window on the side	Move the browser to the right side.

Control	Description
Launch this page in an external browser	Close the internal browser and open the same page in your default Web browser.
Close the Web window	Turn off the internal browser.

When you're exploring various points of interest (POIs; see Chapter 5), you'll often encounter links to Web sites. You can choose to have these Web pages show up in either the integrated browser or your default external Web browser by setting the appropriate option:

1. **Choose Tools⇨Options from the menu.**

2. **Click the General tab (see Figure 2-18).**

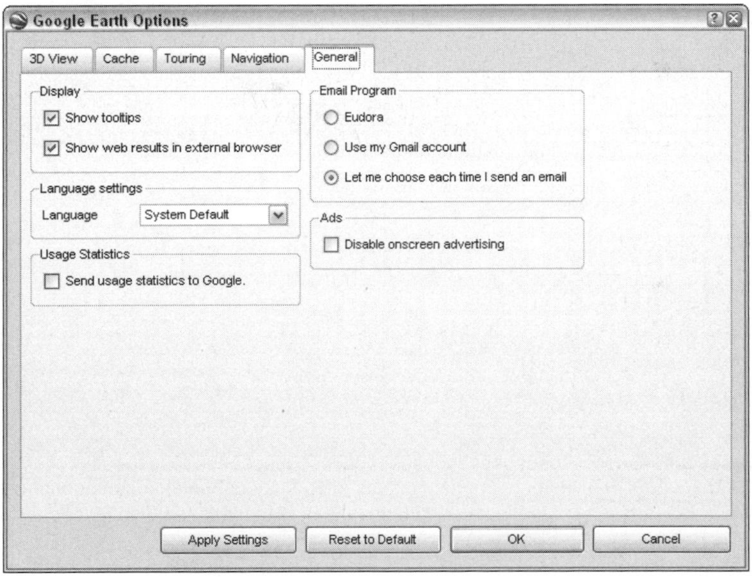

Figure 2-18: Setting the Web browser option.

3. **Choose your display:**

   • Enable the second option under Display — the Show Web Results in External Browser check box.

   or

   • Clear the Show Web Results in External Browser check box to select the integrated browser instead.

4. **Click OK to exit.**

When you next click a Web link in Google Earth, you see the resulting Web page in the browser of your choice. You don't have to open the browser. If you click a link and the browser isn't already open, it opens automatically at the desired Web page.

What if your browser is already open, though? That depends on which you chose. If it's an external browser, like Internet Explorer, a new browser window opens. The integrated browser, however, has only one window, right there in Google Earth, so whatever page is displayed automatically replaces the old one.

Chapter 3

Adjusting Your View on the World

. . . .

In This Chapter

▶ Zooming the map

▶ Using direction and tilt controls

▶ Sizing with the Ruler

. . . .

Google Earth is a lot of fun to use, and a good part of the reason for that is the careful design that went into its interface. It's slick, intuitive, and easy to use. Even when you're using it for serious work, it still feels like you're playing a game.

In this chapter, I take you on a tour of the various ways to modify, measure, and emphasize what you're looking at. I'll show you how to "spin the globe" that's inside Google Earth and the different ways you can choose to zoom in and out or tilt and spin the landscape.

Rock the World: Dragging and Zooming the Map

No matter what your tastes may be, Google Earth has some way of moving things around that'll make you happy. Of the several methods for doing the same things, you can pick and choose the ones you like best. The two major approaches to navigation are using your mouse as a kind of virtual hand or using it to click the navigation controls. The controls are covered in the upcoming section, "Gaining a New Perspective: The Direction and Tilt Controls."

Time to get started with a simple first exploration:

1. **Place your mouse pointer on the globe in the viewing area.**

2. **Press and hold the left mouse button.**

3. **Move the mouse in any direction.**

   The globe follows, allowing you to turn it at will.

 4. **Move the mouse sharply and quickly release the button.**

    The globe continues to move in that direction. To stop it, just click it.

 5. **Double-click the globe.**

    The image begins to zoom in, as if you were descending.

 6. **Click the globe to stop it.**

 7. **Double-click the right mouse button.**

    The image zooms out.

 8. **Click either mouse button to stop it.**

 9. **Turn your mouse's wheel forward and backward.**

    Forward moves the world away from you (as you gain altitude); backward moves it toward you.

If you don't like how the mouse wheel zooms, you can switch its direction. Here's how:

 1. **Choose Tools⇨Options from the menu.**

 2. **Click the Navigation tab.**

 3. **Select the Invert Mouse Wheel Zoom Direction check box, as shown in Figure 3-1.**

 4. **Click OK.**

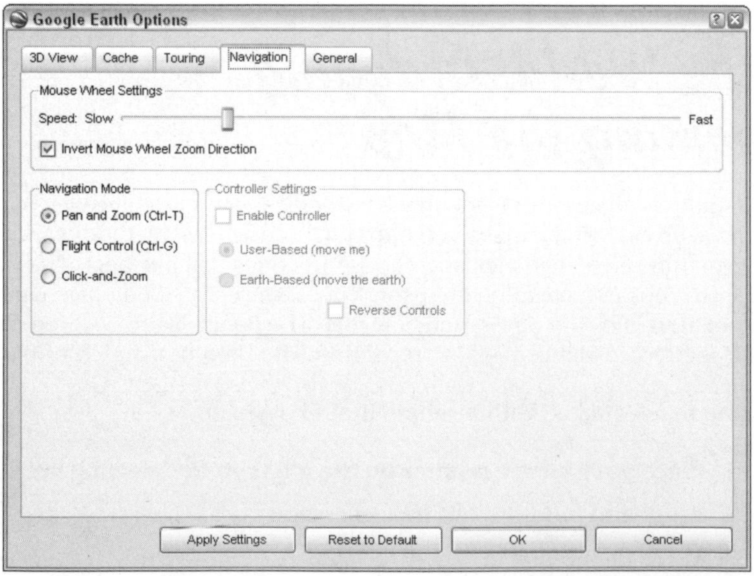

Figure 3-1:
Change the
direction of
your mouse
wheel.

Play with the methods of spinning and zooming for a bit until you're comfortable with them and then try out the full range of possibilities shown in Table 3-1.

Table 3-1	Mouse Navigation
Mouse Action	**Result**
Press and hold left mouse button; move mouse.	Screen image follows mouse movement. A sharp movement followed by the release of the mouse button sets the Earth moving until you click it again.*
Press and hold right mouse button; move mouse.	Screen image zooms in and out. Moving the mouse away from you moves the Earth away from you and vice versa. A sharp movement followed by the release of the mouse button results in a continuous zoom, which can be stopped by clicking in the viewing area.*
Click.	Stops any movement.
Left double-click.	Zooms in.
Right double-click.	Zooms out.
Use mouse wheel.	Zooms in and out. By default, rolling the wheel away moves the Earth away; rolling it toward you does the opposite, but you can reverse this action.
Press wheel or middle button; move mouse.	Movement toward you tilts the scene, away restores it to normal view. Movement left or right rotates the image.

The speed of this sharp movement sets the speed of the continuous scrolling or zooming that results. The faster the mouse movement is, the faster the resulting screen movement will be.

Gaining a New Perspective: The Direction and Tilt Controls

At first glance, the navigation controls can be a bit daunting, but they are quick to learn and easy to use (see Figure 3-2). There are two sliders and a ring. Inside the ring are a few other directional controls.

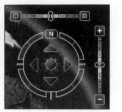

Figure 3-2:
The
navigation
controls.

The horizontal slider is the tilt control. Moving it to the right tilts the scene, and going to the left returns to an overhead view. If you don't feel like using the slider, just double-click the boxes on the ends of the slider. The right one tilts the image all the way, and the left one straightens it up again. A single click on the boxes tilts or untilts just a little bit.

The vertical slider is the zoom control. Moving it up zooms in; moving it down zooms out. Like with the other slider, it has control boxes on its ends as well. A single click on the top one zooms in a small amount and then stops; the bottom one does the same while zooming out. Double-clicking them causes the zoom to continue until you click the viewing area to stop it.

The ring is the rotation control. To use it, click it and hold the mouse button down. Now, move the mouse. Both the ring and the image will rotate.

After you start rotating things, you don't have to keep the mouse pointer on the rotation ring. You can move it anywhere, and the effect will be the same until you release the button.

At the top of the rotation ring is the capital letter N. Of course, this stands for North, but in the process of rotation, North can end up pointing to just about anywhere onscreen. To restore it to its traditional position at the top of the screen, just double-click the N.

The four arrowheads within the rotation ring are directional movement controls. A single click of any of them moves the scene in the opposite direction (or moves your viewpoint in the indicated direction — it's all relative). Double-clicking results in continuous movement; to stop it, just click.

There are, of course, plenty of times when you want to do more than just go left and right, up and down. For those times, the starburst-shaped control in the center works like a joystick. Click it, hold down the mouse button, and then drag it around. You can move in any direction. As with the arrowheads, it is your viewpoint that moves in the direction you pull the control.

The navigation controls only appear when you move your mouse pointer over their screen area (the upper-right corner). To change this behavior, choose View⇨Show Navigation from the menu. The three options are Automatically (the default), Always, and Never.

Three-dimensional viewing

If you've been using the tilt controls, you might not notice much of a difference in the tilted and untilted views unless you have the Terrain feature turned on. Look at your Layers pane and make sure that there's a check mark in the Terrain check box. Then fly on over to some nice mountainous area like the one in Figure 3-3 and tilt things again.

One of the drawbacks to Google Earth (or any satellite view, for that matter) is that you are looking at things from an unfamiliar perspective. Even when looking at your own house or apartment building, the view lacks the "normal" orientation, in which we view things from the ground and buildings rise above the plane of our vision.

Figure 3-3: Mountains spring to life with the Terrain layer and tilt controls.

When you use the tilt controls with the Terrain layer activated, the buildings are still flat images as seen from space.

For the larger cities, Google Earth has an answer: The major buildings have been added as three-dimensional models in a layer of their own. Figure 3-4 shows Manhattan without and with the 3D Buildings layer activated.

Figure 3-4: Tilted view of Manhattan without the 3D Buildings layer (left) and with it (right).

The compass and status bar

The *compass* is the circle in the upper-right corner, with the N at the top. If you'd rather not have it onscreen, choose View➪Compass from the menu.

Turning off the compass does *not* turn off the navigation controls. They will still appear as usual.

The *status bar* is the line of information at the bottom of the screen that provides the

- ✔ Latitude, longitude, and elevation of your mouse pointer
- ✔ Percentage of the image that has so far flowed into your computer
- ✔ Altitude of your viewpoint

To gain a little more screen area, choose View➪Status Bar from the menu. Figure 3-5 shows Google Earth with all possible distractions removed from the viewing area.

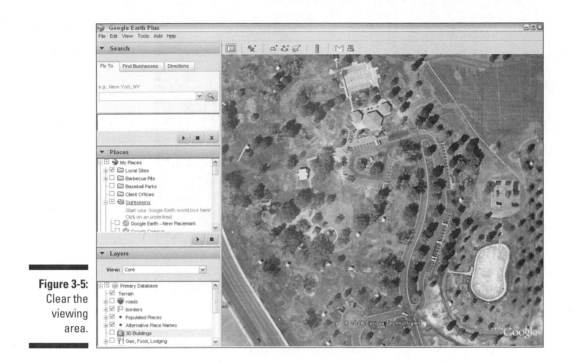

The Bigger They Are: Figuring Sizes with the Scale and Ruler

You have two ways to measure things in Google Earth: the Scale Legend and the Ruler. The Ruler is the more versatile of the two, but the Scale Legend requires no action beyond turning it on.

Using the Scale Legend

Normal maps have a scale printed on them that shows you, for instance, that 100 miles in the real world equals 1 inch on the map. Google Earth has one, too, and it constantly keeps track of the changes in the scale as you zoom in and out (see Figure 3-6). To turn it on (or off), choose View➪Scale Legend from the menu.

Using the Ruler

The Ruler can measure either a line or a path that you draw onscreen. A *path*, in this case, is a series of connected lines.

Figure 3-6:
The Scale
Legend.

Scale Legend

Lines

To measure the distance between two points, you need to use the Line option. Here's how:

1. **Click the Show Ruler button on the toolbar (the vertical ruler icon).**

2. **In the Ruler dialog box that appears (as shown in Figure 3-7), click the Line tab.**

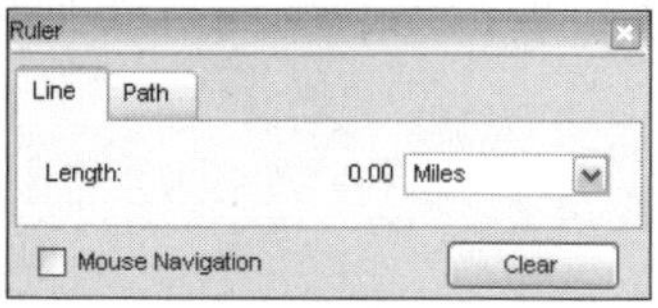

Figure 3-7:
Working
with lines.

3. **Click the start point in the viewing area and then click the end point.**

   A line appears between them with the distance displayed in the Ruler dialog box.

4. **To change the unit of measurement, click the Length drop-down list (see Figure 3-8).**

   You can choose anything from centimeters to nautical miles to smoots.

5. **To erase the line, click the Clear button.**

Miles and meters and smoots. Oh, my!

If you take a careful look at Figure 3-8, you'll see the usual standards of measurement that you're likely at least vaguely familiar with. You know, miles and kilometers, feet and yards, that sort of thing. So what about that last entry? *Smoots?* What?

You can't blame yourself if you don't know how many smoots tall you are or how many meters there are in a smoot. Really. The whole thing started about 50 years ago with a group of young students from MIT as a fraternity prank. One of the students — Oliver R. Smoot, Jr. — was 5'7" (1.702 meters) tall. He was flipped end over end across Harvard Bridge, keeping count just as you might with a yardstick. When the other side was reached, it was scientifically determined that the bridge was slightly more than 364 smoots long.

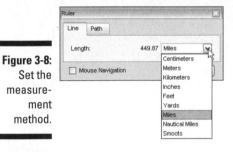

Figure 3-8:
Set the measure-ment method.

You can also just start to draw another line. The first one disappears when you do.

If the Mouse Navigation check box is selected, holding down the mouse button and moving the mouse moves the image as usual. If you deselect it, that same mouse movement simply draws a line while the world stands still. This setting affects the mouse *only* when you're using the Ruler.

Paths

Paths work much the same way as lines do. The exceptions are that in Step 2 of the preceding step list, you click the Path tab and essentially repeat Step 3 several times. To draw a path, you click the starting point, click an intermediate point, click another intermediate point, and so on, defining the waypoints along the path until you finally reach the end point.

As you add new segments to the path, the length of the total path is shown in the Ruler dialog box (see Figure 3-9).

Paths and lines are separate things. Although you can have only one line drawn at a time, you can have both a line and a path onscreen together (see Figure 3-10). Although beginning a new line will delete the old one, the path remains unaffected while you do so.

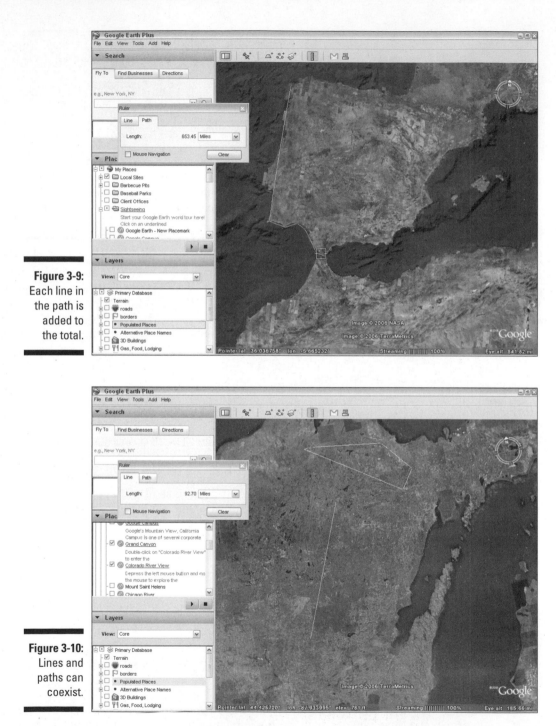

Figure 3-9:
Each line in
the path is
added to
the total.

Figure 3-10:
Lines and
paths can
coexist.

Part II
Personalizing Google Earth

The 5th Wave   By Rich Tennant

"Why don't you try blurring the brimstone and then putting a nice glow effect around the hellfire."

In this part . . .

Chapter 4 shows you how to modify Google Earth's options (such as whether to use meters or feet for measurements) and how to modify the program's screen display to suit yourself.

Chapter 5 digs into one of the program's most powerful features — *layers* — which comprise a series of built-in data points that show the locations of everything from borders and volcanos to ATMs and Italian restaurants. By selecting various combinations of them, you can customize your own map.

Chapter 6 goes on to show how you can add your own data points called *placemarks* — which are to Google Earth what bookmarks are to a Web browser — as well as how to placemark any spot on the planet along with your own notes about it.

Chapter 4

Fine-Tuning the Program

Google Earth works just fine right out of the box, but its creators understand that a lot of us like to monkey with things and customize them just how we like it. You can do lots of things to make Google Earth your own. For example, if you need a bigger Layers pane and don't use the Search pane much, resize them to suit yourself. Want a better look at the big picture? Just go full-screen and admire the view.

Also in this chapter, I show you how to get the most out of your video settings and how to manipulate the elevation of mountains. From measurement options to font choices to language options, this chapter's got you covered.

Relieve the Pane: Manipulating Screen Areas

In Figure 4-1, you can see the main Google Earth window. In the standard configuration, the menu bar and toolbar appear at the top of the window, the sidebar is on the left, and the Viewing pane takes up the rest of the screen.

The toolbar holds eight buttons:

- **Show/Hide Sidebar:** Toggles the sidebar on and off. This gives more screen space to the Viewing pane when you're not using any of the sidebar features.

- **Add Placemark:** Adds a new placemark (see Chapter 6).

- **Add Polygon:** Adds a new polygon (see Chapter 13).

- **Add Path:** Adds a new path (see Chapter 3).

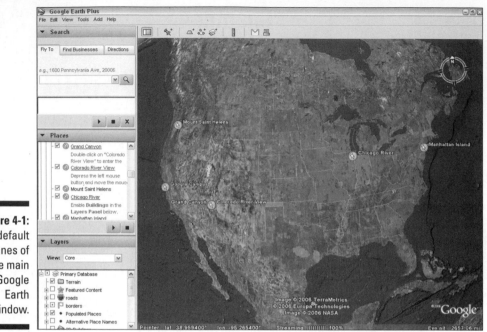

Figure 4-1:
The default
panes of
the main
Google
Earth
window.

✔ **Add Image Overlay:** Adds a new image overlay (see Chapter 9).

✔ **Show Ruler:** Shows the Ruler, which enables you to measure the distance between points in the Viewing pane (see Chapter 3).

✔ **Email:** Uses your e-mail program to send either a placemark to, or an image of, the view on your screen.

✔ **Print:** Prints the image and, optionally, other details. Which options you get when you click this button depends upon the last thing you did:

- *Driving Directions:* You just used the Directions tab in the Search pane. The default is to print the driving directions, but you can select 3D View instead (see Figure 4-2).

Figure 4-2:
Printing
Driving
Directions.

- *3D View + Placemark Details:* You created a placemark before click-ing the Print button. 3D View is available (see Figure 4-3).

- *3D View:* Prints the image at the selected resolution. Available printer resolutions depend upon which version of Google Earth you have and, of course, your printer (see Figure 4-4).

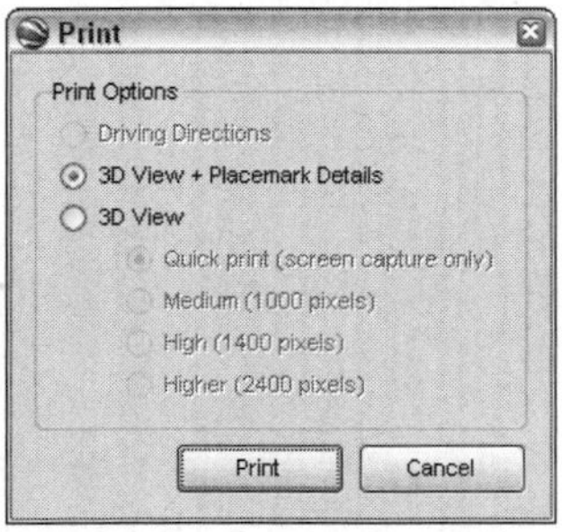

Figure 4-3:
Printing
Placemark
Details.

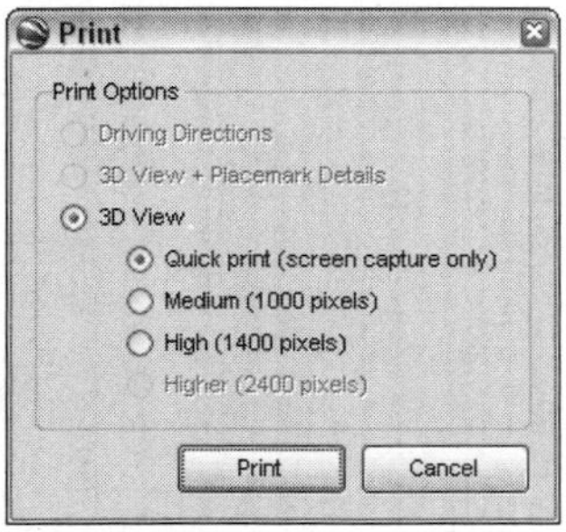

Figure 4-4:
Select the
printer
resolution.

The sidebar contains three smaller panes:

✔ **The Search pane:** Covered in detail in Chapter 2, the Search pane is where you, well, search. Three tabs help you find things:

- *Fly To tab:* This tab is the most fun, in my opinion. Simply type in where you want to go, and you immediately "fly" over the Earth's surface to your destination.

- *Find Businesses tab:* Enter the location and kind of business you're interested in, and Google Earth shows you where they all are. The term *business* should be interpreted loosely because you can also find things like schools and churches from this tab.

- *Directions tab:* This tab gives you detailed driving directions between any two points you enter.

✔ **The Places pane:** See Chapter 6 for more on this.

✔ **The Layers pane:** See Chapter 5 for details.

All these panes can be manipulated to alter Google Earth's appearance or to gain some screen room. For example, you don't have to accept the default proportions of the panes. They can be altered with the stroke of a mouse. To resize a pane, follow these steps:

1. **Place your mouse cursor on the dividing bar between two panes. The cursor changes, as shown in Figure 4-5.**

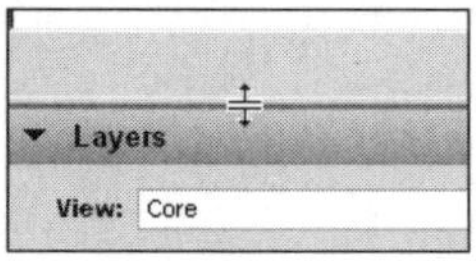

Figure 4-5:
You can
resize
sidebar
panes.

2. **Press and hold the left mouse button.**

3. **Drag the dividing bar to the desired location.**

4. **Release the left mouse button.**

If resizing the panes isn't enough for you, you can *toggle* them — turn them on or off — as well. To do this, click the expand/collapse triangles to the left of the sidebar pane name (Search, Places, or Layers). When a pane is turned off, it takes up almost no space onscreen, thus leaving more room for its neighbors to expand. For example, Figure 4-6 shows that when the Search pane is toggled off, the Places and Layers panes expand to fill the available space.

The sidebar can also be toggled off, thus automatically turning off all three of its panes. When the sidebar is toggled off, the Viewing pane expands to take up the entire screen except for the menu bar and toolbar at the top (see Figure 4-7). To do this, you can click the Show/Hide Sidebar icon in the toolbar, press Ctrl+Alt+B, or choose Tools➪Sidebar from the menu.

TIP

You can switch back and forth between normal view and full-screen mode by pressing F11. The difference between full-screen mode and turning off the sidebar is that the full-screen approach covers the Windows taskbar.

Expand/collapse pane triangles

Figure 4-6:
Turning off
one pane
expands the
others.

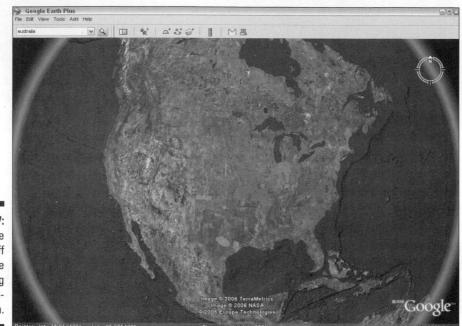

Setting the Options

In addition to monkeying with the screen view, you can go under the hood of Google Earth to change various options to suit yourself. To get started, choose Tools➪Options from the menu. The resulting Options window contains five tabs:

- ✔ 3D View
- ✔ Cache
- ✔ Touring
- ✔ Navigation
- ✔ General

I discuss each of these in greater detail in the sections that follow.

The 3D View tab

The 3D View tab, as shown in Figure 4-8, is the first one you see in the Options window. As you might expect, it offers several choices that affect how you see things.

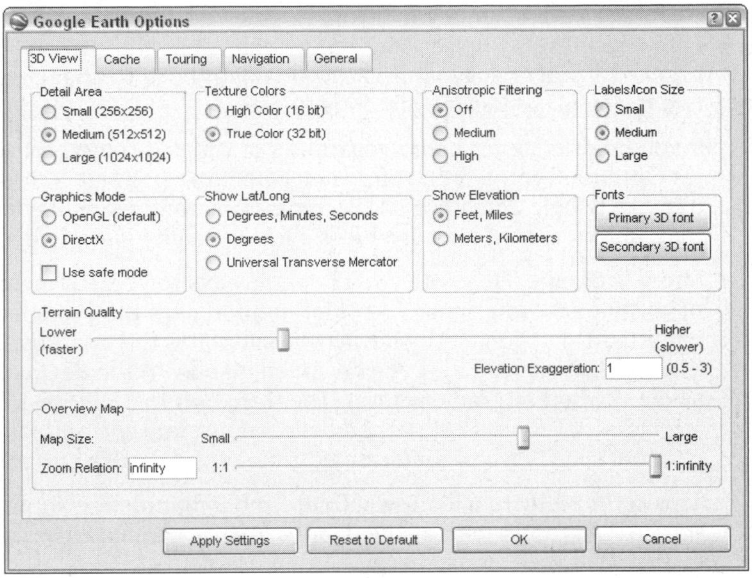

Figure 4-8:
The 3D View tab offers general viewing options.

The various areas on this tab are

- **Detail Area:** The amount of detail that can be shown is dependent upon your video memory. The more detail you need, the more memory that's required. Google Earth solves this problem by providing you with the option to restrict the size of the detail area, which is always at the center of the screen.

  If you select Small, the area of maximum detail is limited to a square of 256 pixels in width and height at the center of the image; the remainder of the image is less detailed. The Medium setting is 512 x 512 pixels, and the Large is 1024 x 1024.

  If the amount of memory in your computer system is too small, the Large option is grayed out (unavailable). Google recommends 32MB of video RAM as a minimum for the Large setting.

- **Texture Colors:** This setting depends upon the quality of your video card. Most computers today have true color (32-bit) cards, but an older video card might require the lower-quality High Color (16-bit) option.

- **Anisotropic Filtering:** This is a highfalutin term for softening the harsh edges along the horizon when you tilt the image onscreen. It's very memory intensive, so go for this only if you've got 32MB of RAM or more. (Anisotropic filtering is available only if you're using the DirectX graphics mode.)

- **Labels/Icon Size:** The default size is Medium. For larger or smaller labels and icons, select the appropriate radio button.

✔ **Graphics Mode:** When you install Google Earth, it chooses what it thinks is the best display option for your system, depending upon your graphics card. If you change your card, you might need to change which of the two major 3-D rendering methods to use.

If you experience problems regardless of which 3-D method your graphics card uses, you have a safety net: Select the Use Safe Mode check box to make Google Earth use a less complex method of displaying things that, unfortunately, also produces a lower-quality viewing experience.

✔ **Show Lat/Long:** There are two common ways to present measurements of latitude and longitude. The older method uses the system of degrees, minutes, and seconds; the newer one simplifies the minutes and seconds to a decimal value. To set the onscreen display to the decimal version, select the Degrees radio button. The third option, Universal Transverse Mercator (UTM), isn't a method of specifying latitude and longitude but one that specifies a predetermined zone of the Earth's surface.

This setting affects only how latitude and longitude are shown on your screen. You can still enter them in the Search pane in either form regardless of what you choose here.

✔ **Show Elevation:** Much like the previous option, this option simply sets whether the onscreen display is in the English or the metric system of linear measurement. To choose the former, select the Feet, Miles radio button; to choose the latter, select the Meters, Kilometers radio button instead.

✔ **Fonts:** If you want to change the lettering that Google Earth uses, follow these steps:

a. *Click the Primary 3D Font button.*

b. *In the resulting dialog box (as shown in Figure 4-9), click the name of the font style that you want (under Font). If necessary, scroll down to locate the name.*

Figure 4-9:
Change your display font here.

![Select Font dialog box showing Font list with Arial selected, Font style options (Normal, Italic, Bold, Bold Italic), Size options, Effects (Strikeout, Underline), Script set to Latin, and a Sample showing AaBbYyZz]

c. *Select the font style by selecting Normal, Italic, Bold, or Bold Italic.*

Some font styles might not be available, depending upon the particular font chosen.

d. *To set the font size, either type in a number in the text box under Size or click the size you want. Scroll down if necessary to locate the desired value.*

e. *(Optional) If you want the letters to appear with* ~~strikethrough~~ *or as* <u>underlined</u>, *select the Strikeout or Underline check box, respectively.*

f. *(Optional) If you want a different alphabet than the default Latin, click the down arrow under Script and select the desired one.*

g. *Click OK.*

The Secondary 3D Font button sets a backup font. This is used if a character cannot be shown in the primary font. Choosing a secondary font is identical to choosing one for the Primary 3D Font setting.

✔ **Terrain Quality:** Drag the slider here to set a compromise between speed and the detail of the terrain. The lower the terrain quality, the faster it displays; the higher the quality, the slower it displays.

• *Elevation Exaggeration:* The default setting of 1 means that the *elevation* — the rise and dip of hills, valleys, and so forth — that you see onscreen is faithfully reproduced. However, sometimes it's helpful to change this and make things look higher than they are in reality. Figure 4-10 shows the same scene with elevation exaggeration set at 1 (left) and at 3 (right). This is a useful technique, for example, for quickly spotting natural water drainage routes.

Many experienced users will set the Elevation Exaggeration to 1.2 or 1.3. This provides a slightly increased perceived height of mountains and depths of valleys. It helps to create a 3-D illusion from the flat images without distorting the landscape too greatly.

The top value possible for Elevation Exaggeration is 3.0, and you can take it all the way down to 0.5.

✔ **Overview Map:** To set the size of the Overview Map, ranging from postage stamp to playing card, drag the Map Size slider to the left for a smaller Overview Map or to the right for a larger one.

The Zoom Relation setting specifies how much of the Earth is shown in the Overview Map. For the whole thing, leave the slider at the default Infinity setting (all the way to the right). To zoom in on a smaller area, move the slider to the left.

For details on using the Overview Map, see Chapter 2.

Figure 4-10:
Exaggerate
the
elevation.

The Cache tab

To get the best performance out of Geographic Information System (GIS) programs, video memory isn't your only concern. The amount of RAM and disk space on your computer system also matters. These values can be adjusted on the Cache tab (see Figure 4-11).

The Memory Cache Size setting is for your RAM.

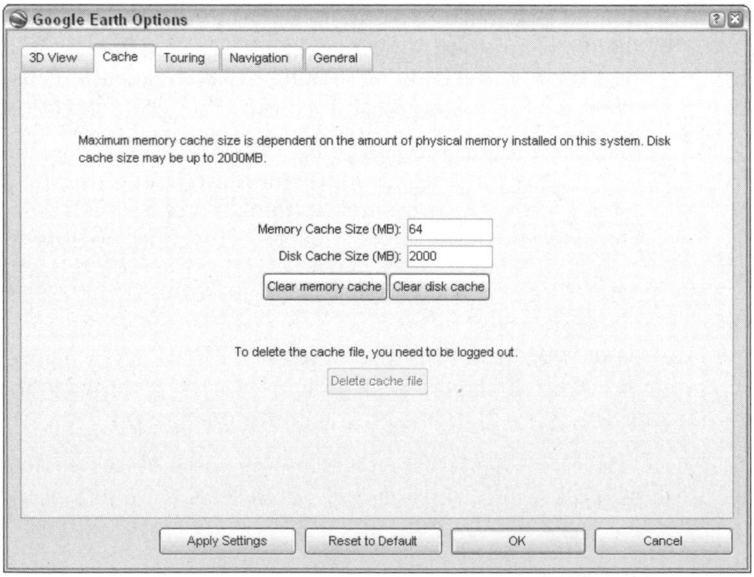

Figure 4-11:
Set the
cache size.

The Disk Cache Size setting is used to supplement the RAM by setting aside a certain amount of space on your hard drive to be used as virtual memory. You can set up to 2000 MB of disk cache, but because disk drives are considerably slower than RAM chips when it comes to memory access, the RAM size is the more important of the two.

Depending on how much memory you have, you can set higher or lower values for both types of cache. Google Earth does not let you set values higher than the amount of memory your computer can sustain.

To erase the current information in either cache, click the Clear Memory Cache or the Clear Disk Cache button. If you're logged out of the Google Earth server (File⇨Server Log Out from the menu), you can also click the Delete Cache File button to not only clear but also erase the disk cache file, which will be re-created the next time you log on.

Occasionally, the imagery in the cache can become corrupted (bad placemark values, interrupted downloading, and so on). When this happens, the view becomes unstable or blurry, or otherwise acts in a peculiar manner. The recommended fix to this abnormal behavior is to use the Delete Cache File button.

The Touring tab

The Touring tab (see Figure 4-12) handles a wide variety of settings relating to movements and camera angles. These settings are outlined as follows:

✔ **Fly-To/Tour Settings:** The Fly-To settings control how you see things when you double-click a placemark in the Places pane, such as how quickly the scenery goes past (see Chapter 2). The Tour settings, on the other hand, affect only the animation of a series of points (see Chapter 7).

- *Fly-To Speed:* Use the slider or type in a specific value to set how fast you fly from place to place. The faster your computer system is *as a whole* — that is, if you have a high-speed Internet connection, a fast microprocessor, lots of RAM, a hot video card, and so forth — the faster you can make this setting. Otherwise, keep it slow, or you'll just be watching a lot of blurry, half-formed images flying past.

- *Tour Speed:* This works the same as Fly-To Speed but affects only the playback of tours.

- *Tour Pause:* This slider controls the amount of time spent waiting at a stop on a tour. You can set this between 0 and 60 seconds.

- *Play Tour:* Use the spinner arrows to set how many times to play a tour in a row. The default is 1, and the top is 9,999.

If you want the tour to loop indefinitely, scroll down from 1 for a setting of Infinite.

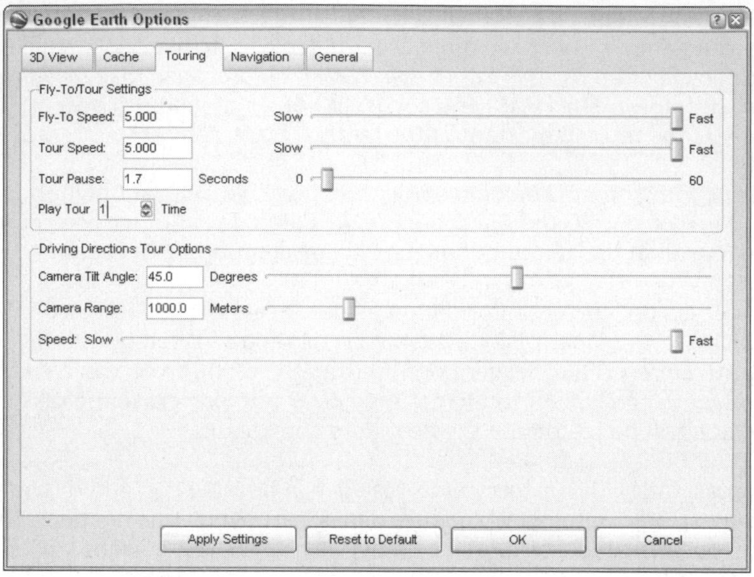

Figure 4-12:
The Touring
tab.

> ✔ **Driving Directions Tour Options:** See Chapter 7 for details on tour procedures.
>
>> • *Camera Tilt Angle:* Use this setting to adjust the degree of tilt at which the scene is shown.
>>
>> • *Camera Range:* This setting specifies how far away the camera (that is, your *viewpoint*) is from the scene.
>>
>> • *Speed:* Slide to the right to step on the gas, and slide to the left to hit the brakes.

The Navigation tab

The Navigation tab, as shown in Figure 4-13, allows you to control the navigation mode produced when you use your mouse as well as to customize the size and content of the Overview Map (see Chapter 2). The settings found here are as follows:

> ✔ **Mouse Wheel Settings:** The default is medium. To slow things down, move the slider to the left; to speed them up, move it to the right.
>
> Select the Invert Mouse Wheel Zoom Direction check box if you'd rather have the Earth move away from you when you roll the mouse wheel away. Deselect it if you prefer to have the Earth move toward you when you roll the mouse wheel away.

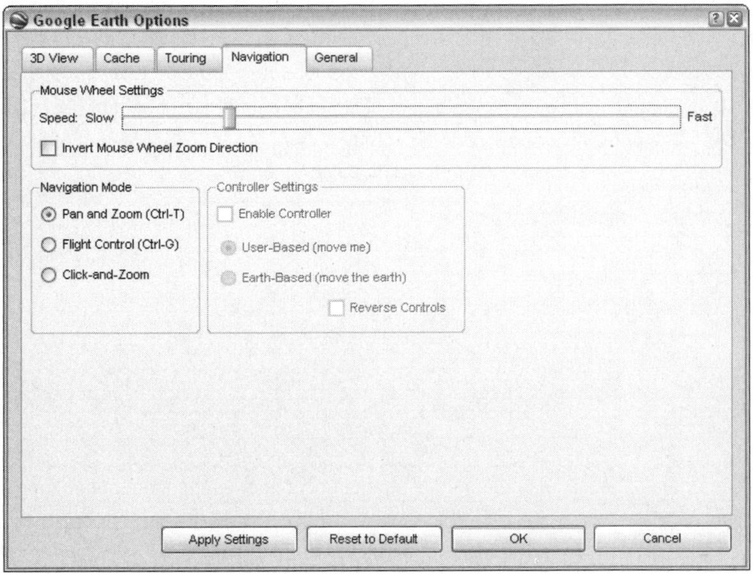

Figure 4-13:
Set navigation and overview options here.

✓ **Navigation Mode:** To set which method of mouse-al manipulation you'd like to use (see Chapter 3 for info on how to use Pan and Zoom, Flight Control, or Click-and-Zoom), select the appropriate radio button.

✓ **Controller Settings:** You can use a controller such as a gamepad, joystick, or flight controller instead of a mouse. If you do, you need to select the Enable Controller check box.

Select the User-Based radio button to move yourself while the Earth remains in place or the Earth-Based radio button to move the Earth instead.

To switch the actions of your joystick or other controller, select the Reverse Controls check box.

The General tab

The General tab (see Figure 4-14) is where you set options covering odds and ends, such as your e-mail preferences. These options are as follows:

✓ **Display:** The check boxes in this section set whether the following options are on:

- *Show Tooltips:* A small, informational pop-up tip shows when you hover your mouse pointer over a control on the Navigation bar.

- *Show Web Results in External Browser:* Use your default Web browser instead of the Google Earth internal browser.

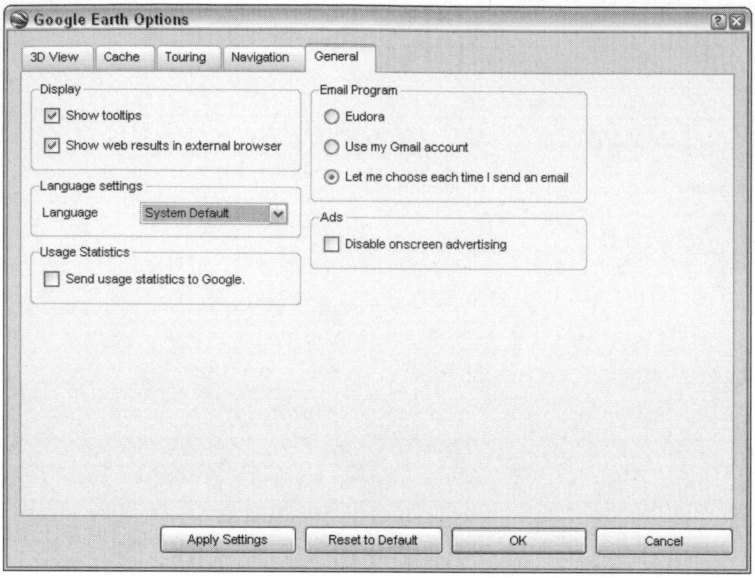

Figure 4-14:
The General
tab.

✔ **Email Program:** This option simply sets which e-mail program Google
Earth calls on when you want to send a placemark to a friend. (See
Chapter 8 for more on sending placemarks.) You can choose to use your
default e-mail software (Google Earth is aware of the major e-mail programs and will select the appropriate one from your system settings),
use your Google Gmail account, or make up your mind each time.

✔ **Language Settings:** Choose from a drop-down list of languages. The
default is, as you might guess, System Default. The supported languages
as of this writing are German, English, Spanish, French, Italian, and
Japanese.

✔ **Usage Statistics:** Google gathers information on how well Google Earth is
working without collecting personal data. Select the Send Usage
Statistics to Google check box to participate in this ongoing study. The
details are at the following URL:

```
http://earth.google.com/support/bin/answer.py?answer=40936&topic=1151
```

✔ **Ads:** If you're using the free Google Earth version, some Google Ads (such
as what you see when using the Google search engine) appear in various
information balloons. If you have Plus or Pro version, you can select the
Disable Onscreen Advertising check box to eliminate those ads.

Chapter 5

Adding Layers and Points of Interest (POIs)

In This Chapter

▶ Understanding layers

▶ Displaying layers

▶ Exploring the various types of POIs

*L*ayers and points of interest (POIs) have a lot in common but also have a couple of important technical differences. Basically, *POIs* are places to go (such as the Eiffel Tower, the Statue of Liberty, or the Sears Tower) — and all the placemarks in the Places pane are POIs. Whether they came with Google Earth or you add them, they exist on your computer.

Layers, on the other hand, exist only on the Google Earth servers. They are forms of information that are added to the basic view in Google Earth — things like national boundaries, crime statistics, or the names of local legislators. Nonetheless, many layers are simply groups of individual locations (such as hospitals, airports, or golf courses). Thus, to the average user of Google Earth, the difference between a placemark in the Places pane and a location that is specified in the Layers pane is often a moot point.

Think of layers as information on a series of transparent sheets. As each sheet is laid on top of the others beneath it (like during an overhead projection), a composite picture emerges.

Peeling the Onion: A Guide to Layers

Layers are added pieces of information above and beyond just the satellite image itself. In fact, everything in Google Earth, except for placemarks, that isn't a photo from space is a layer of some kind. From railroads and highways to airports and eateries, the sheer variety of added layers is what makes Google Earth more than just another peek through an orbiting satellite's lens.

Built-in points of interest

You activate layers by selecting the check boxes next to them in the Layers pane. Depending upon which layer you activate, the resulting display on your screen might change in various ways. For example, if you turn on the Volcanoes layer while looking at Atlanta, Georgia, nothing changes — no volcanoes exist there. Try the same thing in Latin America or the Pacific, however, and your screen is filled with volcano icons, as shown in Figure 5-1.

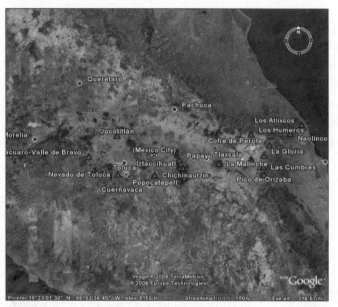

Figure 5-1:
The
Volcanoes
layer in
action.

Likewise, if you select the Populated Places layer, your view of Europe is covered with names (see Figure 5-2); on the other hand, viewing this same layer while looking at North Africa results in a practically bare screen (see Figure 5-3).

Items on the Populated Places layer won't show up on your screen unless your viewing altitude is lower than 2,500 miles (about 4,000 kilometers). The lower you go, the more of them you see.

Figure 5-2:
Europe has
many
populated
places.

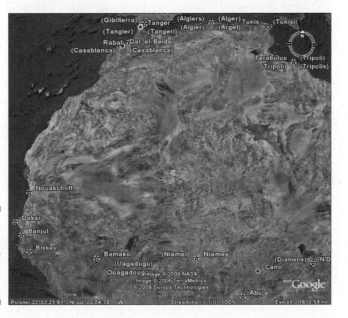

Figure 5-3:
North Africa
is nearly
deserted in
comparison.

Displaying Layers

The Layers pane, of course, shows all the layers and their sublayers (see Figure 5-4). Here, you can turn on or off zillions of settings that alter the volume and type of information included, and thus how things appear on your screen.

Within the Layers pane, the View drop-down list allows you to choose among three display settings (see Figure 5-5):

- **Core:** This setting includes all the layers except for the US Government layer.

- **All Layers:** Cleverly named, this setting shows just that.

- **Now Enabled:** This setting shows only those layers that have either some or all of their elements selected.

Although the amount of information is nearly overwhelming, showing it is quite simple. Each layer has a plus sign and a check box next to it. Click the plus sign to expand the layer, revealing its sublayers. To select all sublayers at once, just select the check box next to its parent layer. To select any sub-layer individually, select the check box next to it. Figure 5-6 shows both methods in action.

Figure 5-4:
The Layers pane has it all.

```
Layers

View:  All Layers                    ▼

⊟ ☑ ✍ Primary Database
  ├ ☑   Terrain
  ├ ☐ 🏢 3D Buildings
  ⊞ ☐ 🏴 borders
  ⊞ ☐ 🛞 roads
  ⊞ ☑ •  Populated Places
  ⊞ ☑ •  Alternative Place Names
  ⊞ ☐ 🍴 Gas, Food, Lodging
  ⊞ ☐ ▢ National Geographic Magazine
  ⊞ ☐ i  Google Earth Community
  ⊞ ☐ 🛒 Shopping and Services
  ⊞ ☐ ⚒ Transportation
  ⊞ ☐ 🏛 Geographic Features
  ⊞ ☐ 🌲 Parks and Recreation Areas
  ⊞ ☐ 🏠 Community Services
  ⊞ ☑ 🗔 US Government
  ⊞ ☐ i  DG Coverage
```

Figure 5-5:
Choose the
Layers
display you
want.

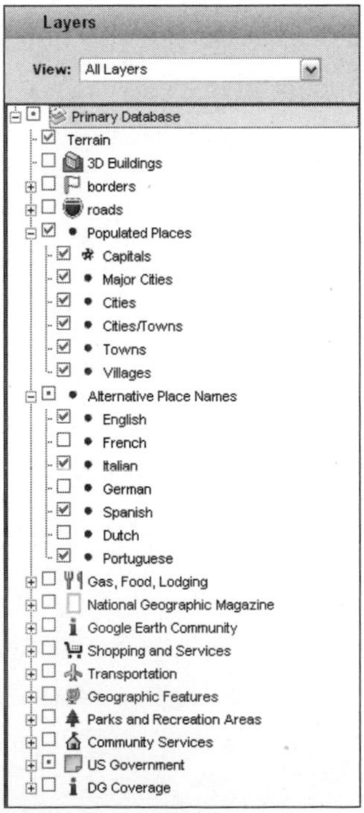

Figure 5-6:
Sublayers
can be
selected as
a whole or
individually.

From School Districts to Earthquakes: Types of Layers

Google Earth offers many different layers, and you can expect new ones to be constantly added. In this section, I show you a sampling of several of the most interesting ones.

A list of all the layers in Google Earth can be found in Appendix B.

The Google Earth Community layer

The Google Earth Community layer is a hodgepodge composed of a number of sublayers. Many users of Google Earth participate in the Google Earth Community forums (see Chapter 8), in which they exchange messages with one another. Some of those messages include placemarks that automatically open in Google Earth. The Google Earth Community layer is the same thing but in reverse order. Instead of the messages linking to the placemarks, the placemarks link to the messages. Sublayers here include Sports and Hobbies, Huge and Unique, Nature and Geography, and Travel Information.

To use this layer, follow these steps:

1. **Select Google Earth Community in the Layers pane (see Figure 5-7).**

   This makes the icons in Figure 5-8 appear in the Viewing area.

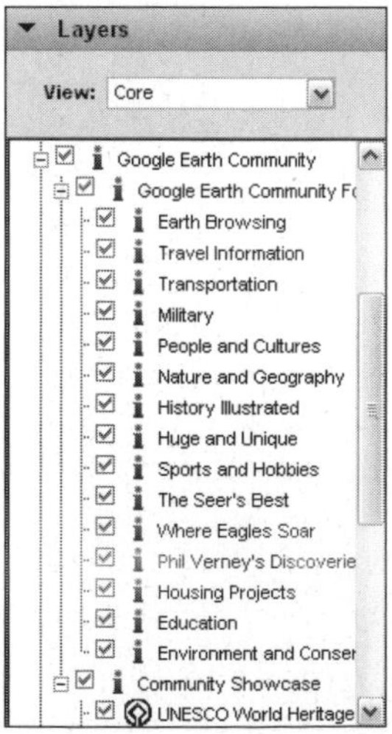

Figure 5-7:
Selecting the Google Earth Community layer.

Figure 5-8:
The Google
Earth
Community
icons
appear.

2. **Place your mouse pointer over one of the icons to see its title (see Figure 5-9).**

Figure 5-9:
Checking
out an
icon's title.

3. Click the icon.

This brings up a text balloon, as shown in Figure 5-10.

The contents of that text balloon might be different from those in this figure, depending upon which icon you chose, but the process is the same.

Figure 5-10:
Clicking
the icon
produces a
text balloon.

4. Click the Click Here for the Post link to read the original message and any replies in the Google Earth Community forums (see Figure 5-11).

Most of these text balloons also have other links you can follow. For example, click the Posted By link for information about the person who posted the message or a link to an outside Web site for additional information.

The Google Earth Community layer can be a bit overwhelming at first. If you simply accept it with every possible sublayer selected (checked), the sheer number of new placemarks that show up onscreen could totally obscure what you're looking at (see Figure 5-12). Again, this depends on the location: New York, for example, has more placemarks than the Gobi desert.

To prevent information overload, I recommend taking a gander at the sublayers and deselecting any that you're not interested in.

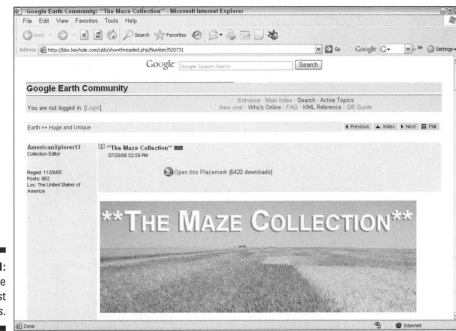

Figure 5-11:
Reading the
original post
and replies.

Figure 5-12:
The Google
Earth
Community
layer
contains
many
sublayers.

Featured Content

The materials in the Featured Content layer come from outside sources, such as *National Geographic* magazine and The Discovery Channel. Although minor variations exist, many of them share the same process that you use for viewing forum messages via the Google Earth Community layer:

1. Click the layer name in the Layers pane.

2. Place your mouse pointer over one of the icons to see its title.

3. Click the icon to bring up the text balloon.

4. Click the links within the text balloon to launch external Web pages.

That's where things can get really different. After you're on the Web and away from Google Earth, there is no standardized user interface to work with. Some of the linked Web pages are fairly static, while others offer a variety of resources ranging from 360-degree panoramic images to film clips and image overlays.

Each external Web site is outside the control of Google Earth and has its own set of procedures to follow. In some cases, for instance, you might need to download QuickTime in order to view online movies. Just remember: When you get there, read the instructions.

National Geographic Magazine layer

When it comes to writing about geography, there's really only one place you can turn — *National Geographic* magazine. This magazine has graced Google Earth with its own special set of layers, including not only links to articles but also live Webcam footage and the *Africa Megaflyover,* a multimedia presentation of a pilot's journey from one tip of the continent to the other. Figure 5-13 shows an example of the wealth of information that's available in this layer.

 If you're not seeing all the Nat Geo stuff, zoom in. Although you can see things like Feature Articles & Photographs and Sights & Sounds icons from way out in space, the Africa Megaflyover is visible only from 2,500 miles (4,000 kilometers) and lower.

UNEP: Atlas of Our Changing Environment layer

The United Nations Environment Programme (UNEP) is right up-front supporting Google Earth and its users. This layer, in addition to providing some interesting information about the ecology, lets you add its image overlays right into Google Earth.

Figure 5-14 shows the UNEP entry for the Florida Everglades ecological region. Near the bottom are two links: Overlay Images on Google Earth and View More Information. The latter is a standard link to another Web site, but the Overlay option works within Google Earth to put the images you're looking at into the Viewing pane (see Figure 5-15). All you have to do is click on it; the rest is automatic.

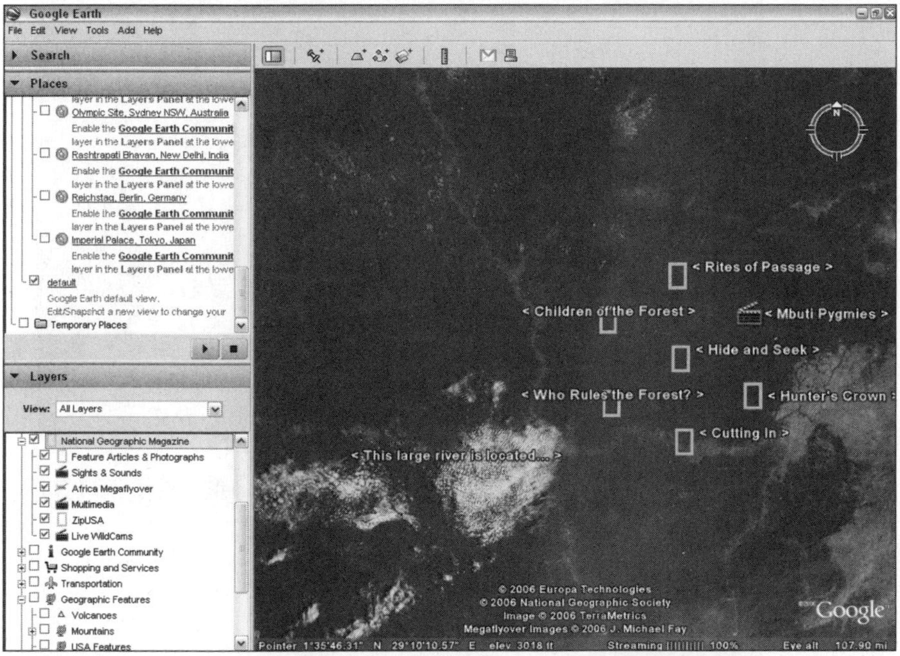

Figure 5-13:
The *National Geographic Magazine* layer is a must-see.

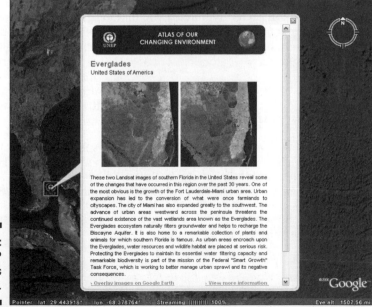

Figure 5-14:
The UNEP Everglades entry.

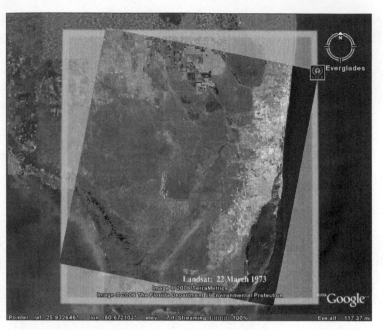

Figure 5-15:
The
Everglades
overlay is
automat-
ically
placed.

Location layers

Several layers can help you find specific locations, ranging from ATMs to churches. The Shopping and Services layer, for example, shows you the locations of groceries, video rentals, drugstores, malls, and much more. The Parks and Recreation Areas layer helps you find everything from the nearest golf course to a quiet spot to take a break (see Figure 5-16). The Community Services layer shows you the location of schools, churches, fire stations, and hospitals, among others.

Boundary layers

Power users will want to check out all the sublayers in the Borders layer. In addition to national borders, you can set options to show state and county borders, coastlines, and the names of nations and islands. As you can see in Figure 5-17, the use of borders can really help you understand exactly what you're looking at.

Figure 5-16:
The Parks/
Recreation
Areas
sublayer
shows you
where the
golf courses
are.

Figure 5-17:
Borders can
enhance
understand-
ing of
locations.

Borders, though, aren't the only kind of boundary line that you can display in Google Earth. Under the US Government layer, you can also scope out everything from postal boundaries to congressional districts. The Community Services layer also includes school district boundaries. For a real-world example of how useful these searching capabilities are, see the upcoming section, "Picking a good place to live."

Geographic/geological layers

A wide variety of geographic and geological layers are available, ranging from volcanoes and earthquake sites to 3-D terrain effects. Here are two of the most striking examples.

Terrain layer

The Terrain layer is one of the most critical in Google Earth. Without it, all you can see of the land is a two-dimensional photograph taken from space. With the Terrain layer, however, you suddenly have all the three-dimensional elevation information that has been gathered all over the planet. Mountains spring to life, and rivers suddenly make more sense as the valleys they run through are carved into the countryside. See the difference the Terrain layer makes in Figure 5-18.

Figure 5-18: The Terrain layer turns the flat image into 3-D.

Water Bodies layer

Selecting the Geographic Features⇨Water Bodies layer adds outline maps of rivers and lakes to your image. The results can be surprising and show that you shouldn't necessarily take the information from just one layer as gospel: In many places, the mapped location of the water and the location shown on the satellite image vary greatly, like the view of the upper Amazon River, as shown in Figure 5-19.

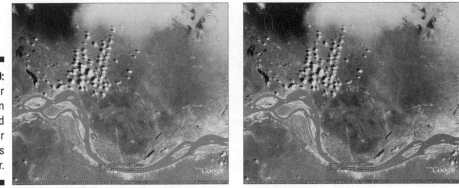

Figure 5-19:
The upper Amazon River and the Water Bodies layer.

There are several reasons for this discrepancy. First of all, the Water Bodies layers (all the layers, actually) are only as good as the data that Google Earth purchases and licenses from various data sources. Like with any other geographic data, the farther you are from major population centers, the sparser and chancier it is. The accuracy of the data sources can vary greatly. And although several mechanisms are in place for users to report data errors, it takes time for them to reach the source, be corrected, updated, and sent back to Google Earth. Then, they wait until there is a large enough group of them to make an update worthwhile. It's imperfect, but it gets a bit better every time.

Also, no matter how carefully maps are geocoded and matched to satellite images, rivers have a way of constantly changing their exact flow. Mark Twain's *Life on the Mississippi* is full of examples of this sort of thing, and the ever-changing nature of rivers is why river pilots — guides who live on a river and keep careful track of its metamorphoses — find ready employment with the captains whose boats travel those rivers.

All it takes is one flood or earthquake to change the course of a river in minutes. The course of the Oxus River in Afghanistan was shifted by an earthquake in ancient times, and the locations of many historically important rivers are mysteries today for a variety of reasons, even the famed Rubicon which Julius Caesar crossed on his way to conquer Rome.

The legend of the Mojave Desert Galleon is another example. It seems a Spanish ship full of conquistadors sailed from the Gulf of Mexico, followed the Rio Grande, and then connected with the rest of the western North American river system. They sailed far north and were never heard from again. An earthquake at that time changed the course of the river they were following, and the ship foundered on dry land as the water disappeared beneath it. Over the centuries, various desert travelers have reported seeing it as the ever-shifting desert sands parted for a time over its grave, but it remains lost to this day.

Transportation layers

Several layers can help you scope out the facts about transportation, whether you need superhighways, railroads, or hiking trails. These layers are as follows:

- ✔ **Transportation:** This layer shows airports, mass transit lines, ferries, and railroads, and tosses in gas stations to boot. There are no options for choosing the type of airport in the Airport category, so in some places, the Transportation layer shows you everything from major international hubs to the local hospital's heliport (see Figure 5-20).

- ✔ **Roads:** The sublayers under Roads allow you to make your own road map based upon your own particular needs. You can select only the major highways, or you can work your way all the way down to mule tracks. In addition to the U.S. road system, Canada and Europe are well covered.

- ✔ **African Roads:** You'll find the info on African roadways under Featured Content⇨Tracks4Africa⇨T4A Roads.

- ✔ **Hiking Trails:** The map of the Great Wide Open is found in the Featured Content⇨US National Parks⇨Trails layer.

Figure 5-20: A view of highways, railroads, and airports can help your travel plans.

Picking a good place to live

A good place to live means different things to different people, of course. For a family with young children, the location of schools might be a priority. For a private pilot, proximity to a small airport could be what tips the balance. Those who prefer mass transit need a subway station or the like nearby. The possibilities are as endless as people are varied, but you can combine the various layers in Google Earth to make the solution to your individual needs show up right on your screen.

As I mention earlier, having too many layers open at the same time can slow the program down, so you will need patience proportional to the number of layers you're viewing at once. The faster your computer and your Internet connection, the better, of course.

Before you get started, give a little thought to what's most important to you. Does your ideal location have to be near a golf course? A church? Perhaps you want to make sure there's a handy gas station around the corner or that a mass transit line goes between there and your office. You might want to consider things like groceries, banks, or particular kinds of restaurants as well. (Do you really want to drive all the way across town for your favorite food?)

While you're at it, consider the things that you *don't* want to live next to. Unless you really like Halloween, for example, you probably wouldn't choose to live too close to a cemetery. Other things are two-edged swords. Although your shopaholic teenager might be thrilled to move in next door to a shopping mall, your elderly parent who wants peace and quiet might have a very different attitude. The same goes for locations such as fire stations and police departments; you have to balance the extra safety or convenience versus the extra noise.

As you think about these things, write them all down so you won't forget anything. When you're ready to check your list out in Google Earth, you'll probably need to activate several different layers. Here's a brief guideline of how to find several things that might be on your list:

- **Community Services layer:** This layer has many items of interest: schools and school districts, places of worship, fire stations, and hospitals.

- **Transportation⇨Transit layer:** If you need access to mass transit, select this layer.

✔ **Boundaries:** When it comes to boundaries, you might need to check several layers. You can find school district boundaries as mentioned in the earlier bullet, or get as detailed as the county boundary level by selecting the Borders layer. You might also want to scroll down to the US Government layer and select the US Congressional Districts, Postal Code Boundaries, and City Boundaries check boxes as well.

✔ **Food:** We all need to eat, but we satisfy this need in different ways. For those who like to dine out formally or chow down on some tender, hot barbecue ribs, the Dining⇨Dining layer (say that five times, fast) is a must. There, you can choose from sublayers including options such as family eateries, pizza parlors, and seafood restaurants (see Figure 5-21). For those who prefer home cooking, check out the Shopping and Services⇨Grocery Stores layer. If you must grab your food on the go, the Convenience Stores layer under Shopping and Services might help, and you'll probably want to select Transportation⇨Gas Stations as well.

✔ **Parks and Recreation Areas layer:** The outdoor or sports enthusiast will want to select at least parts of this layer. In addition to traditional parks, sublayers here include Ski Resorts, Golf, and Sports Venues (major arenas). You might also want to check out Featured Content⇨ US National Parks.

Figure 5-21:
Specifying
a restaurant
is easy.

✔ **US Government layer:** This layer has two other sublayers that are of interest here: Census and Crime Stats. The former provides population and income reports from the 2000 U.S. Census, and the latter does the same for 2000 crime statistics (see Figure 5-22).

Figure 5-22: Census and crime data display in a pop-up.

If both the Census and Crime Stats sublayers are turned on at the same time, their icons might occupy the same space and thus obscure each other. The icon on top is the last one selected in the Layers pane, so you can move the bottom icon to the top simply by clicking its check box twice: once to deselect it, and once to reselect it.

You have to be at a viewing altitude of no more than 40 miles (62 kilometers) to see the Census and Crime Stats icons.

Figure 5-23 shows a neighborhood with several likely layers selected.

What if the things that are important to you just aren't to be found in any of the layers — something exotic like UFO sightings or perhaps something more mundane like statistics on air and water quality? If you'd like to see a new layer in Google Earth, sound off about it in the Google Earth Community. If enough people there seem to like your layer idea, maybe Google will add it.

Speaking of the Google Earth Community, don't forget to activate that layer and then look for any of its icons in the area (see the preceding section). Check out the postings to see whether there's anything you should know in them.

Finally, don't neglect the other tools Google Earth has to offer. Do a search in the Find Businesses tab to locate all sorts of stores, restaurants, and so forth in your target area. And don't forget to use the Directions tab to check out various routes such as between work and home.

Figure 5-23:
Conducting
neighbor-
hood
research.

Chapter 6

Pinning Down Placemarks

· ·

· ·

A *placemark* is to Google Earth what a bookmark is to a Web browser. When you see something interesting while you're wandering the virtual planet and you want to be able to get back there easily, just slap down a placemark, and Google Earth remembers the location for you.

Placemarks are used in Google Earth exactly how pushpins are stuck into physical maps that hang on walls, and that's why its icon looks like one.

Of course, you'll probably end up with more than one placemark as you explore the Earth. And, just like how you probably organize your Web browser's bookmarks in various Favorites folders, you can put placemarks in their own folders as well. Often, people make simple geographic groupings of placemarks — African deserts, North American cities, and so on. There are, however, as many ways to organize Google Earth placemarks as you can imagine.

For example, a sports-involved parent might group the locations of area Little League baseball parks to share with other parents. Or, if you're sick of paying those extra fees for using whatever ATM you can find, why not whip up a map of all the branches of your bank? What if you're in sales? Laying out the locations of this week's upcoming sales calls in Google Earth just might boost your efficiency and save you a bunch of time and trouble on the road. Figure 6-1 shows some possibilities.

Figure 6-1:
Conceptual
groupings
can help
you find
things.

Exploring the Built-in Sightseeing Placemarks

You don't have to wait until you've explored the world to have a few place-marks. Google Earth comes with a ready-to-use selection that includes some great sites like the Eiffel Tower and the Grand Canyon. Here's what you can explore. **Note:** The content is variable, and I expect more to come.

- ✓ **Google Campus:** Google's Mountain View, California site

- ✓ **Grand Canyon:** Arizona's famed landmark

- ✓ **Colorado River View:** Another aspect of the Grand Canyon

- ✓ **Mount Saint Helens:** Washington State's notorious volcano

- ✓ **Chicago River:** Where it meets Lake Michigan

- ✓ **Manhattan Island:** New York's heart

- ✓ **Eiffel Tower and Trocadero:** A triumph of architecture and the gardens of Paris

- ✓ **Nelson's Column:** London's homage to England's naval hero

- ✓ **Red Square:** Moscow's historic district

- ✓ **St. Peter's Basilica:** The Vatican City location of Papal ceremonies

- ✓ **Former Republican Palace:** The palace of Saddam Hussein in Baghdad, Iraq

- ✓ **Union Buildings:** South Africa's governmental center

- ✓ **Forbidden City:** Beijing (Peking), China's palace of the Ming Dynasty

- ✓ **Olympic Site:** Sports complex that hosted the 2000 Summer Olympics in Sydney, Australia

- ✓ **Rashtrapati Bhavan:** The palace of the President of India in New Delhi

- ✓ **Reichstag:** Germany's parliamentary building in Berlin

- ✓ **Imperial Palace:** The home of Japan's emperor in Tokyo

Some of these Sightseeing placemarks include in the description suggestions for an enhanced experience, such as enabling the 3D Building layer for a more impressive skyline or tapping into the vast commentary of the Google Earth Community for the kind of information you don't find in the travel books.

To get familiar with your placemarks, follow these steps:

1. In the Places pane, scroll down to Sightseeing (see Figure 6-2).

If necessary, click the plus sign to expand the list of Sightseeing placemarks so that you can see them. (The plus sign toggles to a minus sign when the list is expanded.)

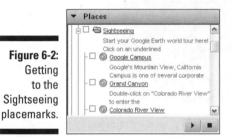

Figure 6-2: Getting to the Sightseeing placemarks.

If your sidebar is turned off so that you can't see the Places pane, you can bring it back by pressing Ctrl+Alt+B.

2. If you can't read the full description in the Places pane, click the placemark (don't double-click).

This opens up a text balloon in which the whole description is shown (see Figure 6-3).

3. To see a placemark, double-click it.

Google Earth automatically flies you to the placemark. During the flight, the text balloon shows the description of the location and remains there after you arrive.

To remove the text balloon from your screen, click anywhere else in the program after you arrive. Or, you can get proactive and click the X in the upper-right corner to close it during flight.

You can optionally click the To Here or From Here links (in the text balloon) if you're looking for travel directions. (See Chapter 7 for more on touring.) The To Here and From Here links work only with placemarks.

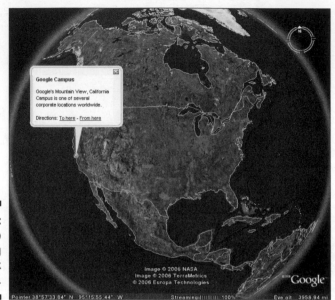

Figure 6-3:
Click to
open long
placemark
descriptions.

X Marks the Spot: Creating and Naming Placemarks

Although the placemarks that come with Google Earth are a great place to start, you're bound to end up making some placemarks of your own. Here are four ways to create a placemark:

- **From the Add menu:** Choose Add⇨Placemark or Add⇨Folder.

- **With a key combination:** The key combination for a new placemark is Ctrl+Shift+P. For a new (placemark) folder, it's Ctrl+Shift+N.

- **The Add Placemark button:** Just click this toolbar button, which looks like a pushpin.

- **Places pane entry:** Right-click an entry in the Places pane, and then choose Add⇨Placemark or Add⇨Folder from the resulting pop-up menu.

Each method takes you to the same place but with minor variations in the journey.

Folders are created the same way as placemarks except that there is no Folder option when you use the toolbar's Add Placemark button.

Most likely, however, you'll be doing things the easiest way — adding placemarks from the toolbar. You handle that by following these steps:

1. **Click the Add Placemark button (the second button from the left — it looks like a pushpin) as shown in Figure 6-4.**

   The placemark goes in the center of the Viewing area, so position your image accordingly before you add a placemark.

2. **In the New Placemark dialog box that opens, enter a name for the item you're creating in the Name text box at the top (see Figure 6-5).**

   The latitude and longitude are already entered for you.

3. **In the Description text area, enter any notes you want to make about the item you're placemarking.**

   The first few words of this description appear under the item in the Places pane. I recommend including some short mention of what the place is and perhaps a note on why you find it interesting; this can be very helpful when you find a forgotten placemark later on and wonder why you made it.

Add Placemark button

Figure 6-4: Make a new placemark.

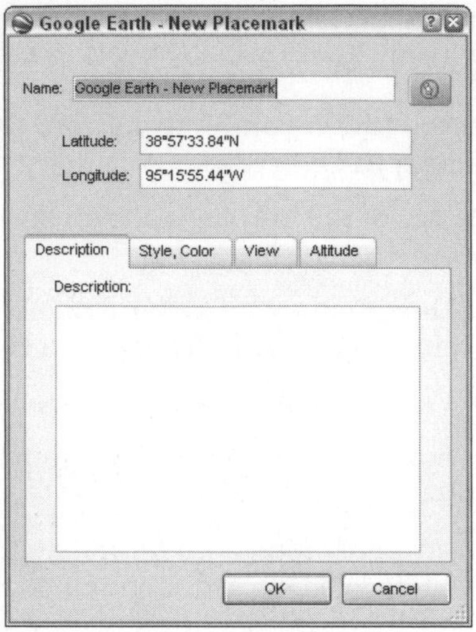

Figure 6-5:
Name your
placemark
here.

4. **If all you want is to quickly create a placemark, give it a name, save it, and click OK.**

   Your new placemark or folder appears in the My Places folder in the Places pane, represented by a pushpin icon (see Figure 6-6).

5. **(Optional) On the other hand, if you want to explore all your options, just leave things here as they are and move on to the next section.**

All your placemarks in the My Places folder load whenever you start Google Earth. The more placemarks you have, the longer it takes to get going. If you want to disable them all at once, just click the My Places folder at the top of the Places pane so that it is deselected.

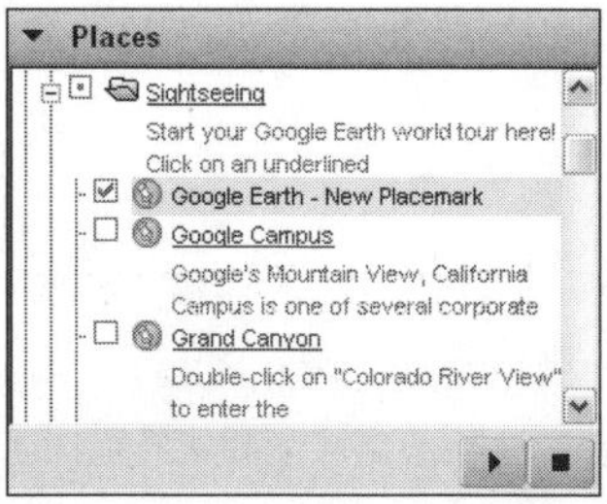

Figure 6-6:
The new
placemark
in the
Places
pane.

Editing Placemarks

After you add a placemark, you can change anything in it from its name to the camera angle used to view it:

1. **Right-click the placemark, either in the Places pane or its icon in the Viewing area.**

2. **Choose Properties from the contextual menu.**

   The Edit Placemark dialog box appears.

   You're off and running.

The following sections discuss each of the tabs present in the Edit Placemark dialog box.

The Edit Placemark dialog box is identical to the New Placemark dialog box described in the preceding section on creating and naming placemarks. Setting the advanced options for either placemarks or folders is identical, the only exception being that folders have only the Description and View tabs.

Customizing styles and colors

Beyond the basic creation and naming of a placemark, you have a variety of options you can set that affect the placemark's appearance. The Style, Color tab (see Figure 6-7) has settings that affect how the placemark displays on the map. The settings are for the color, size, and opacity of either two or three items:

- ✔ **Lines:** This option appears only if you choose the Extend to Ground option on the Altitude tab and put your placemark higher than the ground. (See the section, "Setting the altitude," later in this chapter.) These lines extend from the placemark down to the ground. If you want the lines, select this option; otherwise, deselect it.

- ✔ **Label:** This is the name that you gave the placemark when you created it or when you last edited it.

- ✔ **Icon:** This is the pushpin icon.

Here's how to set the options for each of these:

1. **To set the color for any of these items, click the Color square next to it.**

   The Select Color dialog box appears. (See Figure 6-8.)

2. **Make your color choice by clicking one of the Basic Colors.**

   If none of these basic colors suits you, you can click in the mixing box to the right to interactively create a color. You can also specify a color by manually entering its values in the text boxes below the mixing box. If you want to use this custom color in the future, click the Add to Custom Colors button. Then you can select this color any time by just clicking its square under Custom Colors.

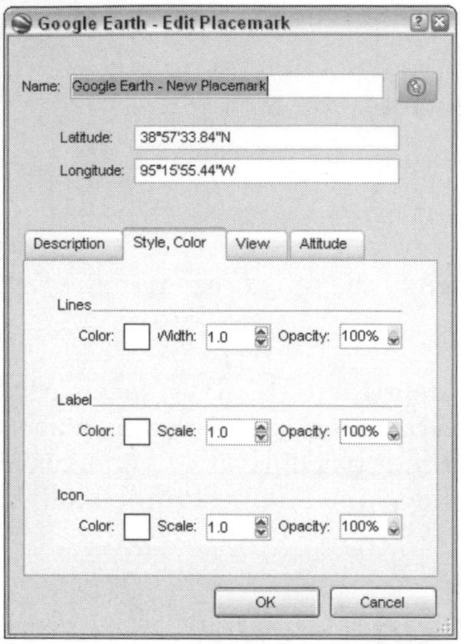

Figure 6-7:
Change
placemark
color, size,
and opacity
here.

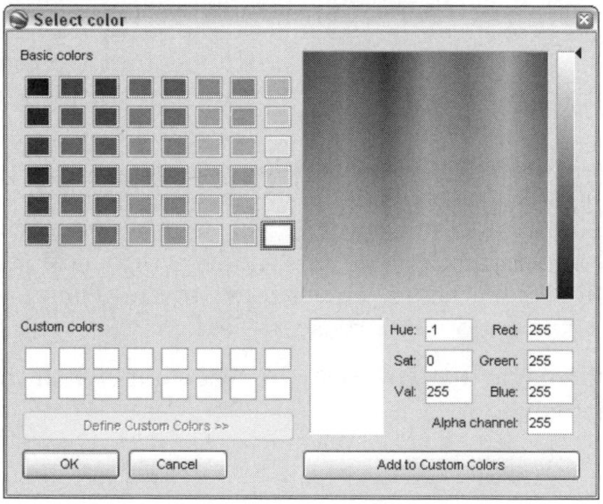

Figure 6-8:
Set
placemark
color here.

3. **Click OK to return to the Style, Color tab.**

4. **Specify either the width of a line or the scale (both height and width at once) of the icon or label by either typing the value into the text box or scrolling the numbers up and down with arrows, as shown in Figure 6-9.**

   Permissible values range from 0.0 to 4.0.

5. **Set *opacity* (the presence or lack of transparency) in exactly the same way you set the width/scale, except that the limits fall between 0% (totally transparent) and 100% (totally opaque).**

6. **The effects of these changes are immediately visible but aren't yet cast in stone. To save them, click OK button; to cancel them, just click Cancel.**

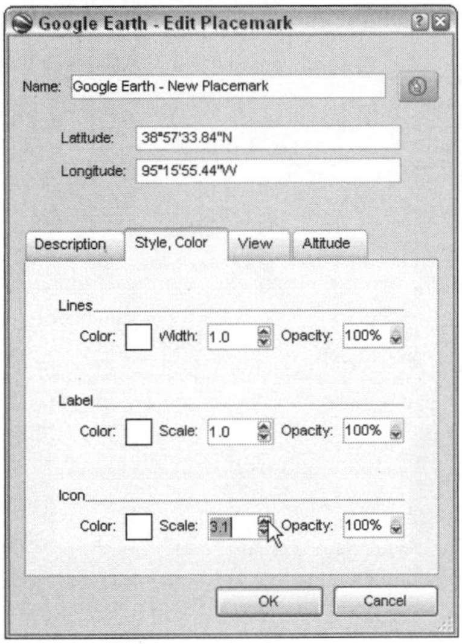

Figure 6-9:
Use the
scroller to
set scale.

Changing the placemark icon

The preceding section shows you how to change the properties of the pushpin icon, but you can also change the icon itself. Google Earth comes with a pretty good selection of icons — golf flags, silverware, and airplanes, for example — but you can go even beyond that and specify your own artwork instead.

There are lots of reasons to use a custom icon instead of the standard push-pin. You might need to signify different kinds of resources; varying ages of archaeological sites; or types of roads, bridges, or other infrastructure items. Maybe you simply want to mark an important intersection with a special sign.

There isn't anything on the Style, Color tab that will help you do this; instead, it's that little button in the upper right of the Edit Placemark dialog box (see Figure 6-10).

Here's how to use it:

1. **Click the Change Icon button.**

   This brings up an options box with lots of icons you can choose from (see Figure 6-11).

2. **If one of these icons is to your liking, click it to choose it. Or, click the word None at the bottom of the icons to have no icon. To use your own image, click the word Custom instead.**

   The new icon immediately appears in place of the pushpin in the Edit Placemark dialog box as well as in the viewing area, as shown in Figure 6-12. If you choose None, no image will show in either place.

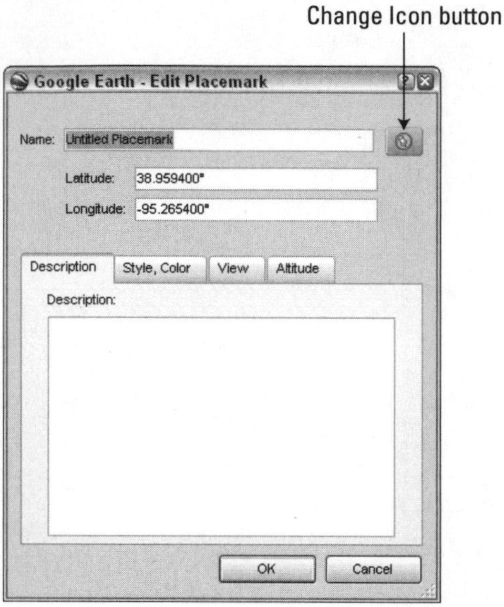

Change Icon button

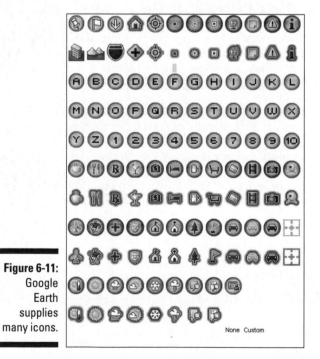

Figure 6-10:
The Change
Icon button.

Figure 6-11:
Google
Earth
supplies
many icons.

The new image becomes the default icon instantly. If you want the traditional pushpin back, you have to reselect it when you create a new placemark.

3. **If you chose Custom in the preceding step, you see the dialog box shown in Figure 6-13. Click Browse to locate your file.**

The image file used for a custom icon must be of a standard type: `.jpg` (or `.jpeg`), `.bmp`, `.tif` (or `.tiff`), `.tga`, `.png`, or `.gif`.

4. **Navigate to the location of the file (see Figure 6-14), click its name, and then click Open.**

This takes you back to the dialog box shown in Figure 6-13.

5. **Click OK to accept the icon file and return to the Edit Placemark dialog box.**

6. **Click OK.**

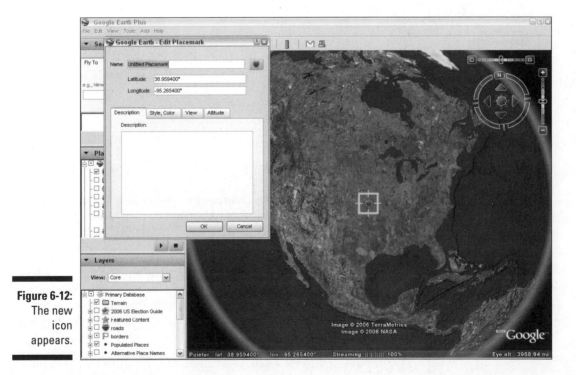

Figure 6-12: The new icon appears.

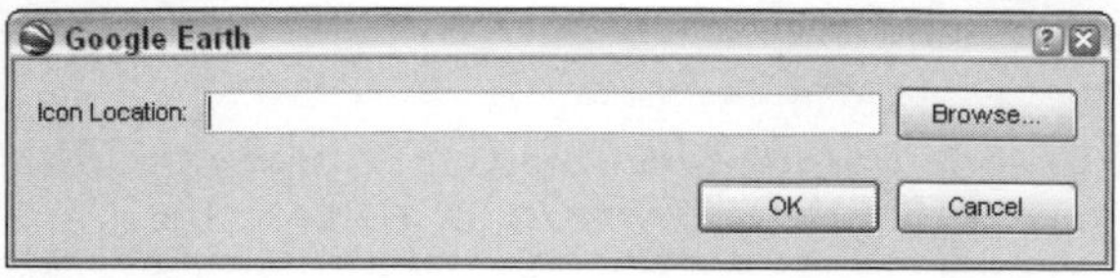

Figure 6-13:
Picking a
custom
placemark
icon file.

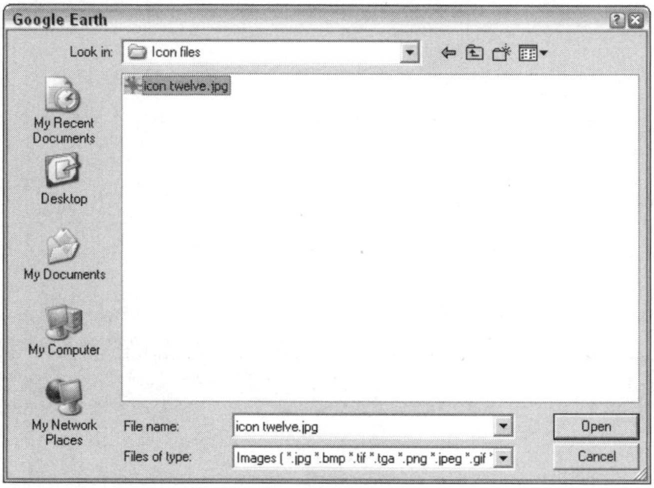

Figure 6-14:
Navigate to
the custom
pushpin file.

Adjusting the view

In the View tab (see Figure 6-15), you can set from what location, angle, and altitude you view a given placemark. It is important to distinguish this from the location and altitude of the placemark itself. The view settings determine how the placemark is shown in Google Earth.

The first option you run into here is the Center in View check box. When you select this, how you work with icons in the Viewing area changes. Normally, if you click and drag an icon, the icon itself moves. With this option selected, however, the icon remains fixed in the center of the screen while you move the Earth behind it.

When setting values on the View tab, you can enter the values by hand, but it is much easier to use the navigation tools to find a viewpoint you like (see Chapter 3), edit the placemark, and click the Snapshot Current View button. This automatically changes all the settings to conform to the ones in the Viewing area. To change back, click the Reset button. Table 6-1 explains the meaning of each setting:

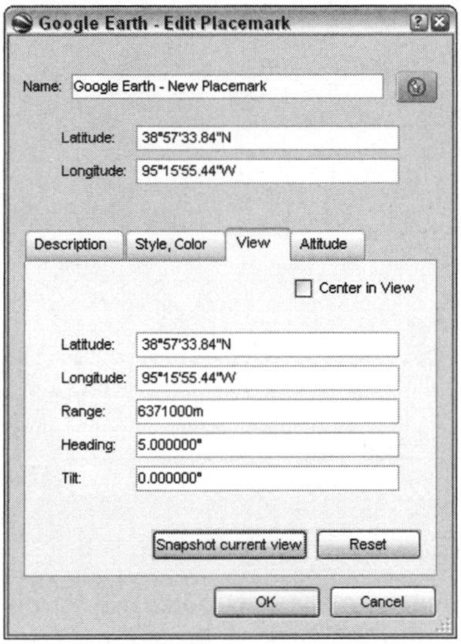

Figure 6-15:
The View
tab sets
options for
looking at
the
placemark.

Table 6-1	View Settings
Setting	**Description**
Latitude	Position north or south of the equator.
Longitude	Position east or west of the Prime Meridian.
Range	Distance from the placemark.
Heading	Direction in which you are facing. (0 is north, 90 is east, 180 is south, and 270 is west.)
Tilt	The angle of view as set by the Tilt controls in the Navigation bar.

Setting the altitude

If you want to create a striking visual display, you can specify the placemark icon's height above the ground via the Altitude tab, as shown in Figure 6-16. You might want to pursue a few other options here.

Altitude here is shown in meters regardless of the Elevation measurement settings you chose in Options, which you can read about in Chapter 4.

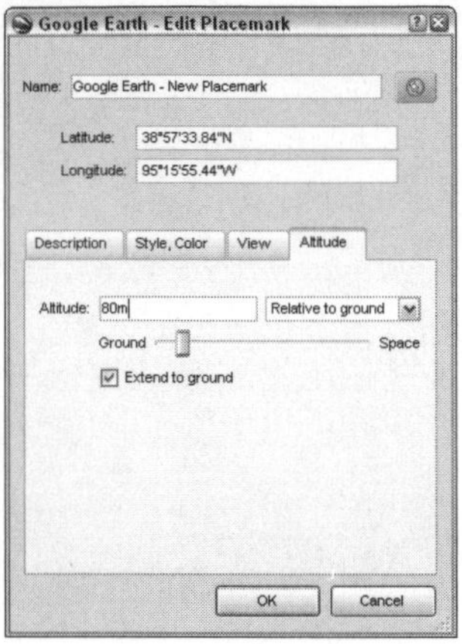

Figure 6-16:
The Altitude
tab
specifies
the icon's
height
above the
ground.

The altitude can be entered manually into the text box, or it can be set by using the Ground/Space slider: Ground is 0 meters high, and Space is 800,000 meters high.

The instant you move the slider from Ground, the Clamped to Ground setting suddenly changes to Relative to Ground. The converse is true as well: If you move the slider all the way back to the left, the setting reverts to Clamped to Ground. You can also click this drop-down list to choose a setting of Absolute. Table 6-2 gives the details of the various choices in this list:

Table 6-2	Altitude Settings
Setting	*Description*
Clamped to Ground	The default altitude method. The item is on the ground at whatever elevation ground level occupies. The altitude setting for this is always 0 (zero) because anything else would be above the ground.
Relative to Ground	This option places the item above the ground level by the amount specified in the Altitude setting.
Absolute	This works the same as Relative to Ground except that the Altitude setting places the item at that height above sea level rather than ground level.

If you choose either the Relative to Ground or the Absolute altitude setting, you get another option (which is grayed out if you're using Clamp to Ground): Extend to Ground. This is useful when you have a placemark hovering over some landmark (see Figure 6-17).

Figure 6-17:
The connecting line helps pinpoint place-marked locations.

The color and width of these lines is set in the Style, Color tab, which I cover in the earlier section, "Customizing styles and colors."

Organizing Placemarks

Say you have the Statue of Liberty as a placemark. Maybe you want to put that placemark in two folders: one for world monuments and another for American history. Doing so is easy; after you create a placemark or a folder, you can copy, paste, or cut it just like you're used to doing with files and folders on your hard drive.

In this section, I take a look at how to manage your placemarks after you add some to your collection.

You can work with placemarks in the Places pane pretty much the same way you do with files on your hard drive. In other words, you can rename, cut, copy, paste, delete them, and so forth. You can also save particular placemarks or even entire folders separately from the main listing.

Saving files

Everything you place in the My Places folder (which is every placemark you make, ultimately) is automatically saved in one big file that loads every time you start Google Earth. There are times — like when you want to share some placemarks with a friend — when you'll want to save just a placemark, or perhaps a folder full of placemarks, as a separate file. To do so, follow these steps:

1. **Right-click the folder or placemark that you want to save.**

2. **From the contextual menu, choose Save As.**

3. **Navigate to the folder on your computer where you want to save the file (see Figure 6-18).**

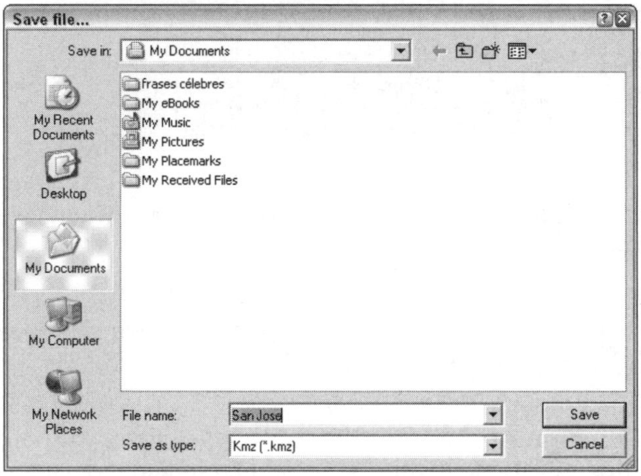

Figure 6-18:
Saving a
placemark.

4. **(Optional) Enter a new name in the File Name text box.**

5. **Click the Save as Type list down arrow and select KML if you don't want to save the file in the default KMZ file format.**

   The two formats both save the same information, but KMZ files are zipped and therefore usually smaller. (See Chapter 10 for more information on the Keyhole Markup Language [KML] used by Google Earth.)

6. **Click Save to finish the job.**

You can save the image in the viewing area, too. To do that, choose File➪ Save➪Save Image from the menu (or just press Ctrl+Alt+S). The shot will be saved in the JPEG graphic format.

To rename a placemark or folder, right-click it, choose Rename from the contextual menu, and have at it.

There is, however, no Move command on the contextual menu. So what do you do if you want to move a placemark from one folder into another one? Or if you need to move a folder into another folder so that it becomes a subfolder of that one? It's easy, and you can do both things in a few different ways. Here's the simplest approach:

1. **Click the placemark or folder that you want to move.**

2. **Hold the left mouse button and drag the item to its new folder.**

3. **Release the mouse button.**

   The placemark or folder shows up in its new location (see Figure 6-19).

Figure 6-19:
Putting a placemark into a new folder.

If you prefer working with menus, you can also move an item this way:

1. **Right-click the placemark or folder that you want to move.**

2. **Choose Cut from the contextual menu.**

   The placemark or folder is removed from the Places pane.

3. **Right-click the folder where you want to relocate the item, as shown in Figure 6-20.**

4. **Select Paste from the contextual menu.**

   The placemark or folder appears in its new location.

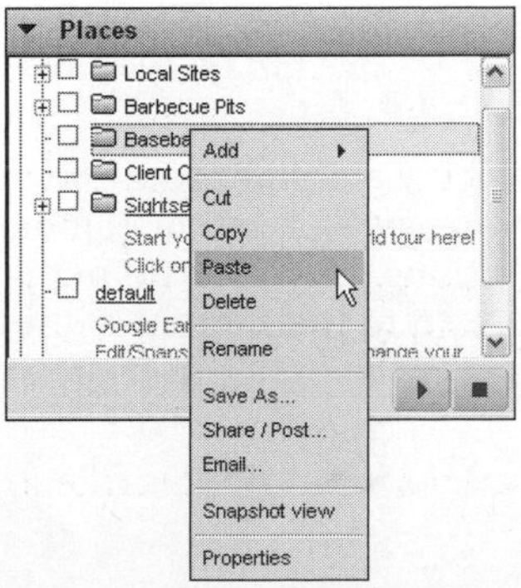

Figure 6-20:
Pasting a placemark.

You could also use key combinations to speed things along. To do this, just click the item you want to work on and press Ctrl+X to cut the item or Ctrl+V to paste it into its new location.

If you want to put the same placemark in two different folders, just use the Copy menu option (or Ctrl+C) in Step 2 above instead of using Cut.

Sorting — by hand!

With everything else that Google Earth has going for it, the lack of a sort feature for placemarks is a bit of a shocker (one that will be fixed soon, probably before you read this). In the meantime, every placemark or folder that you create comes in at the top of the list.

Thus, a new placemark shows up first in whatever folder it's created in, copied to, or moved to via cut and paste. Whatever folder you create shows up first in its parent folder as well, regardless of whether that folder is the main My Places folder or one that you created yourself.

There is nothing above the My Places folder; therefore, you cannot create any folder outside it.

The solution is simple albeit tedious. You use pretty much the same procedure as for moving a placemark into a folder, only you don't drop it on a folder icon. Instead, you just drop it below the point where you want it to go, as shown in Figure 6-21.

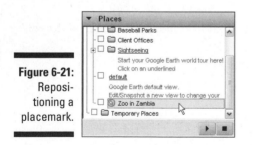

Figure 6-21: Repositioning a placemark.

Suppose you've already got everything nicely alphabetized, and you just added a placemark for something cool you saw — a zoo in Zambia — and there it is, Z, coming before A. There's nothing for you to do but grit your teeth and drag your new placemark on down to the bottom of the list. If you've got a lot of placemarks, make a sandwich first.

Part III
Becoming a Cybertourist

In this part . . .

Chapter 7 shows you how to set up your own *tours,* which are pathways from one place to another. You can let the program create a tour by giving you driving directions between two locations, or you can set up your own custom tour by placing your placemarks in the order you choose.

Chapter 8 introduces you to the Google Earth Community, which is the huge and fast-growing group of users who love to share their adventures with others and are there to help answer your questions.

Chapter 9 shows you how to use external input to enhance your Google Earth experience. You can, for instance, import scanned map images and use them as image overlays on top of the existing satellite imagery. It also shows how to use your GPS (Global Positioning System) device to add custom data to Google Earth. (This feature is available only in the Google Earth Plus or Pro versions.)

Chapter 10 opens up the mysterious world under Google Earth's hood and shows you how to use *KML,* the native markup language of Google Earth files. KML is very similar to HTML, so if you know anything at all about creating Web pages, you'll be modifying your placemarks in no time.

Chapter 7

Going on Tour

Maybe you're planning to hop in the old jalopy and see what there is to see out on the open road. Or it could be that you're not interested in where the roads go at all, but you'd still like to show where several things are in relation to each other for one reason or another.

In Google Earth, *tours* are the solution to these kinds of needs. A tour is an animation of a journey along a series of points, and those points are up to you. That journey might follow a nice smooth highway, or it might soar high over places where even a 4-wheel drive or a mule would have trouble.

Real Roads: Getting Route Info

You can use the search results that Google Earth gives you as the basis for a tour. When you use the Directions tab, for instance, you get not only a series of placemarks but a slightly different way of marking things, called the *Route*. Check it out and see them both in action:

1. **In the Search pane, click the Directions tab.**

2. **Enter a value in the From text box and another in the To text box.**

   For example, you might want to put Chicago in the former and Detroit in the latter, as shown in Figure 7-1.

3. **Click the Begin Search button.**

   The results appear in the Search pane (see Figure 7-2).

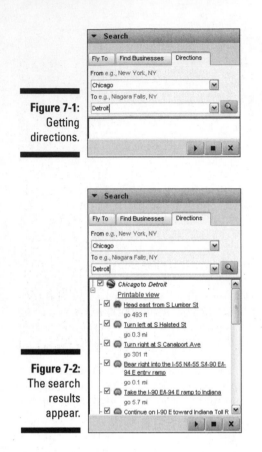

Figure 7-1:
Getting
directions.

Figure 7-2:
The search
results
appear.

After you have something to work with, take a look at a couple of different ways of using it. The results in the Search pane consist of a series of steps (such as turn left here, go this far, turn left again, continue for two miles, and so on). Each step in the process is also a temporary placemark.

These Directions placemarks use an automobile icon that is green for the first step, amber for intermediate steps, and red for the conclusion of the journey.

To play the tour:

1. **Click the top level heading under the Search results.**

2. **Click the Play Tour button (described in the following section).**

    The viewing area flies to each placemark, showing each of them in the order in which they are listed, as shown in Figure 7-3.

Search results are designed to be *ephemeral* in Google Earth; that is, they're automatically deleted whenever you exit the program. If you want to keep the results of a search you have performed, however, it's simple to do. Those temporary placemarks in the Search pane can be moved to the Places pane, where they will be automatically saved when you exit Google Earth instead of being automatically deleted. Here's how:

1. **Choose the item you want to move.**

    • *To move the whole set of directions:* Right-click the direction set's top level (the one that says *wherever* to *wherever*).

    • To move an individual placemark: Right-click it only.

2. **Choose Save to My Places from the pop-up menu (see Figure 7-4).**

    That's all there is to it.

If you don't like using menus, you can also drag and drop items from the Search pane to the Places pane.

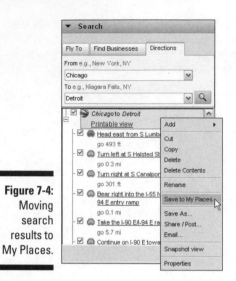

Animating placemarks and routes

In both the Search pane and the Places pane (see Figure 7-5) are two buttons for touring: Play Tour and Stop Tour. The third button in the Search pane, by the way, is for deleting search results and has nothing to do with tours.

Play Tour buttons Delete Search Result button

Figure 7-5:
The Play
Tour and
Stop Tour
buttons are
duplicated.

Stop Tour buttons

Although they serve the same function, each Play Tour button controls only those items within its own pane. This means that you can't select a folder in the Places pane and then click the Search pane's Play Tour button or vice versa. If you do, you get a Tour Failed error message, as shown in Figure 7-6.

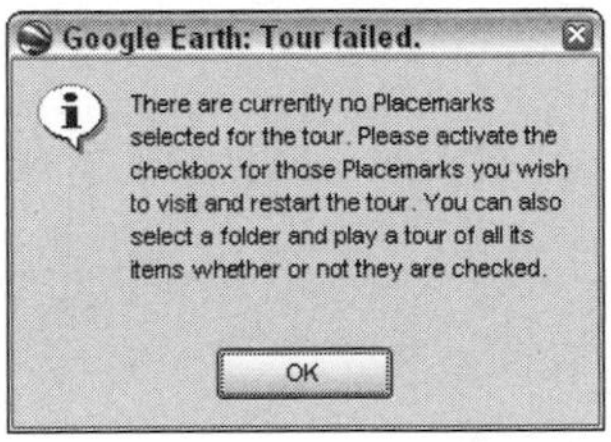

Figure 7-6:
The Tour Failed error box means that you clicked the wrong Play Tour button.

> **Google Earth: Tour failed.**
>
> There are currently no Placemarks selected for the tour. Please activate the checkbox for those Placemarks you wish to visit and restart the tour. You can also select a folder and play a tour of all its items whether or not they are checked.
>
> OK

To solve this, just click OK in the error message box and then click the correct Play Tour button.

This problem, by the way, doesn't exist with the Stop Tour buttons. It doesn't matter which pane your tour started from; click either of the Stop Tour buttons, and the tour will stop. No problems and no error messages.

Clicking the viewing area will stop a tour, also, just like it stops any other motion, such as a fly-to or a zoom.

Touring a path

If you scroll down to the end of the Driving Directions placemarks, just beyond the final automobile icon (the red one), you find one more item — simply called *Route,* as shown in Figure 7-7. Click it and then click the Play Tour button.

Right away, you notice the difference in the way the tour plays. Instead of going to a placemark, pausing there, and then going to the next one and pausing again, the scene just starts at the beginning and keeps moving until it reaches the end. This is because the scene isn't a series of placemarks but rather a *path*.

I discuss paths in Chapter 3.

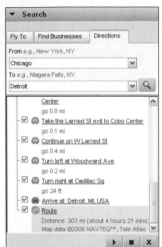

Figure 7-7:
The Route
variation is
another way
to tour.

Although paths that you create in Google Earth are found under the Places
pane, they still act just like the Driving Directions Routes do in the Search pane.
This means — you guessed it — the options you use for Driving Directions are
also the ones that will control how a path-based tour is shown on your screen.
(See the upcoming section, "Driving Directions Tour options.")

Working the Touring Tab

Two sets of options let you control how the different display methods work.
Both are on the Touring tab, which I touch on briefly in Chapter 4. To get
there, choose Tools➪Options from the menu and then click the Touring tab.

This time, play around a bit with the settings to see exactly how they interact
with one another as well as what the strengths and weaknesses of each are.

Feel free to fearlessly fool around with these settings. No matter how far you
get from where you started, you can just click the Reset to Default button to
return everything to its pristine state.

Fly-To/Tour settings

The Fly-To Speed determines how quickly you get from place to place when
you're clicking placemarks in the Places pane or finding locations via the Fly
To or Find Businesses tabs in the Search pane (the Directions tab is dealt
with in the next section). The Tour Speed, on the other hand, sets the pace

at which tours are displayed. Not only can you can set them independently of one another, but there's another nice touch as well: the ability to use a slider and to manually enter precise speeds.

Figure 7-8 shows the Speed slider at its default setting. Drag it to the left for a slower speed and to the right for a faster one. The default speed is 0.119. The minimum is 0.0, and the maximum speed you can have is 5.0. You can, of course, type in a higher number, but Google Earth automatically resets it to 5.0 when you click OK.

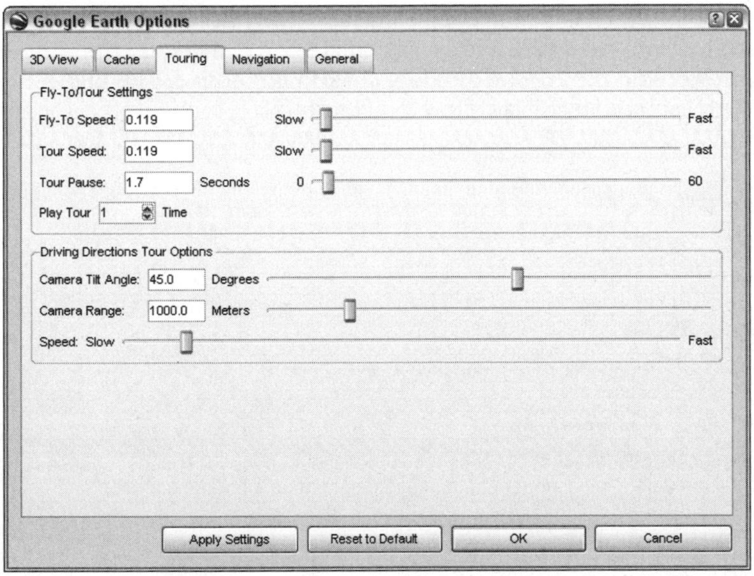

Figure 7-8: Set the Speed slider.

At the maximum Fast setting, there is actually no fly-to experience; rather than watching the intervening land and sea zoom past on the way to your destination, the location simply appears onscreen instantly.

Here, you can also set two other factors affecting the tour: Tour Pause and Play Tour *x* Times. This, by the way, is an example of the careful attention to detail Google lavished on this program. The interface actually changes to say "Time" if you select 1 and "Times" if you choose 2 or more plays.

The Tour Pause value is 1.7 seconds by default, but can range from 0 (no pause at the placemark) to 60 (a one-minute pause). Unfortunately, you cannot set individual pause times for each of the placemarks in a tour; instead, this is a universally applied selection. The number of times to play the tour can range from 1 to 9,999, or you can scroll below 1 to find the Infinite setting.

Driving Directions Tour options

You can use the search results that Google Earth gives you as the basis for a tour. When you use the Directions tab as shown in the opening part of this chapter, for instance, these are the option settings that influence how you see the *Route* part of that tour. They have no effect on a normal placemark-based tour.

The first two settings use the metaphor of a camera hanging in the sky. You get to aim the camera and position it. The Camera Tilt Angle is, by default, 45 degrees, which is a nice compromise halfway between flat on the ground and straight up and down. The lowest angle you can get, by the way, is 0, just as if you were on the ground and looking straight ahead. The highest isn't 90 degrees, but only 80, as shown in Figure 7-9.

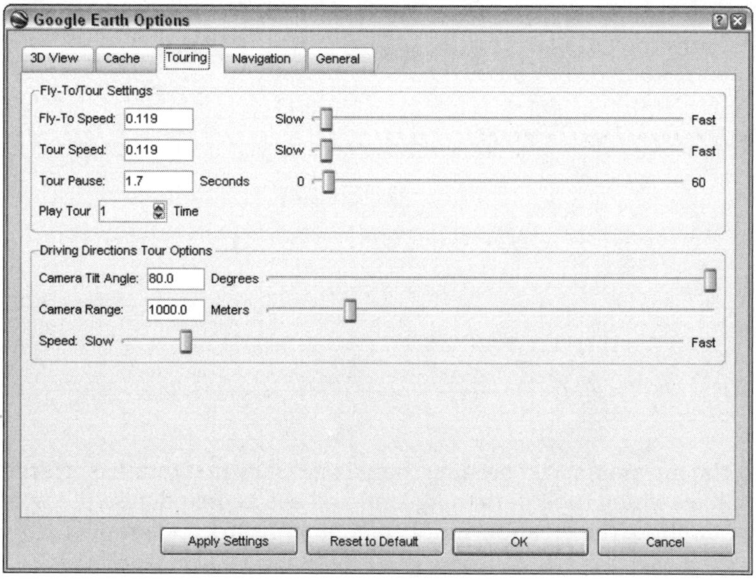

Figure 7-9: The highest Camera Tilt Angle is 80 degrees.

The Camera Range tells Google Earth how far the camera is from the tour it's showing. The farther away, the more area you can see but with less detail, so you might want to experiment with this to find the best balance for your tour's purposes. The default value is 1,000 meters, with the lowest being 150 meters and the highest possible at 5,000 meters.

The Camera Range setting is always in meters regardless of your measurement options settings in Google Earth. In case you're not familiar with the metric system, a *meter* is roughly equivalent to three feet, measuring about 1.1 yards. A kilometer, or 1,000 meters, is about 0.6 miles long and a mile, conversely, is 1.6 kilometers long. Another way to look at it is that five kilometers is roughly three miles.

The Speed slider works just as the others do. To go faster, move to the right; slower is to the left. Again, this slider has no effect on placemark-based tours but only on Routes and paths.

Making Custom Tours

When it comes to touring in Google Earth, you aren't limited to following real roads. You can take off and go anywhere, look at anything from any perspective you want, in whatever order you want.

Planning your tours

You can just slap a bunch of placemarks together, click the Play Tour button, and be done. Technically, that's a tour. But after you're past the basics, put a bit of thought into your tour.

What is the purpose of your tour? What kinds of information are you trying to provide, and to whom? What's the best way to accomplish your goals? There are as many answers to those questions as there are situations that prompt them, of course, and each situation is unique.

In some cases, the lay of the land is automatically your friend. In others, it goes against you. For instance, say you're interested in showing off the natural features of some spot. City or countryside, it's a matter of chance exactly how well those features will show up on satellite photos. You can usually count on the Terrain layer's elevation to provide a good sense of drama in motion during a tour, but the area you're working with might not lend itself to that sort of thing. Kansas and Florida, for instance, just don't have that kind of change in elevation.

Look at things from several angles. Rotate and tilt. Zoom in and out. Get a good feel for all the possibilities as you look for the one that clicks best. After you settle on that, you need to determine the best sequence of placemarks for the tour.

The majority of times, you find some sort of natural order implicit in the tour itself. A simple set of driving directions, for example, has to be used pretty much as is because any change in the order or number of steps could render it useless.

In fact, most tours will follow some sort of geographical basis, even if they aren't representing an actual ground or air journey. For example, if you want to show the wonders of each continent, jumping around at random is pretty chaotic. You wouldn't normally show the Egyptian pyramids, jump next to the Great Wall of China, and then rush back to show the Suez Canal, for instance. Both aesthetically and in terms of program performance, moving in shorter jumps makes more sense.

Constructing the tour

Start off with making a place to put the tour, creating the placemarks for the tour, and then saving the whole thing as a unit. Begin by making a new folder:

1. **In the Places pane, right-click My Places (scroll up if necessary to see My Places).**

2. **Choose Add⇨Folder from the pop-up menus, as shown in Figure 7-10.**

Figure 7-10:
Making a
folder to
contain your
tour.

3. **Type a name in the Name text box (see Figure 7-11), perhaps something like TourOne.**

4. **Enter a description in the Description text box.**

You can use HTML in the description if you want to add italics or even a link to a Web site.

5. **Click OK to finish.**

The folder appears at the top of the My Places folder, as shown in Figure 7-12.

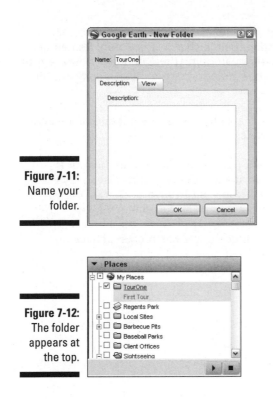

Figure 7-11:
Name your
folder.

Figure 7-12:
The folder
appears at
the top.

Your course of action depends on whether the placemarks you want to add to the tour already exist. If they do, then you simply need to follow one of two procedures to add them to the TourOne folder. You can:

✔ **Drag them from their current locations and drop them into the TourOne folder.** This permanently removes them from their old locations.

✔ **Copy them from their old locations and paste those copies into the TourOne folder.** This leaves the original versions intact.

These procedures are detailed in Chapter 6.

If the placemarks for your tour haven't already been created, you need to go to each location in Google Earth one by one and make a new placemark for each stop on the tour. To make them automatically go into the TourOne folder as you create them, simply click TourOne before you create the new placemarks. If you forget to do that and end up with parts of your tour elsewhere, you can solve that problem by just dragging them into TourOne.

Speaking of dragging and dropping, you can also rearrange the placemarks within the TourOne folder by dragging them into a new position. Remember that they play in top-down order, so repositioning them changes how the tour works. Thus, if you decide to add a new item to the tour, it's an easy matter to slip it into whatever position you want.

You're all set. To play the tour, just click its folder to select it and then click the Play Tour button in the Places pane.

As things stand, the TourOne folder is a part of My Places, and the tour is automatically saved to your hard drive along with everything else in My Places the next time you close Google Earth. If you want to save a separate copy right away, right-click the folder and select Save As from the pop-up menu.

If you want to share your tours with other Google Earth users, check out Chapter 8 to see how it's done.

Chapter 8

Mingling with the Community

As of this writing, about 600,000 people have signed up for membership in the Google Earth Community (the official Web site for users of Google Earth), and more than a thousand join every day, sharing their latest discoveries with one another and helping each other out in countless ways. This number reflects only those users who are active participants in the forums, but you don't have to join if you don't want to. If you'd rather be a "lurker" and just read the members' posts, that's okay. The actual number of people who use Google Earth but haven't signed up for the forum is anyone's guess — but there are more than 100,000,000 unique IPs (Internet computer addresses) using Google Earth, so it's probably safe to say "a lot."

Using the Keyhole Forums

The Google Earth Community on the Web can be reached in two ways. From within Google Earth, you can simply choose Help⇨Google Earth Community from the menu. When you do this, your Web browser automatically opens with the Google Earth Community's forums page already loaded (see Figure 8-1).

If you want to go there without firing up Google Earth first, just start your Web browser and enter the URL as with any other Web site:

```
http://bbs.keyhole.com/ubb/ubbthreads.php/Cat/0
```

Whatever way you get there, you'll notice that you're not at a Google.com Web site but one run by Keyhole.com. Don't be confused: That's the company that originated the program that would later be called Google Earth, and it's also why the internal language of Google Earth is called *KML,* which is short for Keyhole Markup Language (see Chapter 10). The user forums were already in existence at Keyhole.com when Google bought the program, and Google apparently took the wise approach of, "If it ain't broke, don't fix it," choosing to leave the existing forums intact rather than make the users switch over to some new site and learn a whole new way of interacting with one another.

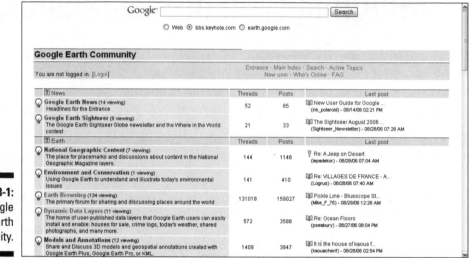

Figure 8-1:
The Google
Earth
Community.

There are also several other points of entry you might want to add to your Web browser's Favorites listing. Some of these are accessible from any Keyhole page by clicking the links on the upper-right side. Here are the URLs of the various Keyhole pages:

✔ **Login**

```
http://bbs.keyhole.com/ubb/login.php
```

The page for registered forum participants to enter their user name and password.

✔ **Forum Threads**

```
http://bbs.keyhole.com/ubb/ubbthreads.php/Cat/0
```

The same page you get from Google Earth's Help menu. (See "Browsing the forums" later in this chapter.)

✔ **Entrance**

```
http://bbs.keyhole.com/entrance.php
```

Contains Google Earth news, a variety of useful links, and a log on for registered participants.

✔ **Main Index**

```
http://bbs.keyhole.com/ubb/categories.php/Cat/0
```

Messages broken down by category, such as Discovery Club and Education.

✔ **Search**

```
http://bbs.keyhole.com/ubb/search.php
```

Search for keywords in forums. (See "Searching the forums" later in this chapter.)

✔ **Active Topics**

```
http://bbs.keyhole.com/ubb/dosearch.php?Cat=0&Forum=
          All_Forums&Words=&daterange=1&newertype=
          d&newerval=1&Limit=25&topic=1&fromsearch=1
```

Listing of all topics that have had an entry within the last 24 hours.

✔ **New User**

```
http://bbs.keyhole.com/ubb/newuser.php
```

Signup page for becoming a member of the Google Earth Community. (See "Joining the Google Earth Community," later in this chapter.)

✔ **Who's Online**

```
http://bbs.keyhole.com/ubb/online.php?Cat=0
```

List of currently active users.

FAQ

```
http://bbs.keyhole.com/ubb/faq.php?Cat=0
```

```
http://bbs.keyhole.com/ubb/postlist.php/Cat/0/Board/SupportFAQ
```

```
http://bbs.keyhole.com/ubb/postlist.php/Cat/0/Board/wisdom
```

Frequently Asked Questions.

Joining the Google Earth Community

Once again, you don't have to officially join the Google Earth Community in order to benefit from it. You can still read the posts, view the images, download the files, and so forth. Still, there are some important things you can't do, like starting a new topic of discussion. If you want to just take a look around, you can skip this section and jump ahead to the next one. However, if you find that you're ready to shed your lurker status and want to become an active participant in the Google Earth Community, it's a simple and painless process:

1. **Open your Web browser and go to the New User page at**
   `http://bbs.keyhole.com/ubb/newuser.php` (see Figure 8-2).

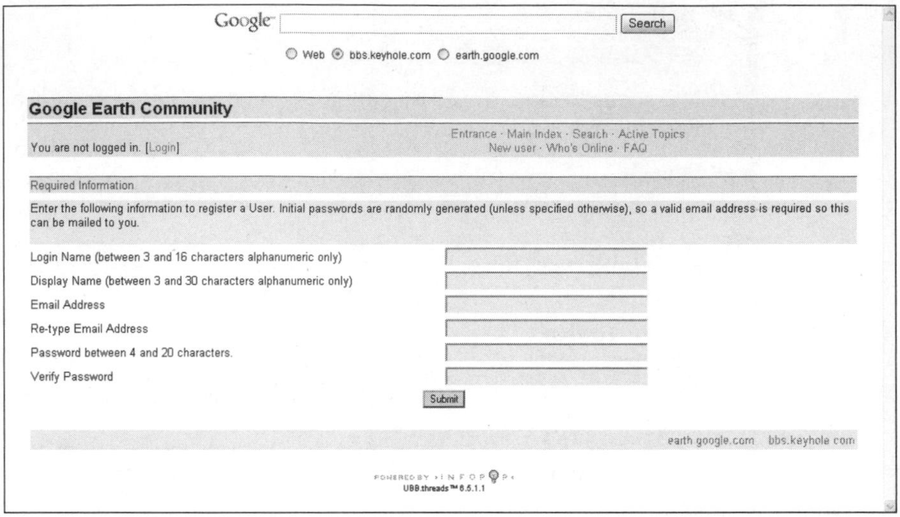

Figure 8-2:
Sign up on
the New
User page.

Alternatively, if you have Google Earth running, you can choose Help⇨ Google Earth Community.

2. **When the Forum Threads page appears, click the New User link at the top right.**

3. **Enter a name in the Login Name text box.**

   This name is what you use as your user name when you log in.

4. **Type another name in the Display Name text box.**

   This name is the one by which the other users in the Google Earth Community know you.

5. **Type your e-mail address in the next two text boxes.**

   You have to enter it twice as an error-checking measure.

6. **Type your password in the final two text boxes.**

7. **Click the Submit button.**

   If there are any problems (such as mismatching e-mail addresses or trying to choose an existing user's login name), you will be asked to correct them and resubmit. Otherwise, you get a page saying that you have registered.

8. **Check your e-mail for a message asking you to confirm your registration. Click the link in that message to confirm your registration.**

   If your e-mail software doesn't support embedded Web links, copy the URL and paste it into the Address bar in your Web browser.

Signing on to the forums

After you register, you're ready to log on. How you log on varies depending upon your point of entry to the Google Earth Community. (See the preceding section for details.) If you get there via the Google Earth Help menu, you need to click the Login link (upper left of the screen), which takes you to another page (see Figure 8-3) where you enter your user name and password. The same is true for the Main Index and every other page except for the Entrance. If you go in via the Entrance, use the logon box at the upper right, where you can enter that information without having to go anywhere else first.

These forums use cookies to manage your sessions, so you need to make sure that your Web browser is set to accept them before you log in.

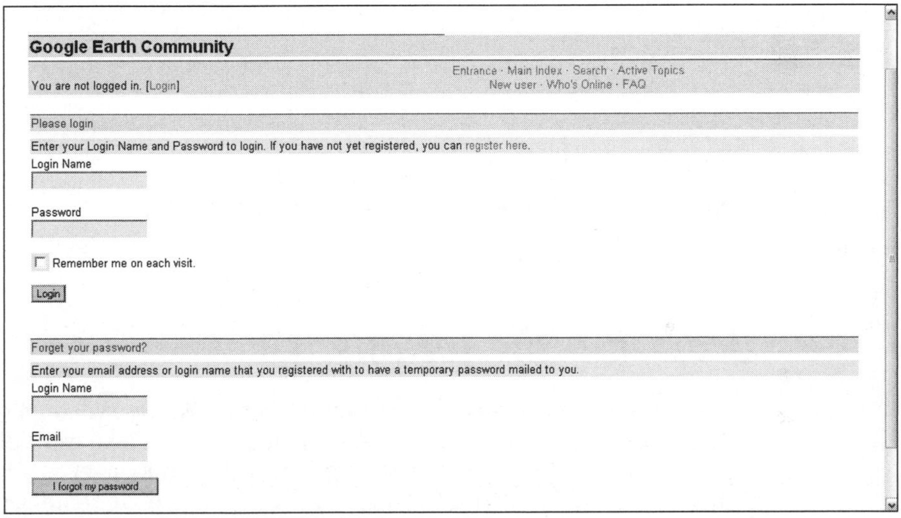

Google Earth Community

Entrance · Main Index · Search · Active Topics
New user · Who's Online · FAQ

You are not logged in. [Login]

Please login

Enter your Login Name and Password to login. If you have not yet registered, you can register here.

Login Name

Password

☐ Remember me on each visit.

[Login]

Forget your password?

Enter your email address or login name that you registered with to have a temporary password mailed to you.

Login Name

Email

[I forgot my password]

Figure 8-3:
The Login
page.

After you enter the appropriate info in the Login Name and Password text boxes, click the Login button. You're in.

If you want to have the site set a cookie on your system so you don't have to type the info in every time you go there, select the Remember Me on Each Visit check box.

If you forgot your password, scroll down and enter your Login Name and e-mail address in the text boxes at the bottom of the page; then click the I Forgot My Password button.

After you log on, you'll find yourself looking at a Web page like the one in Figure 8-4. This is My Home, and you'll notice that there's also a new link along with the standard Keyhole pages — My Home. Whenever you're logged on, that link takes you to your account management page from any other page you might be viewing.

Browsing the forums

There are a variety of ways to get to the forum postings. You can get to them via the Main Index or Search pages, for instance. For these examples, start where Google Earth starts you off: the Forum Threads page, as shown in Figure 8-5, which is the page you reach when you choose Help⇨Google Earth Community from the Google Earth menu.

The main categories are shown on the left side: News, Earth, Other Planets, Discovery Club, Education, and so on. These are the same as the ones on the Main Index page, but they are expanded here to also show their subcategories, thus saving you an extra step (although eating up a bit more screen space). For example, the Education category shows subheadings of Students, Educators, and Tools. To get a look at the messages in those areas, just click the heading.

Also note the links on the right side that take you instantly to the most recently posted message in each forum.

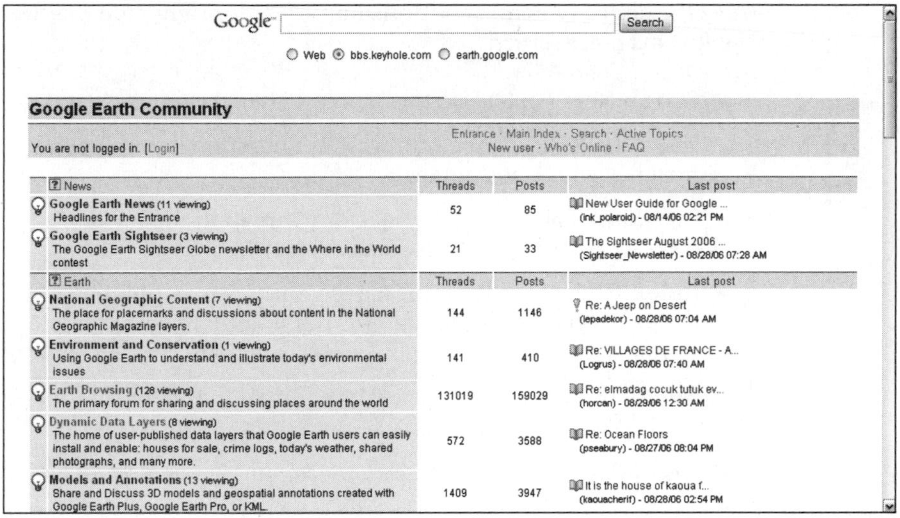

Figure 8-5:
The Forum
Threads
page.

After you select a forum, you'll find yourself looking at a complete list of threads, such as the one shown in Figure 8-6. A *thread* is a series of messages on the same topic. Thus, if you post a new message and someone replies to it, both of those messages are parts of the same thread.

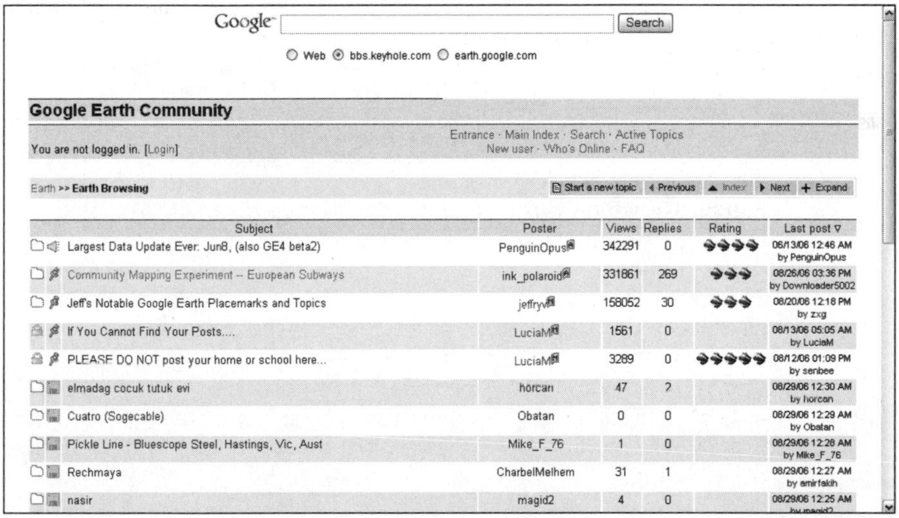

Figure 8-6:
A thread
listing.

Note the series of control buttons on the upper-right side that let you handle the forums more easily:

✔ **Start a New Topic:** Use this to send your own message to the forum.

The Start a New Topic button won't function unless you're a registered member who is logged in.

✔ **Previous:** This takes you back one thread in the forum (unless you are on the first topic in the forum).

✔ **Index:** This has a ToolTip (place your mouse's pointer over the button to see it) that reads Main Index, but it actually takes you to the Forum Threads page.

✔ **Next:** This takes you forward one thread in the forum (unless you are on the last topic in the forum).

✔ **Expand:** This turns the listing of threads or topics into a complete list of every message.

When you do this, the Expand button toggles to the Collapse button (see Figure 8-7). Clicking the Collapse button makes the listing revert to topics only (and the button, of course, goes back to Expand).

Beneath these buttons, each column has a heading showing things like the subject and who posted the original message. If you click those headings, the page is re-sorted. For example, if you click the Subject heading, the subjects show up in reverse alphabetical order; click the same heading again, and they show up in alphabetical order.

Figure 8-7:
Expand the
threads.

Google™ [   ] [Search]

○ Web ⦿ bbs.keyhole.com ○ earth.google.com

Google Earth Community

You are not logged in. [Login]

Entrance · Main Index · Search · Active Topics
New user · Who's Online · FAQ

Earth >> **Earth Browsing**   📄 Start a new topic ◀ Previous ▲ Index ▶ Next ━ Collapse

Subject

📁 Largest Data Update Ever: Jun8, (also GE4 beta2)

📁 Community Mapping Experiment -- European Subways

　📁 Philadelphia, USA transit map
　📁 New York City, USA subway map
　　📁 Example 3D Grand Central map
　📁 Frankfurt /Main, Germany
　　📁 Does New York have a subway map?
　　📁 Metro-map of Istanbul
　　　📁 Re: Metro-map of Istanbul: Metro Map of ANKARA
　　📁 Hram Svete Trojice
　　　📁 Gradska trznica
　　　　📁 Re: Community Mapping Experiment -- European Subways

When you click a thread, you get a page like the one in Figure 8-8. This shows the original post at the top and a listing of all the replies to it (and replies to the replies, because they also form part of the thread). To see them, simply scroll down and click any that interest you.

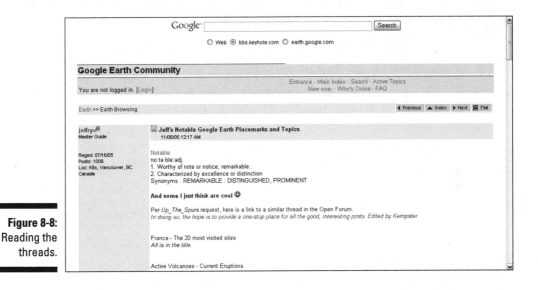

Figure 8-8:
Reading the threads.

The Expand/Collapse button also changes to Flat. If you click it, the listing of the replies at the bottom disappears. Instead of just the list of messages, you get all the messages displayed fully on the same page. The button now reads `Threaded`, and if you click it, the original listing will return.

If you're a registered and logged-on user, you'll see Reply and Quote buttons along with each message you view. They both generate a reply: The first one gives you a blank text area, and the second quotes the message you're responding to, just like in traditional e-mail messages.

Searching the forums

Although browsing through the forums is a fascinating activity, you might prefer to use the search feature instead. It can save you hours of wasted time by focusing your reading to only those messages that have certain keywords in them. It's also a lot less complex than browsing. Here's how it's done:

1. **Go to the Search page (see Figure 8-9).**

   • *If you're already on one of the Google Earth Community's Web pages:* Click the Search link at the upper right to get there.

- *If you're not already on one of the Google Earth Community's Web pages:* Use your Web browser to go to `http://bbs.keyhole.com/ubb/search.php`.

2. **Choose which forum to search in the (you guessed it) Forums to search listing on the left side. Scroll down if necessary to find the one you want.**

   If you want to search everything, leave things at the default All Forums setting. If you want to search more than one forum but not all of them, hold down your Ctrl key as you click the forum names.

3. **Enter the words you want to look for in the Keyword Search Terms text box.**

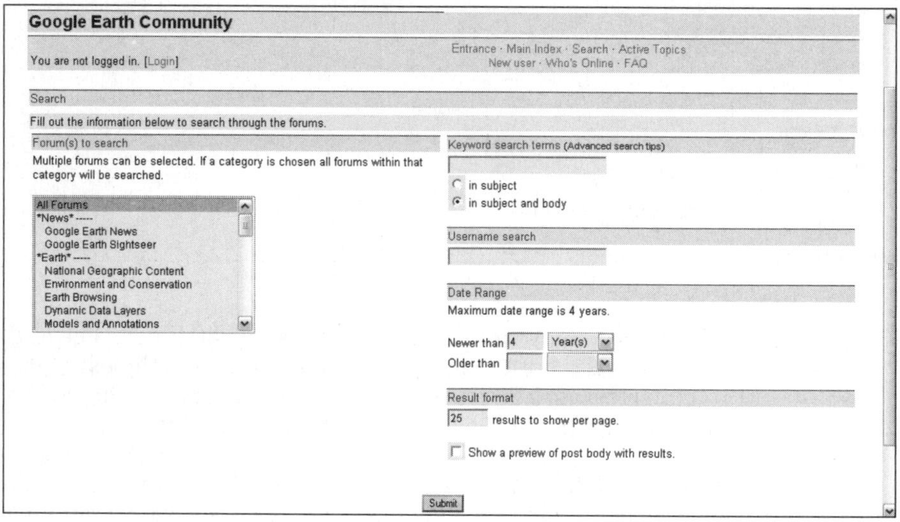

Google Earth Community

You are not logged in. [Login]

Entrance · Main Index · Search · Active Topics
New user · Who's Online · FAQ

Search

Fill out the information below to search through the forums.

Forum(s) to search

Multiple forums can be selected. If a category is chosen all forums within that category will be searched.

> All Forums
> "News" -----
>   Google Earth News
>   Google Earth Sightseer
> "Earth" -----
>   National Geographic Content
>   Environment and Conservation
>   Earth Browsing
>   Dynamic Data Layers
>   Models and Annotations

Keyword search terms (Advanced search tips)

◯ in subject
◉ in subject and body

Username search

Date Range

Maximum date range is 4 years.

Newer than 4 Year(s)
Older than

Result format

25 results to show per page.

☐ Show a preview of post body with results.

Submit

Figure 8-9:
The Keyhole
Search
page.

---

4. **Select where to search:**

   - *To look for those terms only in the titles of messages:* Select the In Subject radio button.

   - *To look for them in both the title and text:* Make sure that the In Subject and Body radio button is selected instead.

5. **To limit the search results to only those messages written by a particular person, enter that name in the Username Search text box.**

   To find every message written by a particular user, skip Step 3 and just enter that name with no search terms.

6. **To limit the results to a particular time frame, enter a number in either the Newer Than or the Older Than text box, and then choose Day(s), Week(s), Month(s), or Year(s) from the drop-down list next to it.**

   For instance, if you want to find a message you saw within the past two weeks, you enter a **2** in the Newer Than text box and then choose Week(s).

7. **In the Result Format text box, type the number of search results you want on each of the results page.**

   The default value is 25, and the maximum is 99.

8. **Select the Show a Preview of Post Body with Results check box to make the results page includes the first line of the message; otherwise, you get only the subject listed.**

9. **Click Submit.**

   The results appear on a Web page like the one in Figure 8-10.

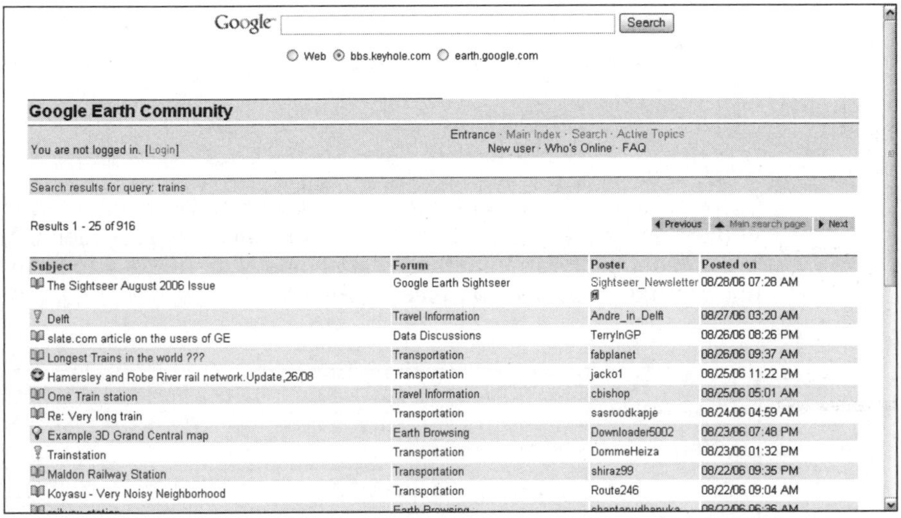

Figure 8-10: A Search results page.

Getting Help

The Google Earth Community itself is a real boon to users of the program. The Help menu within Google Earth itself, however, is another matter. There really isn't much in the way of help available in the program — it's all on the Web.

When you choose Help➪Help Center Website, you get the Web page shown in Figure 8-11, and it's not as helpful as you might need. It's more of a simple FAQ (list of Frequently Asked Questions) mixed in with some info about billing and a few technical details.

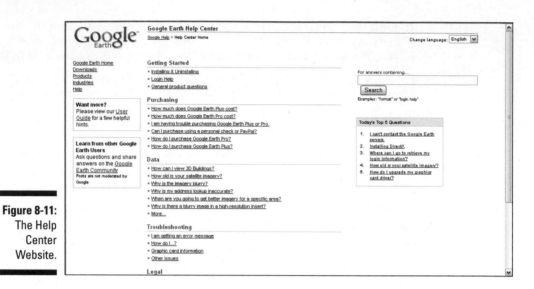

Figure 8-11:
The Help
Center
Website.

You can go there from outside Google Earth by entering the following Web address into your browser:

```
http://earth.google.com/support
```

Where you'll find real help is in the Google Earth User Guide, which is, of course, accessed by choosing Help⇨User Guide from the menu. This is a much fuller exploration of the program and is more likely to have the answers you're looking for (see Figure 8-12).

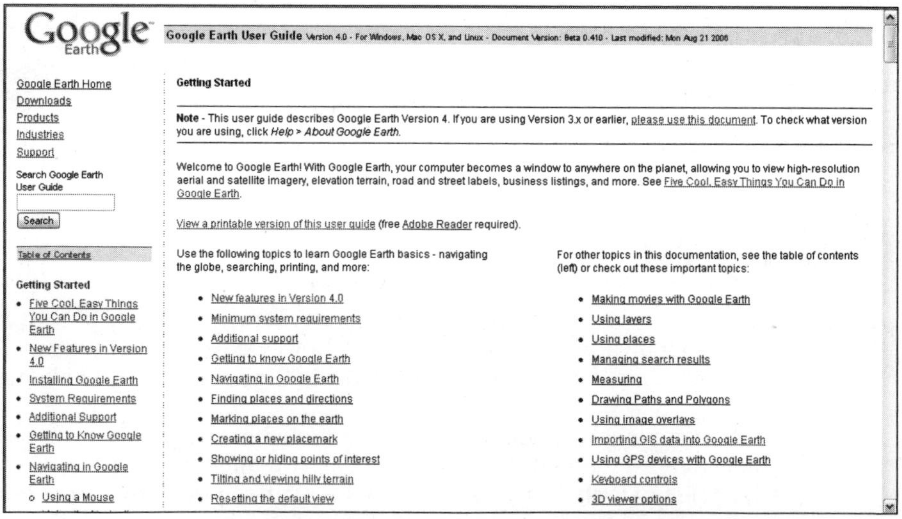

Figure 8-12:
The Google
Earth User
Guide.

You can go there in your Web browser by entering this address:

```
http://earth.google.com/userguide/v4/index.html
```

You can download an Adobe PDF version if you'd rather keep the whole User Guide on your own computer. You can find it at

```
http://earth.google.com/userguide/v4/google_earth_user_guide.pdf
```

If you bought the Google Earth Pro subscription, you also get tech support via phone.

Exploring Outside

Although the official Google Earth Community is quite an impressive site, it's far from the only place supporting Google Earth users or enhancing their experience. There are an ever-increasing number of sites like Google Earth Hacks (see Figure 8-13) that you can enjoy exploring. Although a full survey of Google Earth-related sites would need a whole new book, Table 8-1 gives you a nice start, listing several sites that deal with Google Earth.

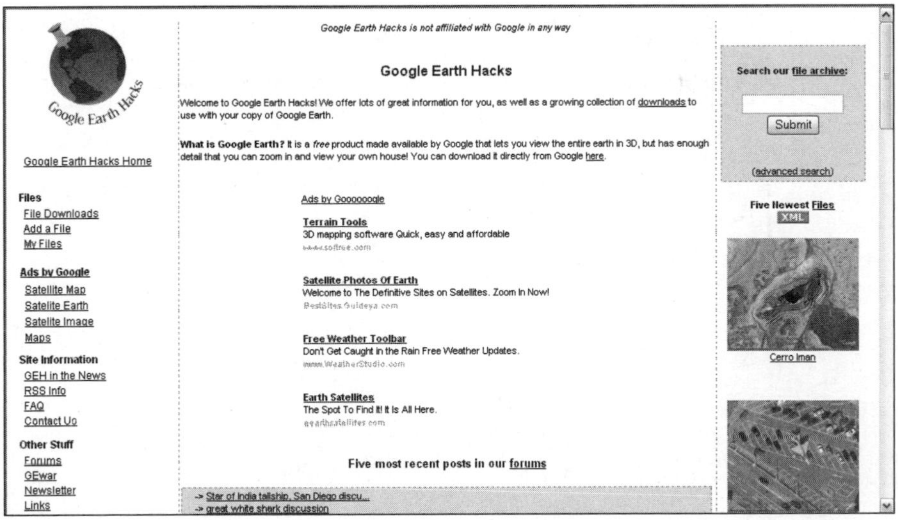

Figure 8-13: Google Earth Hacks is one of many useful third-party sites.

Table 8-1	Unofficial Google Earth Web Sites
Web Page	**Address**
Geocaching.com	www.geocaching.com
Google Earth Blog	www.gearthblog.com
Google Earth Cool Places	www.googleearthcoolplaces.com
Google Earth Explorer	http://explorer.altopix.com
Google Earth Guide Book	http://google-earth.guide-book.co.uk
Google Earth Hacks	www.googleearthhacks.com
Google Earth Lessons Blog	http://gelessons.com/blog/
Google Earth Placemarks	www.earthplacemarks.com
Google Sightseeing	www.googlesightseeing.com
Google Talk Forum	www.googletalkforum.com/google-earth-google-maps
Juicy Geography's Google Earth Page for Teachers	www.juicygeography.co.uk/googleearth.htm
Maphacks	www.gisuser.com/maphacks
Ogle Earth	www.ogleearth.com

Chapter 9

Importing Data and Images

· ·

· ·

Although Google Earth is an awesome combination of both software and data, sometimes you just have to go outside the program to get something you need, such as more detailed demographic data or a historical map. Just for the sake of argument, say you live someplace (or just want to research it) that isn't on the lists of the most desirable real estate on the planet. Well, Google Earth (like everything else) pays the most attention to the squeakiest wheels, and it's a simple fact that your uncle's farm in the boonies just doesn't compete with the heart of Manhattan's high-rent district.

Where do you turn if you need (or just want) something better than Google Earth has to offer in some area? Or what if you have some kind of specialized data that's really important to you but not of much interest to the rest of the world? Don't toss out Google Earth; it can still accommodate your needs.

Adding Custom Data to Google Earth

Say you've got something that you're particularly interested in — something that you just can't find in the current version of Google Earth. Perhaps it's information like annual rainfall patterns in your home county or the incidence of different types of malaria in 19th-century Africa, or maybe you'd like to lay a drawing of a proposed housing development on top of some vacant lots.

Are you lost? Is there nothing you can do? Fortunately, the answer is a resounding, "NO!" Google Earth is fully capable of accommodating your needs. All you've got to do is to tell it where to find the data, and it'll add it. Chapter 14 tells you where to find it, and this chapter tells you how to add it.

Using image overlays

Probably the most common type of data you'll want to add is an *image overlay,* which is just what it sounds like — a picture or drawing that you put on top of the base image in the viewing area. You can easily drop these image files into Google Earth. The drawback to using image overlays is the same as for any other addition you make: They take up some of your computer resources; and, the more you add, the greater the drain.

To help lessen the strain, use the smallest file size that will do the job. Convert a TIFF file to a JPEG, for instance, to save space. Google recommends that you never use a file larger than 2,000 pixels square.

Here's how to add an image overlay:

1. **Navigate in Google Earth to where you want to add the overlay.**

   Make sure that the scene in Google Earth matches as closely as possible the one in the image you're going to lay over it. Depending upon your source image, you might need to zoom in or out, drag the scene around, or adjust the tilt angle, for example.

2. **When you've got the right spot in the Viewing area, click the Add Image icon on the toolbar (see Figure 9-1).**

   Alternatively, you can choose Add⇨Image Overlay from the menu or use the keyboard combination Ctrl+Shift+O.

3. **In the resulting New Image Overlay dialog box (see Figure 9-2), type a name for the overlay into the Name text box.**

4. **Click the Browse button and navigate to the image file you want to open as an overlay (see Figure 9-3).**

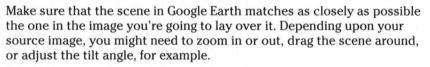

   You can use image files only in the following formats:

File Type	Extension
Bitmap	`.bmp`
GIF	`.gif`
JPEG	`.jpg` or `.jpeg`
PNG	`.png`
Targa	`.tga`
TIFF	`.tif` or `.tiff`

5. **Double-click the name of the desired file, or just click it and then click Open.**

   The image displays in Google Earth, as shown in Figure 9-4.

Add Image icon

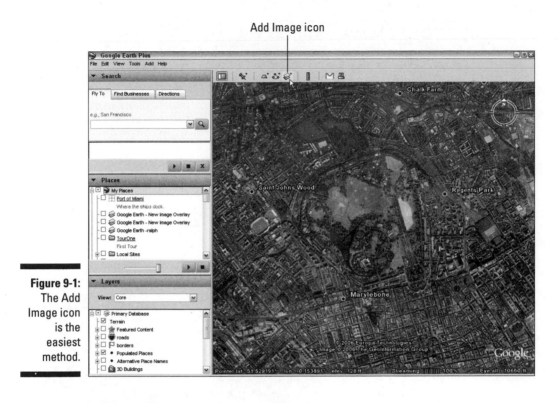

Figure 9-1:
The Add
Image icon
is the
easiest
method.

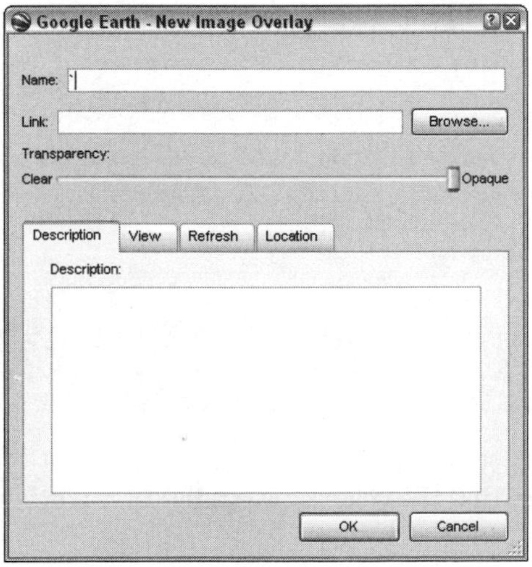

Figure 9-2:
Name your
overlay.

6. **(Optional) Enter a description in the Description text area.**

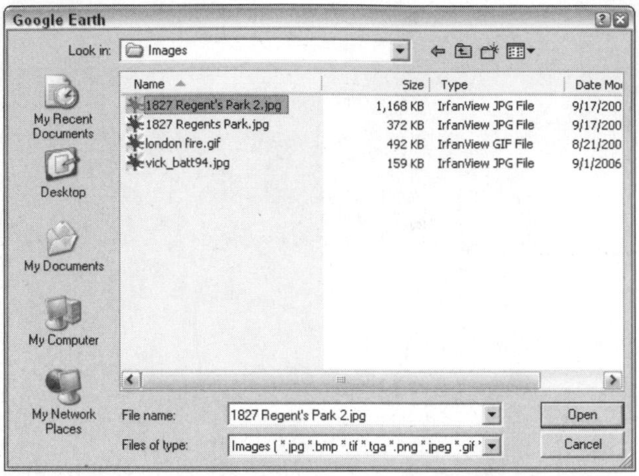

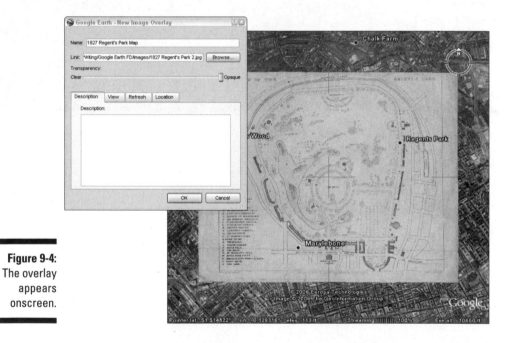

Figure 9-3:
Select the
image file.

Figure 9-4:
The overlay
appears
onscreen.

7. **Click OK to make sure that the overlay is added to the other resources in My Places.**

   If you feel like working without a net, you can go ahead and work with the overlay without saving it first. (See the upcoming section, "Positioning, rotating, and scaling.")

If you take the daring route, skip ahead to the following section. If you play it safe, the image overlay you just added is listed at the top of My Places, but the New Image Overlay dialog box disappears from your screen, and you need to get it back before going on.

   a. Right-click the new overlay listing in My Places.

   b. Choose Properties from the pop-up menu (see Figure 9-5).

This brings up the Edit Image Overlay dialog box, which is identical to the New Image Overlay dialog box.

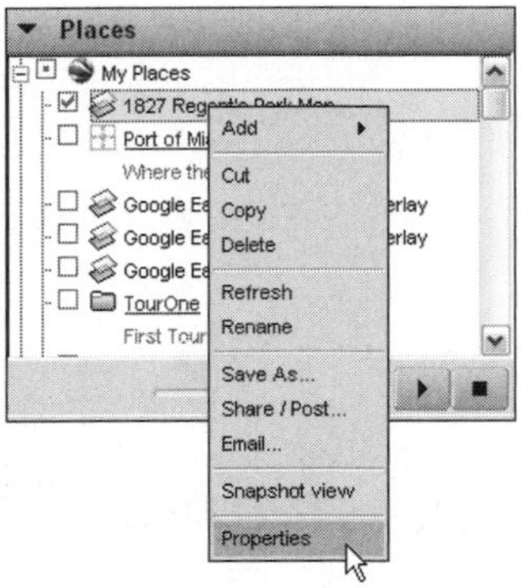

Figure 9-5:
Modifying
properties.

Transparency

Before you can position an image overlay precisely, you need to make the image at least slightly transparent so that you can see what's underneath it. Feel free to vary this setting as needed while you work with the image overlay. You can turn it off when you're done.

Setting the transparency is about as simple as it gets. Just click the Transparency slider and drag it (see Figure 9-6).

Dragging the slider to the left (Clear) increases the transparency; dragging it to the right (Opaque) makes the image overlay increasingly (you guessed it again) opaque. At the far right, you can't see anything behind the image overlay. At the far left, the overlay itself disappears because it becomes completely transparent. It's still there as an object in Google Earth; it's just an invisible one.

The opacity of an image overlay is only in relation to the underlying satellite imagery. Layers like roads and water bodies still appear on top of it, regardless of its transparency setting.

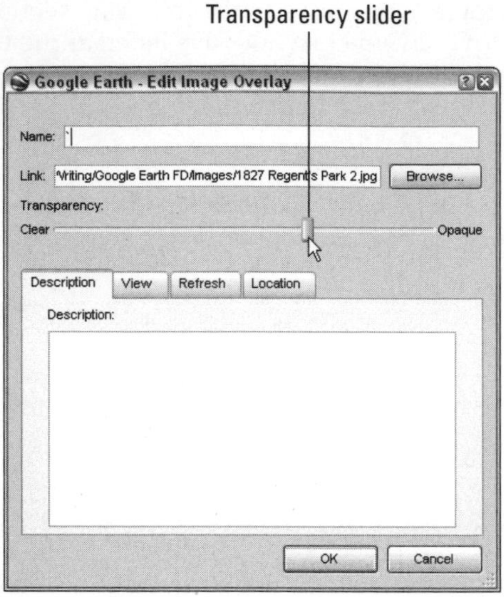

Transparency slider

Figure 9-6:
Working the
Transpar-
ency slider.

Positioning, rotating, and scaling

Odds are pretty good that the image you import won't be an absolutely
perfect fit for the view you've got in Google Earth. That means you have to
monkey with it a bit to get things just the way you want them, like rotating
or scaling the image.

Unless the area you're working with is perfectly flat, make sure that Terrain is
turned on in the Layers pane. That way, the image overlay drapes itself over
the shape of the land and blends in perfectly.

If the New Image Overlay/Edit Image Overlay dialog box is getting in your
way, move it to the side by clicking and dragging the dialog box's title bar.

Assuming that you've got your image overlay loaded approximately where you
want it and you have the Edit Image Overlay dialog box open, here's what you
need to do next, starting by looking at the image overlay. It has a series of
green markings on it (see Figure 9-7). Each of these is a control for positioning
the overlay.

If the green handles don't appear, either the Edit Image Overlay dialog box
isn't open, or the image overlay's transparency is set to Clear.

1. **Move your mouse pointer until it's over the green plus mark in the
   center of the image.**

   When you're in the right spot, the pointer changes from an open hand to
   a pointing index finger.

Green markings

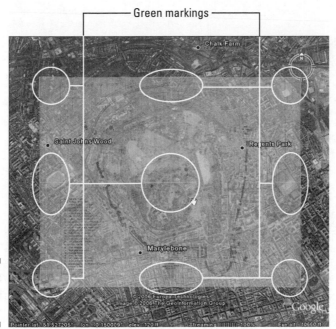

Figure 9-7:
Positioning
the overlay.

2. **Press and hold the mouse to move the pointer.**

   The image follows the movement, allowing you to position it precisely
   where you want it.

3. **Resize the image overlay.**

   • Click one of the green L-shaped markers at the corners of the image
   and drag them to resize the image's height and width simultaneously.

   You probably want to resize the image overlay *proportionally* in most
   cases — that is, you want it to retain the same relationship of height
   and width that it originally had as you stretch and shrink it — so you
   need to hold down your Shift key as you resize it. Otherwise, you end
   up with some distortion of the original image's proportions. When
   you do this, your mouse pointer changes to a quadruple arrow.

   • Click one of the T-shaped markers on the sides to stretch the
   image vertically or horizontally with the double-arrow cursor.

   Figure 9-8 illustrates the image being resized from the right side marker.

   The left side marker is different from the other three side markers — note
   the diamond-shaped control at the end of it. This is the final repositioning
   tool, which you use for rotating the image overlay. Your mouse pointer
   becomes a pointing hand when it's over the rotation tool. Click it; while
   holding down the mouse button, move the pointer up to rotate the image
   overlay clockwise and down to rotate it counterclockwise (see Figure 9-9).

Double-arrow

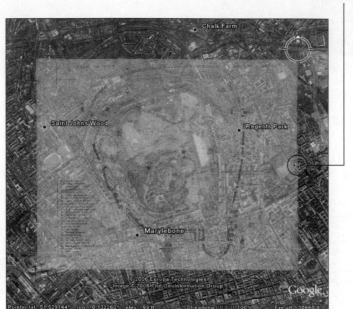

Figure 9-8:
Resizing
from the
right side.

You can use these various resizing/repositioning controls in combination to put the image overlay just where you want it. Typically, you would first resize the image proportionally to make it fit the underlying area, and then rotate it as needed to align the various features in the image overlay with the screen display in Google Earth. You might also need to move one or more of the sides in to make the two images coincide and then perhaps to move the image just a tad in one direction or other until you're finally satisfied that it's a good fit.

Precision location

Although you can do a lot with the tools already covered, visual approaches don't allow you to have really pinpoint control over your image overlay. Google has thought of that, though, and you can set the location with mathematical precision if you have an overlay where you know the exact location of its edges (such as when you're overlaying with an image of a map done by a professional surveyor).

1. **Choose Tools⇨Options.**

2. **On the Location Tab (see Figure 9-10), enter the precise latitudes in the North and South text boxes and the longitudes in the East and West text boxes.**

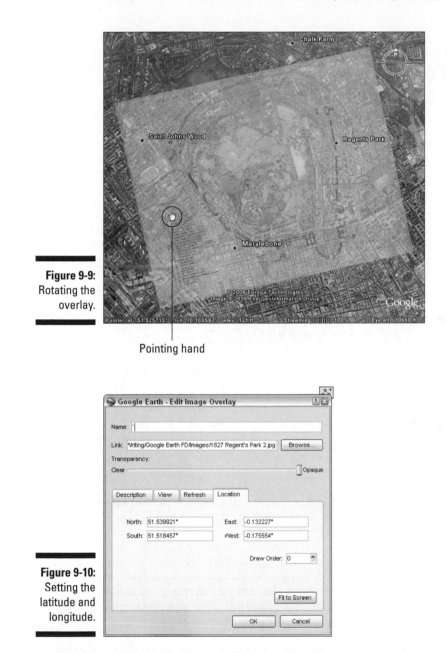

Figure 9-9:
Rotating the
overlay.

Pointing hand

Figure 9-10:
Setting the
latitude and
longitude.

3. **Click OK.**

You're all set; the image overlay will be fit to those exact settings.

Sometimes you get lucky and get your hands on *georeferenced overlays,* which are images that have their corner location data (in latitude and longitude) embedded within the image. This allows Google Earth to read the info and properly place the image: It will automatically size and place a georeferenced overlay. Of the Web sites that perform this service, `www.gpsvisualizer.com/kml_overlay` is a primary one.

Use the Draw Order setting when you have multiple image overlays that all fit into the same place. In most such cases, which one is on top matters, and the Draw Order number determines this. The image overlay with the value of 0 is on the bottom, 1 is on top of it, 2 is on top of that, and so forth.

The bad news is that this feature is active only in the Google Earth Pro version. If you're using the freebie or the Plus version, though, you can still set the draw order. Simply add the bottom overlay first, the second level next, and so on until you're done. The Draw Order number for all of them is officially 0, but they'll still show up in the order you added them.

Importing from GPS Devices

Google Earth is a product of the modern world, after all. As such, it recognizes that people go wandering about the planet with modern gadgetry, like Global Positioning System (GPS) devices.

GPS users rely upon a system of artificial satellites in orbit around the Earth. The radio signals from these satellites, when combined, can tell a GPS receiver exactly where it's located in terms of longitude and latitude as well as exactly how high it is above sea level.

Exactly which GPS devices Google Earth works with is kind of up in the air, but certainly most of them made by the two most popular manufacturers, Garmin and Magellan, have been tested successfully.

Even if you don't own a Garmin or Magellan unit, however, you can probably still use your GPS device with Google Earth. Even if your device won't directly connect with the program, the odds are pretty good that it comes with some kind of software interface that will allow you to save its data as one of the common GPS file types, such as `.loc` or `.gpx`.

After you do that, Google Earth can then simply import that data from your computer without having to ever have been connected to the non-supported GPS device. All you have to do is

1. **Choose File⇨Open.**

2. **In the Open dialog box, as shown in Figure 9-11, choose Gps from the Files of Type drop-down list.**

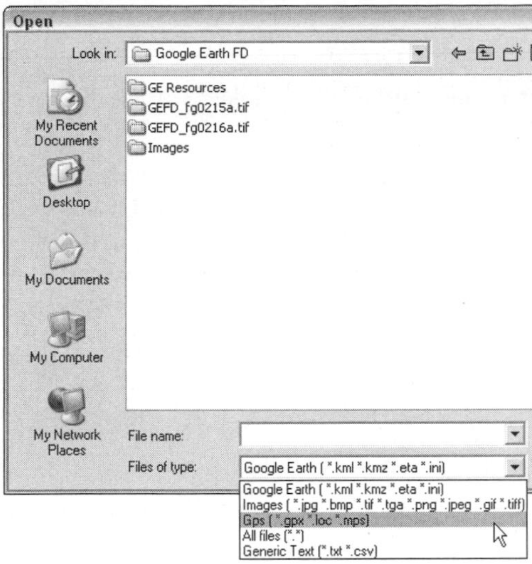

Figure 9-11:
Importing
GPS data.

3. **Navigate to the location of the file you want to import.**

4. **Double-click the name of the desired file (or just click it and then click Open).**

This same technique, with the exception of the type of file chosen in Step 2, is used to open all types of external data files that Google Earth can import.

If you do have a Garmin or Magellan GPS device, you can transmit its data directly into Google Earth without having to save it first:

1. **Connect your GPS device to your computer with the cable that came with it for this purpose.**

2. **Turn on the GPS device.**

3. **In Google Earth, choose Tools⇨GPS.**

4. **In the resulting GPS dialog box, as shown in Figure 9-12, select either Garmin or Magellan in the GPS Manufacturer panel.**

5. **In the Import panel, enable the check box(es) to select what points to import.**

6. **In the bottom portion of the dialog box are three more check boxes used for setting the way the imported information is displayed in Google Earth. They're pretty self-explanatory:**

- *Draw Icons at Track and Route Points:* Adds a graphical symbol at each imported point.

- *Draw Lines for Tracks and Routes:* Makes Google Earth connect all the dots.

- *Adjust Altitudes to Ground Height:* Ignores any altitude information that was imported and makes the points (and connecting lines, if you chose that option) hug the terrain. You might, for instance, have data that you recorded while flying over the terrain but want to show the path of the flight as a line on the ground.

Figure 9-12:
Choosing the manu-
facturer.

> GPS
>
> Select the manufacturer of your GPS device, turn the device on, and press OK.
>
> GPS Manufacturer
> ◉ Garmin
> ○ Magellan
>
> Import
> ☑ Waypoints
> ☑ Tracks
> ☑ Routes
>
> ☐ Draw icons at track and route points
> ☑ Draw lines for tracks and routes
> ☑ Adjust altitudes to ground height
>
> OK   Cancel

7. **Click OK.**

   Google Earth first checks for a USB cable connecting to the GPS device; if it doesn't find one, it cycles through all your serial ports looking for the device's connection.

   If you're properly connected and Google Earth still can't find your GPS device, make sure that the software drivers for it are installed. Typically, this means that you need to install the software that came with your GPS device.

8. **After the GPS device is found, Google Earth begins downloading the data from it.**

   When it's finished, you'll see the dialog box shown in Figure 9-13.

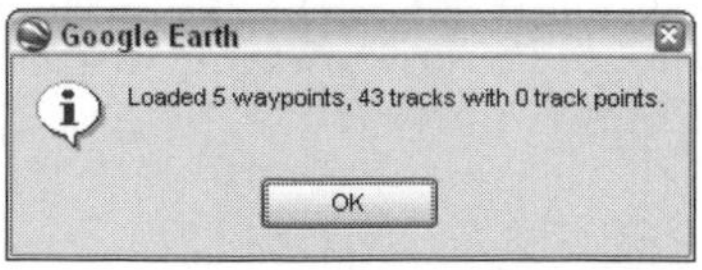

Figure 9-13:
Finishing the process.

> Google Earth
>
> ⓘ Loaded 5 waypoints, 43 tracks with 0 track points.
>
> OK

9. **Click OK to finish.**

Successfully downloaded information shows up at the bottom of the Places pane under Temporary Places, with a default name of Garmin (or Magellan) GPS Device (see Figure 9-14). It works just like any other set of placemarks.

Figure 9-14:
The GPS data is shown under Temporary Places.

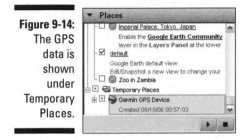

Chapter 10

KML: It's Sorta Like HTML

Among the ever-expanding alphabet soup of markup languages — HTML, XML, and so forth — there's a newcomer you're going to want to know. It's KML, short for the Keyhole Markup Language, and it's at the heart of Google Earth.

Markup languages like HTML (HyperText Markup Language, used to make Web pages) have a different intent from programming languages. Although these definitions are a bit arbitrary, markup is used only to define how things are shown on a computer screen. (Programming is used to define processes that take place in a computer.) You don't have to worry about programming Google Earth, but you can do a lot about defining the view it gives you.

Keyhole.com, by the way, was the company that originated the program that would later be called Google Earth, and it's also why the internal language of Google Earth is called Keyhole Markup Language — KML.

Creating and Saving KML Files

Fortunately, working with KML doesn't require any kind of specialized software. You can use any kind of text editor, even Notepad, which comes with Windows. However, if you're really serious about it, you might want to try HomeSite+ for Windows or Barebones' BBEdit for the Mac.

Do not use a word processor as your text editor. Word processing programs, such as Microsoft Word, add their own formatting to the saved file, and this interferes with your KML code.

The process is about as simple as it gets. I'll use Windows Notepad in the following example:

1. **Open your text editor.**

2. **Type in the KML code (that you'll work with later in this chapter), as shown in Figure 10-1.**

Figure 10-1:
A plain text editor like Notepad is all you need to write KML.

```
Untitled - Notepad
File  Edit  Format  View  Help
<Placemark>

    <name>Hollywood Bowl with Snippet</name>

    <Snippet>A natural formation with seats added</Snippet>

    <visibility>0</visibility>

    <LookAt>
        <longitude>-118.3390383230917</longitude>
        <latitude>34.11230602728949</latitude>
        <altitude>0</altitude>
        <range>272.1817526117454</range>
        <tilt>1.4859072944678418e-010</tilt>
        <heading>-0.004589114879398169</heading>
    </LookAt>

    <Point>
        <coordinates>-118.3390383230917,34.11230602728949,0</coordinates>
    </Point>

</Placemark>
```

3. **When you're finished, choose File⌐Save from the menu (or use the Ctrl+S key combination) and then navigate to the folder where you want to save the file.**

4. **In the File Name text box, type the filename *including* the .kml extension, as shown in Figure 10-2.**

That last part is critical. If you don't add the extension yourself, Notepad automatically adds a .txt extension instead.

5. **Click Save.**

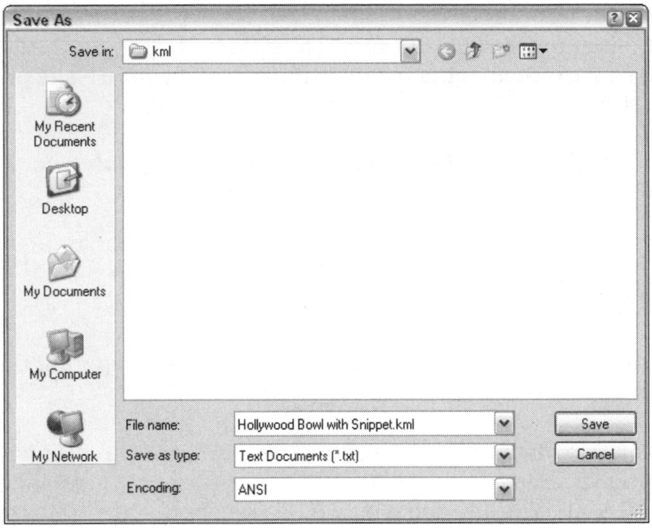

Figure 10-2:
Saving the
KML file.

Mastering the Syntax

If you've ever worked with any kind of computer code, even if it's just HTML, you'll find KML familiar territory. It's very much like HTML, in fact, so don't let the idea of getting under the hood and playing with Google Earth intimidate you.

Nonetheless, if you try to use a malformed KML file with Google Earth, all you'll get is an error message for your trouble, so it's worth paying a bit of attention to the details before you get started.

Tags and elements

KML works like other markup languages, using tags to specify which elements to use. An *element* is one of the basic building blocks of the language, and a *tag* is the manner in which that element is represented in a bit of KML code.

For example, the `Placemark` element is represented by the `<Placemark>` tag. Tags are always delineated by these double brackets, and every element requires both a beginning and an ending tag. Thus, a `Placemark` element is always represented like this example:

```
<Placemark>placemark data</Placemark>
```

Don't worry for now about the `placemark data` part — that's just a place-holder for either an *attribute* of the `<Placemark>` tag or another nested element. I cover attributes in the next section and the whole issue of nesting elements later on.

You'll notice that the start tag and the end tag differ in only one way — the end tag includes a slash before the element's name.

Attributes

Elements tell Google Earth what something is, but *attributes* tell the program what to display.

Say, for instance, that you have two different addresses to deal with. You would — you've already guessed this, I'm sure — use two instances of the `address` element. Within each, you would specify the attributes — the actual street address, for example.

If you wanted to show the addresses of the White House in Washington and of Google in California, the tags and attributes would read as follows:

```
<address>1600 Pennsylvania Avenue, Washington, DC</address>
<address>1600 Amphitheater Pkwy, Mountain View, CA</address>
```

Despite the similarity of the first part of the addresses, these two locations are on opposite sides of the continent, and their differences are specified in the simple and standardized information contained in the tags' attributes. (See the section on the `Address` tag later in this chapter.)

Containers

Everything in KML, just as in HTML, is involved in what is technically known as a *container* relationship. Attributes, for example, must be contained within the elements themselves. Moving outward from there, one element can be contained by another element, which can be contained by another, and so forth. To phrase it another way, everything in a KML file must be *nested* within something else.

This containment is sometimes referred to as a *parent/child* relationship. Any element that contains another element is the *parent,* and the elements that it contains are the *child* elements.

If you violate this parent/child relationship, your KML files won't work properly. Failure to properly contain elements is perhaps the single most important factor that generates annoying errors when you try to import your homemade KML files into Google Earth.

To build upon the earlier examples, a `Placemark` element would be the parent of an `address` element, which would, in turn, be the child of the `Placemark` element. It is customary to indent the child element in the code listing in order to distinguish it from its parent element, like this:

```
<Placemark>
    <address>1600 Pennsylvania Avenue, Washington, DC</address>
</Placemark>
```

Capitalization matters in KML. If you try for a `<Placemark>` tag or an `<address>` tag, things won't work.

Of course, this containment can't go on forever; after all, there has to be something at the top that contains everything else, and there is. The top-level element in this hierarchical relationship is the *root element,* and only four root elements are possible in KML.

The root element

When you create a KML file, the first thing you need to do is to specify its root element. If you're dealing with a simple situation like a single location you want to show, you would likely use the `Placemark` element, but three other possibilities exist, as I mention in the preceding section.

The other three are `KML`, `Document`, and `Folder`. So, how do you choose which root element to use in a particular situation? It depends on what child elements it needs to contain. Here's the hierarchy: `KML`, `Document`, `Folder`, `Placemark`. If you're putting several placemarks together, you want to have a folder as the root. Several folders should, in turn, have a document as their root, and `KML` is the granddaddy that can contain all the others. You'll see how it all works as the example code in this chapter develops.

Comments

Even when you're working with short KML files, I recommend annotating what you're doing with *comments,* which are short pieces of text you type right into the source code for your file. You might know every detail of the file and understand exactly why you did everything you did — today, that is. But what about when you look at that file a year from now? Trust me, by then, it'll just be another piece of a lost past. Comments are also a great help if you're planning to send the file to somebody else, and you want to help him understand what he's looking at.

Thankfully, you don't have to keep a written journal of your efforts in order to keep a reminder. KML comments come to your rescue. Two special symbols work much like the start and end tags of elements: A comment opens with `<!--` and ends with `-->`. Here's how it looks as a line of code:

```
<!-- Comment goes here -->
```

Of course, you don't type the `Comment goes here` part but replace that with whatever it is you want to say.

Comments not only serve as memory joggers for you, but they can help you to find a file on your computer — just search for files containing the words you used in the comments.

The Most Useful KML Tags

This section starts with simple tags and their attributes. Each builds upon the other to show how to do more complex things.

Placemarks

Try one of the most familiar features of Google Earth — the good old placemark. The start and end tags for it are

```
<Placemark> </Placemark>
```

When you send a placemark to a friend, you're really sending her a short KML file, and there's a lot of information that can be included between those two tags. Here's a bare bones version of the KML code for a simple placemark:

```
<Placemark>

   <name>Hollywood Bowl</name>

   <description>The Los Angeles Philharmonic's amphitheater</description>

   <visibility>0</visibility>

   <LookAt>
      <longitude>-118.3390383230917</longitude>
      <latitude>34.11230602728949</latitude>
      <altitude>0</altitude>
```

```
        <range>272.1817526117454</range>
        <tilt>1.485907294467841e-010</tilt>
        <heading>-0.004589114879398169</heading>
    </LookAt>

    <Point>
        <coordinates>-118.3390383230917,34.11230602728949,0</coordinates>
    </Point>

</Placemark>
```

Figure 10-3 shows this placemark in Google Earth:

The name and description elements

The `name` element corresponds to the Name text box when you're creating or editing a placemark (see Figure 10-4). Likewise, the `description` element and the Description text area contain the same information. In fact, this part of the Google Earth interface is designed to gather the data to place in the KML code for the placemark; when you type anything here or alter any settings on any of these tabs, the result is ultimately written to KML.

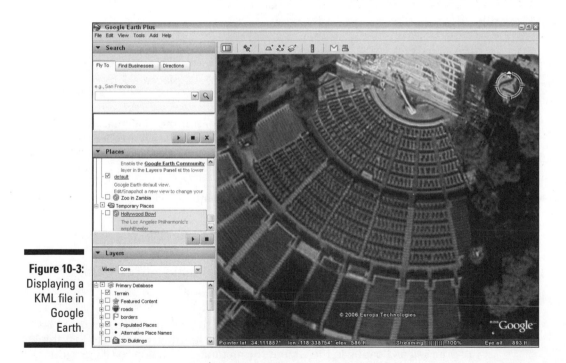

Figure 10-3:
Displaying a KML file in Google Earth.

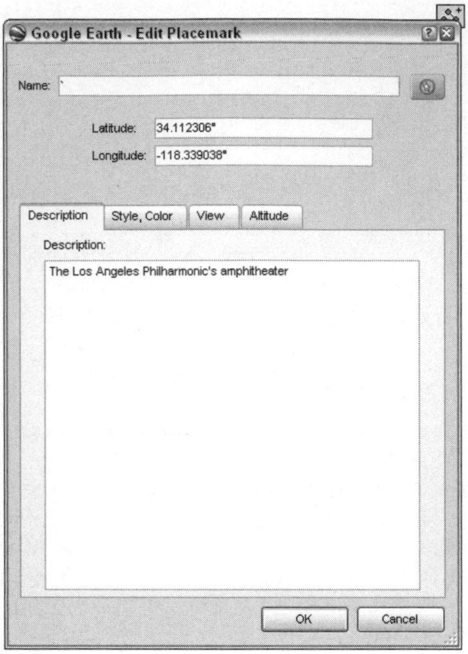

Figure 10-4:
Google
Earth
gathers info
for its KML
files from
forms.

The visibility element

Within Google Earth, you control the visibility of a placemark by selecting its check box to either select it (make it visible) or deselect it (make it invisible).

The `visibility` element controls whether or not the placemark's icon is visible *at the time you load the placemark's KML file*. It has no effect whatsoever on what happens after that point — you can click the placemark's check box to deselect it anytime you want.

To set the placemark so that its icon is automatically visible on loading, like the one in Figure 10-5, use this code:

```
<visibility>1</visibility>
```

To make the icon invisible on loading, just change the 1 to a 0 (zero).

The LookAt element

With the `LookAt` element, it's pretty obvious that what you're looking at is the placemark. But who's doing the looking? It's perhaps easiest to just think of yourself as floating in the air, but the metaphor common to GIS programs, including Google Earth, is that of a camera which floats in the air and sends us a view of what's in front of its lens.

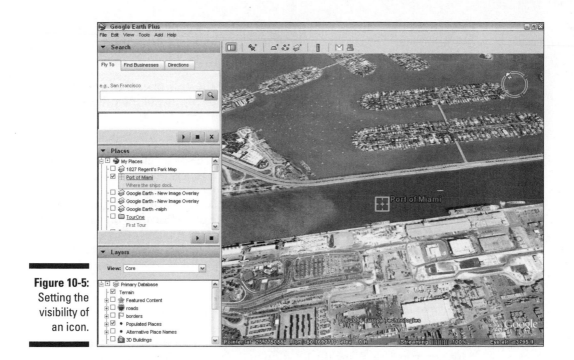

Figure 10-5:
Setting the
visibility of
an icon.

The six child elements of the `LookAt` element basically represent two sets of elements that are used to specify the location of the placemark and the camera that's looking at it. In each case, you need to specify three specific measurements.

```
<LookAt>

    <longitude>-118.3390383230917</longitude>
    <latitude>34.11230602728949</latitude>
    <altitude>0</altitude>

    <range>272.1817526117454</range>
    <tilt>1.485907294467841e-010</tilt>
    <heading>-0.004589114879398169</heading>

</LookAt>
```

Locating the placemark: The longitude, latitude, and altitude elements

In order to locate a placemark, you have to give its longitude, latitude, and altitude. As you can read in Chapter 2, *longitude* and *latitude* are the lines that crisscross maps, specifying how far away a place is from the prime meridian and the equator.

This means that you are telling Google Earth how far east or west a point is with the `longitude` value, how far north or south it is with the `latitude` value, and how high it is with the `altitude` value.

The `longitude` and `latitude` elements are the only ones that are actually required to make `LookAt` work. If you don't specify any of the others, they will all default to `0` (zero).

The `altitude` element, you will note, is set to `0` in this code. However, the Hollywood Bowl is something like 600 feet above sea level, and the placemark isn't 600 feet below the ground. The reason for this is that in the absence of instructions to the contrary, Google Earth takes any altitude value to mean the same as Clamped to Ground (see Figure 10-6). This, for most purposes, is fine. However, if you know the exact altitude of the location and want the placemark to float above it, you can override this. You'll need to get a bit more specific about how you want altitude handled by setting the values in the `altitudeMode` element. (See the section entitled "Altitude and altitudeMode" later in this chapter.)

Positioning the camera: The range, tilt, and heading elements

The camera needs to be located in three-dimensional space just as much as the placemark that it's viewing does. The method for doing this is a little bit different from specifying the location of the placemark, though. You're not trying to specify a point within the longitude/latitude/altitude system but rather a point that exists relative to the placemark.

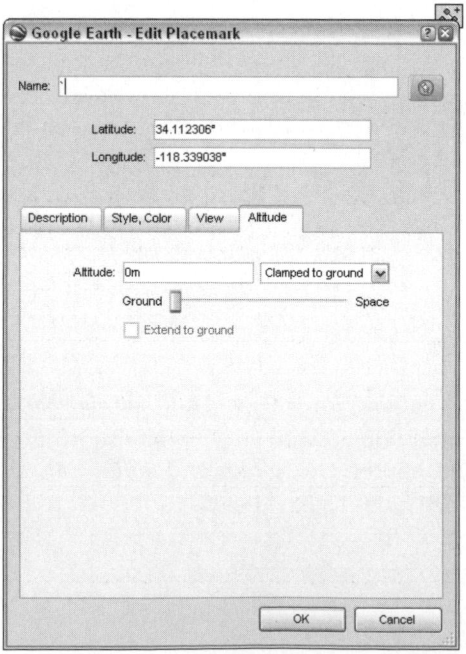

Figure 10-6:
Altitude settings are automatically clamped to ground level.

First, you need to tell Google Earth how far away from the placemark the camera is. This is done via the `range` element. This works as if you had a camera on the end of a rope. The other end of the rope is figuratively tied to the ground at the location you specified for your placemark, and the `range` value tells how long the rope is.

After you know how far you are from your placemark, you've still got a lot of room to move around that center. Say that rope is a mile long; the camera could be a mile east of the placemark or a mile west of it, or anywhere in between, and it could be lying on the ground or a mile in the air.

So, even though you've established the range, you've got only one of the three pieces of information you need to position the camera.

That's where the `tilt` and `heading` elements come into play. The `tilt` value tells Google Earth what the angle of the camera is. Now that it knows the distance (range) and the angle (tilt), it can figure out the altitude of the camera. However, that still leaves a very large circle in which the camera can be located.

Now, you have to tell Google Earth the last bit of information: what direction the camera is pointing in. That's the job of the `heading` element. A `heading` value is given in *degrees,* a concept which is not hard to grasp. Remember that every circle is divided into 360 degrees? There's an imaginary circle — usually represented by a compass rose on a map — in which north is at the top, or at a heading of 0 degrees. South is at the bottom — half a circle away, at 180 degrees. East (on the right) and west (on the left) are, respectively, at 90 degrees and 270 degrees.

So, what if you want to point your camera toward the south? You'd use a `heading` value of `180`. Toward the east? `90`. And so forth. Table 10-1 shows the degree values for the major subdivisions of common directions:

Table 10-1	Degree Values for Common Direction Names
Direction	**Degrees**
North (N)	0
East (E)	90
South (S)	180
West (W)	270
Northeast (NE)	45
Southeast (SE)	135

(continued)

Table 10-1 *(continued)*

Direction	Degrees
Southwest (SW)	225
Northwest (NW)	315
North northeast (NNE)	22.5
North northwest (NNW)	337.5
East northeast (ENE)	67.5
East southeast (ESE)	112.5
South southeast (SSE)	157.5
South southwest (SSW)	202.5
West southwest (WSW)	247.5
West northwest (WNW)	292.5

When you're pointing the camera toward one direction, you're looking from its opposite. For example, if the camera's heading is toward the east, you're looking from the west. Figures 10-7 and 10-8 show the same scene from opposite camera headings.

Figure 10-7:
Facing east.

Figure 10-8:
Facing west.

You can also specify negative degrees, if you're so inclined. In that case, west would be –90 instead of 270, and east would be –270 instead of 90. South would be –180 instead of 180, but north will always be 0. To get the negative degree value of a heading, subtract 360 from it.

Pinning the icon: The Point element

The Point element tells Google Earth where to put your placemark's icon. If you leave it out, you won't see one. Normally, of course, the icon should go exactly where the placemark itself is located, so you'll see the same longitude, latitude, and altitude values as are found in that placemark's LookAt element.

However, they're handled a little bit differently. Instead of separate elements for those three values, a single element combines them all: the coordinates element. In this example, it looks like this:

```
<Point>

    <coordinates>-118.3390383230917,34.11230602728949,0</coordinates>

</Point>
```

The order is important in the Point element. You have to enter the longitude, latitude, and altitude in that order. When specifying location in the LookAt element, it doesn't matter which comes first. Although they were listed in order of longitude, latitude, and then altitude, they didn't have to be. The following code is just as valid as the example one:

```
<LookAt>

    <latitude>34.11230602728949</latitude>
    <altitude>0</altitude>
    <longitude>-118.3390383230917</longitude>
       ...

</LookAt>
```

If you try that with the `coordinates` element, though, you'll end up with things in the wrong place.

The `coordinates` element *cannot* be used as a child of `LookAt`; you must use the separate `longitude`, `latitude`, and `altitude` elements there instead.

The Snippet element

You're already familiar with the `name` and `description` elements, but here's one more way to add some written information to your placemark — one that you just can't do inside Google Earth. That's the `Snippet` element, and it works a little strangely.

Like the `name` element, it accepts only plain text; you can't embed any HTML code within it. Like the `description` element, it can show up under the placemark in My Places, but it can also show up elsewhere, and even elbow a competing description aside.

The code couldn't be simpler:

```
<Snippet>text goes here</Snippet>
```

Just type in whatever you want in place of *text goes here*, and you're all set.

But what do you want to see when you load the placemark? Check out the options. First, redo the example so that it has a snippet in place of the description, as in the following modification. The name has also been changed to reflect the purpose of the example; other than that, everything is the same.

```
<Placemark>

  <name>Hollywood Bowl with Snippet</name>

  <Snippet>A natural formation with seats added</Snippet>

  <visibility>0</visibility>
```

```
<LookAt>
    <longitude>-118.3390383230917</longitude>
    <latitude>34.11230602728949</latitude>
    <altitude>0</altitude>
    <range>272.1817526117454</range>
    <tilt>1.485907294467841e-010</tilt>
    <heading>-0.004589114879398169</heading>
</LookAt>

<Point>
    <coordinates>-118.3390383230917,34.11230602728949,0</coordinates>
</Point>

</Placemark>
```

Normally, you see the description's text under the placemark's icon, but if you leave out the description, you'll see the snippet's text there instead. Here's one other odd thing you'll notice — there's no link to the placemark (see Figure 10-9). This doesn't mean that the placemark doesn't work; the link is to the description, which is what is shown in the text balloon. No description equals no link.

Figure 10-9:
No description means no text balloon link.

However, you can have both working at the same time as well. If you add the description element back into the code while leaving the snippet, too, as in the following code sample, you get a different result — the link is back.

```
<Placemark>
    <name>Hollywood Bowl with Snippet</name>
    <description>Description added back in.</description>
    <Snippet>A natural formation with seats added</Snippet>
    <visibility>0</visibility>
    <LookAt>
        <longitude>-118.3390383230917</longitude>
        <latitude>34.11230602728949</latitude>
        <altitude>0</altitude>
        <range>272.1817526117454</range>
        <tilt>1.485907294467841e-010</tilt>
        <heading>-0.004589114879398169</heading>
    </LookAt>
    <Point>
        <coordinates>-118.3390383230917,34.11230602728949,0</coordinates>
    </Point>
</Placemark>
```

The snippet's text still shows under the placemark in the Places pane, but the description's text is available by clicking the placemark's link to display the text balloon (see Figure 10-10).

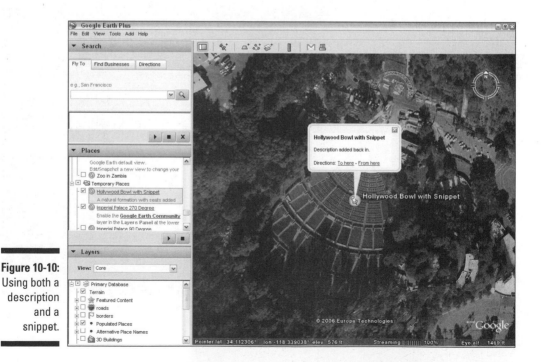

Figure 10-10:
Using both a description and a snippet.

Altitude and altitudeMode

If you've read this chapter to this point, you've seen the `altitude` element as a child of the `LookAt` element. As you might recall, the value is automatically set to the same as ground level unless you tell Google Earth to do things differently. The way you do so is via the `altitudeMode` element.

This has three possible values, each of which corresponds to the same settings on the Altitude tab in Google Earth (see Figure 10-11).

As I mention in Chapter 6, there are three different methods for displaying the placemark's icon:

- ✔ **Clamped to Ground:** The same level as the ground.
- ✔ **Relative to Ground:** `altitude` value added to the ground's altitude.
- ✔ **Absolute:** Not really absolute at all — it's actually just relative to sea level instead of ground level.

The Google Earth option Clamped to Ground becomes the value `clampToGround`, Relative to Ground becomes `relativeToGround`, and Absolute is `absolute`. Thus, if you wanted to choose the second option, you'd use this code:

```
<altitudeMode>relativeToGround</altitudeMode>
```

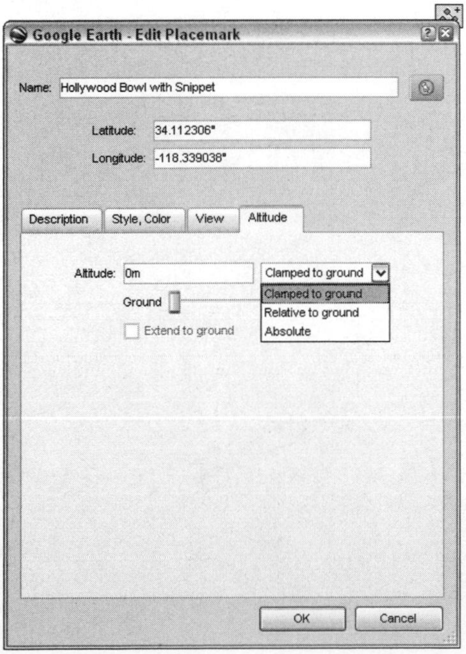

Figure 10-11:
The settings correspond to the Altitude tab.

You don't really need to use the `clampToGround` value. If you want things clamped to the ground, just don't specify any `altitudeMode` at all.

The address element

If you've read this chapter to this point, you're already familiar with the `longitude`, `latitude`, and `coordinates` elements, but here's another way to specify a location that's a little bit more to the taste of the average person — a street address. As you might guess, you use the `address` element to do that.

As usual in KML, the process is a simple one. The drawback is that it's limited to locations in the United States, Canada, and the United Kingdom. If that area covers the turf you're working with, here's how to go about it.

You can use any usual form of address as the value for the `address` element. Thus, you may have something like this:

```
<address>123 Main Street, Smalltown, KS</address>
```

You can also use a ZIP code (or Canadian or British postal code) either as a part of the address or as a standalone value. In the latter case, the exact point will be more or less in the geographical center of that ZIP code area (see Figure 10-12):

```
<address>90210</address>
```

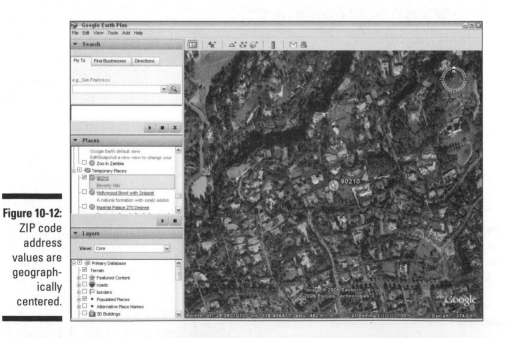

Figure 10-12: ZIP code address values are geographically centered.

Working with Styles

Although earlier versions of KML supported local *styles* (embedded within individual placemarks), they are now deprecated in favor of a global style environment. In this section, I show you how to work at a higher level of file — not just a simple placemark, but a folder which contains several placemarks.

You can extend these concepts to include even larger KML files.

First off, you're going to go all the way up in the root element department. When working with a complex file, it's best to play it as safe as possible in order to avoid any possibility of generating errors. So this is the most complex piece of KML code you've seen so far. Still, start off small and build from there:

```
<?xml version="1.0" encoding="UTF-8"?>
<kml xmlns="http://earth.google.com/kml/2.1">
    <Document>
        <Folder>
            <Placemark>
            </Placemark>
            <Placemark>
            </Placemark>
        </Folder>
    </Document>
</kml>
```

The opening two lines of this segment specify some technical details that you don't need to worry about but that are very helpful to Google Earth (or any other program that can read KML files). They tell that program that this file is done in KML version 2.1, which falls under the XML version 1.0 standard, and that it uses standard text encoding methods.

The second line is also the real beginning of the file as far as your display is concerned. That's the top-level <kml> element, which will contain everything else as a child element. Notice that the last thing in the file is the </kml> closing tag, in order to keep things tidy.

Within this set of tags, the next level is the Document element, which will contain any and all folders you assign to this file. (For this example, you're keeping it down to only one folder.)

The next level represents the Placemark elements that will reside in the folder. This is the basic skeleton of the file you'll be creating. Now, all that remains is to fill it in with all the good stuff.

The Style element

The `Style` element itself is the parent for everything you'll want to do style-wise. Everything from the size and color of text to which icon shows up onscreen is handled here. In this section, you'll explore several ways to use it to spruce up your Google Earth experience.

To get things started, add it in the appropriate location. A global style definition can be a part of the `Document` element or the `Folder` element, and is available to all that element's children. In this example, put it in the document itself to make it available to all folders that might be added to this file in the future. Thus, you need to amend the code example to read:

```
<?xml version="1.0" encoding="UTF-8"?>
<kml xmlns="http://earth.google.com/kml/2.1">
    <Document>
        <Style>
        </Style>
        <Folder>
            <Placemark>
            </Placemark>
            <Placemark>
            </Placemark>
        </Folder>
    </Document>
</kml>
```

Note that the `Style` and `Folder` elements are at the same level, equal children of their parent document. This style of indenting each element to signify its position in the container relationship is meant to make the code easier to understand.

The styleUrl element

When you create a style, you give it a name, but it's called an `id` here instead. This name can then be used to reference the style you've created whenever you need to use it. The `id` value must be unique, of course, so that Google Earth can tell which style you mean when you call on it.

Expand the code example by adding a second `Style` element and giving them two names:

```
<?xml version="1.0" encoding="UTF-8"?>
<kml xmlns="http://earth.google.com/kml/2.1">
    <Document>
        <Style id="StyleOne">
        </Style>
```

```
        <Style id="StyleTwo">
        </Style>
        <Folder>
            <Placemark>
            </Placemark>
            <Placemark>
            </Placemark>
        </Folder>
    </Document>
</kml>
```

From now on, anytime you want to apply one style or the other, all you have to do is give their names. For example, say you want to apply StyleOne to the first placemark. You simply add the styleUrl element to the placemark like this:

```
<Placemark>
    <styleUrl>#StyleOne</styleUrl>
</Placemark>
```

That little # tells Google Earth to look inside this file for a style definition named StyleOne. You can use styles from another file as well, but you have to specify the URL so that Google Earth can find it. For example, if you're looking for a style called RainbowSunset on a distant Web server, you might use something like this:

```
<Placemark>
    <styleUrl>http://www.notinthisfile.edu/
        butinthisone.xml#RainbowSunset</styleUrl>
</Placemark>
```

After you understand how to name and reference a style definition, you're ready to do some styling!

LabelStyle

The LabelStyle element corresponds to the Label settings on the Style, Color tab (see Figure 10-13). The Color and Opacity settings are combined into a single color element here, while the scale is set by the scale element.

The color value is one of the easiest concepts to understand, of course. Unfortunately, it's also one of the most difficult to handle in KML. This is because it requires hexadecimal numbers for input. The numbers you're probably used to working with everyday are in base 10, but hexadecimal (hex) numbers are in base 16, which uses the numbers from 0 through 9 normally and then substitutes the letters A through F for numbers 10 through 15 and then wraps things up by using the number 10 for 16.

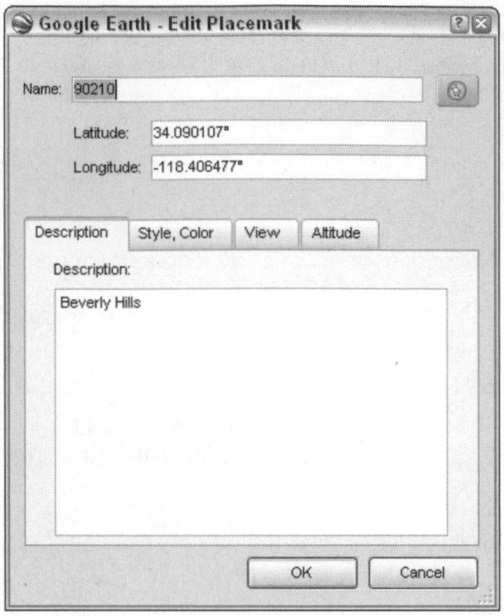

Figure 10-13:
Setting the
label values.

Although professional programmers have long been used to this, they're pretty much Greek to the average Google Earth user. What can be even more confusing is that these numbers, which specify four different settings, are all run together into one long number.

Here's how it looks:

```
<color>ff0055ff</color>
```

If you were to break it all out, you would see that there are actually four numbers here: ff, 00, 55, and ff. In normal decimal notation, they are 255, 0, 85, and 255, respectively. The first one sets the *alpha* (or opacity) value. The remaining three specify the amount of blue, green, and red, in that order.

For all these values, the hex notation ff is the highest possible (255 decimal). Thus, if you want something totally opaque and red, you set it like this:

```
<color>ff0000ff</color>
```

Translation: complete opacity (ff), no blue (00), no green (00), complete red (ff).

To help you through this potentially bewildering mathematical maze, Table 10-2 gives the hexadecimal values for various levels of opacity, and Table 10-3 lists those for some common colors.

Table 10-2   Hexadecimal Values for Various Opacities

Color	Value
10%	19
20%	32
25%	3F
30%	4C
40%	65
50%	7F
60%	99
70%	B2
75%	BF
80%	CC
90%	E5
100%	FF

Table 10-3   Hexadecimal Values for Common Colors

Color	Value
Aqua	FFFF00
Black	000000
Blue	FF0000
Fuchsia	FF00FF
Gray	808080
Green	008000
Lime	00FF00
Maroon	000080
Navy	800000
Olive	008080
Purple	800080

(continued)

Table 10-3 *(continued)*

Color	Value
Red	0000FF
Silver	C0C0C0
Teal	808000
White	FFFFFF
Yellow	00FFFF

As you can see, the opacity values are two characters each, and the colors have six characters. The latter are, of course, pairs of numbers representing the same three colors to mix that you dealt with before (blue, green, red), so you can just plug them in right away. All you have to do is to put the opacity value in, followed by the color value. Thus, if you want to create a color that is 80% opaque and of an olive hue, you take the CC from Table 10-2 and add it to the 008080 from Table 10-3 to get

```
<color>cc008080</color>
```

To set the size of a label, you use the `scale` element. The following code, for example, makes the label twice its size — in both dimensions. The label is twice as high *and* twice as long. This means that the actual result is that the label takes up four times the area it will at a setting of 1.0 (normal size).

```
<scale>2.0</scale>
```

Allowable values for the scale range from 0.0 to 4.0.

Aside from the standard settings you can manage within Google Earth, you can toss one more thing into the mix if you like strange and unpredictable effects: The `colorMode` element allows you to randomize the colors, using a different one each time. To do this, you simply add this line to your color definition:

```
<colorMode>random</colorMode>
```

Add all that into the developing file's source code in the part that defines the options for `StyleOne`:

```
<Style id="StyleOne">
   <LabelStyle>
      <color>cc808000</color>
      <scale>2.0</scale>
      <colorMode>random</colorMode>
   </LabelStyle>
</Style>
```

Now, whenever this style is applied to a placemark, the placemark's labels assume all these properties.

IconStyle

The `IconStyle` element is much like the `LabelStyle` one except that, of course, it applies to the placemark's icon itself instead of the lettering next to it. It uses the same `color`, `colorMode`, and `scale` child elements but adds two more as well: `icon` and `heading`.

The `icon` element is used to specify which image to use for the icon. This is a required child element of `IconStyle`, so even if you're going to use the regular `icon`, you need to say so. Assuming that you want to leave the colors and the scale as they were in the preceding example, here's how to do that:

```
<IconStyle>
    <color>cc808000</color>
    <scale>2.0</scale>
    <colorMode>random</colorMode>
    <Icon>
        <href>root://icons/palette-3.png</href>
    </Icon>
</IconStyle>
```

To change the icon to any other, simply substitute its location in the `Icon` element's `href` child element.

The `heading` element determines which way the placemark's icon is facing. It works just like the same thing in the `LookAt` element: A value of `0` aims the icon to the north, `90` to the east, `180` to the south, `270` to the west, and so forth. (See Table 10-1 for a listing of directions and their degree values.)

Here's a version of the preceding that uses a custom icon and points it toward the eastern horizon:

```
<IconStyle>
    <color>cc808000</color>
    <scale>2.0</scale>
    <colorMode>random</colorMode>
    <Icon>
        <href>c:/GoogleEarthIcons/MyOwnIcon002.jpg</href>
    </Icon>
    <heading>90</heading>
</IconStyle>
```

Go ahead and add this new code to the example as part of the second style definition:

```xml
<?xml version="1.0" encoding="UTF-8"?>
<kml xmlns="http://earth.google.com/kml/2.1">

   <Document>

      <Style id="StyleOne">
         <LabelStyle>
            <color>cc808000</color>
            <scale>2.0</scale>
            <colorMode>random</colorMode>
         </LabelStyle>
      </Style>

      <Style id="StyleTwo">
         <IconStyle>
            <color>cc808000</color>
            <scale>2.0</scale>
            <colorMode>random</colorMode>
            <Icon>
                 <href>c:/GoogleEarthIcons/MyOwnIcon002.jpg</href>
            </Icon>
            <heading>90</heading>
         </IconStyle>
      </Style>

      <Folder>

         <Placemark>
         </Placemark>
         <Placemark>
         </Placemark>

      </Folder>

   </Document>

</kml>
```

Radio buttons and check boxes (listStyle)

After you have two different style definitions set up, turn to the folder you created but haven't developed yet. The first step is to give it a name and description. Go ahead and modify that part of the source code so that it reads something like this:

```
<Folder>

    <name>StyleExample</name>
    <description>Shows different styles being applied</description>

    <Placemark>
    </Placemark>
    <Placemark>
    </Placemark>

</Folder>
```

If you wanted to, you could just go ahead to the placemarks now, but you'll want to explore a couple of other things first. One is the `open` element. This is similar to the `visibility` element used for placemarks in that it sets the manner in which the folder is shown at first. Here's how it works:

```
<Folder>
    <open>0</open>
</Folder>
```

A value of 0 means that the folder is closed, and you have to click the plus sign next to it to see what it contains. Change the value to 1, however, and the folder is initially shown with everything in it showing as well.

The other thing to explore is another way of changing the appearance of the listings in the Places pane using the `listItemType` and `listStyle` elements. Normally, the folders have check boxes next to them that you use to activate or deactivate the contents. By changing the list style in which the placemarks are displayed, you also alter the behavior of a click. With the default check box style, you can simultaneously select two or more placemarks. If you replace the check boxes with radio buttons, however, each placemark you select is *exclusive;* choosing one shuts off the other. Figures 10-14 and 10-15 show how the two methods work.

Figure 10-14:
The default
check box
style.

The two values that create these are, respectively, `checkHideChildren` and `radioFolder`. You simply create a style with either value in it, and you're off and running. To set a folder for radio buttons, for example, you would do this:

```
<Style id="buttonsNotBoxes">
    <ListStyle>
        <listItemType>radioFolder</listItemType>
    </ListStyle>
</Style>
```

You don't ever need to specify the `checkHideChildren` value. Because it's the default display method, it's already active if you don't specify `radioFolder` instead. Go ahead and add this style to the example, along with the other things I just covered:

```
<?xml version="1.0" encoding="UTF-8"?>
<kml xmlns="http://earth.google.com/kml/2.1">
    <Document>

        <Style id="StyleOne">
            <LabelStyle>
                <color>cc808000</color>
                <scale>2.0</scale>
                <colorMode>random</colorMode>
            </LabelStyle>
        </Style>

        <Style id="StyleTwo">
            <IconStyle>
                <color>cc808000</color>
                <scale>2.0</scale>
                <colorMode>random</colorMode>
                <Icon>
                    <href>c:/GoogleEarthIcons/MyOwnIcon002.jpg</href>
                </Icon>
                <heading>90</heading>
            </IconStyle>
        </Style>
```

```
     <Style id="buttonsNotBoxes">
        <ListStyle>
           <listItemType>radioFolder</listItemType>
        </ListStyle>
     </Style>

     <Folder>
        <name>StyleExample</name>
        <description>Shows different styles being applied</description>
        <open>1</open>

        <Placemark>
        </Placemark>
        <Placemark>
        </Placemark>

     </Folder>

  </Document>
</kml>
```

You're almost done now. Other than adding a couple of placemarks, all you
have to do is to reference those styles in the appropriate places. Start with
the folder and style it with the buttonsNotBoxes style. Do that by adding
a line right under the opening tag, <Folder>, like this:

```
     <Folder>
        <styleUrl>#buttonsNotBoxes</styleUrl>

        <name>StyleExample</name>
        <description>Shows different styles being applied</description>
        <open>1</open>

        <Placemark>
        </Placemark>
        <Placemark>
        </Placemark>

     </Folder>
```

Now it's time to apply each of the other two remaining styles to one of the
placemarks, like this:

```
        <Placemark>
        <styleUrl>#StyleOne</styleUrl>
        </Placemark>

        <Placemark>
        <styleUrl>#StyleTwo</styleUrl>
        </Placemark>
```

Finally, toss in the placemark data, and here's the final version of the KML code example, with a few comments thrown in to remind you what's what:

```
<?xml version="1.0" encoding="UTF-8"?>
<kml xmlns="http://earth.google.com/kml/2.1">

    <Document>

        <Style id="StyleOne">
            <LabelStyle>
<!-- This sets an olive color with 80% opacity. -->
                <color>cc808000</color>
<!-- Covers four times the area of 1.0. -->
                <scale>2.0</scale>
<!-- Sets the color to change with each use -->
                <colorMode>random</colorMode>
            </LabelStyle>
        </Style>

        <Style id="StyleTwo">
            <IconStyle>
                <color>cc808000</color>
                <scale>2.0</scale>
                <colorMode>random</colorMode>
<!-- Gives the location of a custom icon. -->
                <Icon>
                    <href>c:/GoogleEarthIcons/MyOwnIcon002.jpg</href>
                </Icon>
<!-- The icon faces east. -->
                <heading>90</heading>
            </IconStyle>
        </Style>

        <Style id="buttonsNotBoxes">
            <ListStyle>
<!-- Changes the default check boxes to radio buttons. -->
                <listItemType>radioFolder</listItemType>
            </ListStyle>
        </Style>

        <Folder>

<!-- Ties the style to this folder. -->
            <styleUrl>#buttonsNotBoxes</styleUrl>
            <name>StyleExample</name>
            <description>Shows different styles being applied</description>
<!-- Makes the folder show its contents at opening. -->
            <open>1</open>

            <Placemark>
```

```
            <styleUrl>#StyleOne</styleUrl>
            <name>Hollywood Bowl with Snippet</name>
   <description>The Los Angeles Philharmonic's amphitheater</description>
<!-- This moves the description into the text balloon. -->
            <Snippet>A natural formation with seats added</Snippet>
<!-- Makes the icon invisible at opening. -->
            <visibility>0</visibility>
<!-- Specifies the location of the placemark and the camera. -->
            <LookAt>
                <longitude>-118.3390383230917</longitude>
                <latitude>34.11230602728949</latitude>
                <altitude>0</altitude>
                <range>272.1817526117454</range>
                <tilt>1.485907294467841e-010</tilt>
                <heading>-0.004589114879398169</heading>
            </LookAt>
            <Point>
                <coordinates>-118.3390383230917,34.11230602728949,0</coordinates>
            </Point>
        </Placemark>

        <Placemark>
            <styleUrl>#StyleTwo</styleUrl>
            <name>Port of Miami</name>
                <description>Where the ships dock.</description>
<!-- Makes the icon visible at opening. -->
            <visibility>1</visibility>
            <LookAt>
                <longitude>-80.16927921121973</longitude>
                <latitude>25.77781453124814</latitude>
                <altitude>0</altitude>
                <range>1416.675283716215</range>
                <tilt>37.92222918159425</tilt>
                <heading>34.4116436411719</heading>
            </LookAt>
            <Point>
                <coordinates>-80.16927921121975,25.77781453124814,0</coordinates>
            </Point>
        </Placemark>

    </Folder>

  </Document>

</kml>
```

Part IV
Advanced Features

The 5th Wave   By Rich Tennant

"This is amazing. You can stop looking for Derek. According to a Google Earth search I did, he's hiding behind the dryer in the basement."

In this part . . .

Chapter 11 introduces you to an important companion program — Google SketchUp — which allows you to create 3-D models for importation into Google Earth.

Chapter 12 goes into more depth about the uses of Google SketchUp and shows you how to create a 3-D model.

Chapter 13 shows you how to create polygons and join shapes.

Chapter 14 goes into advanced SketchUp topics like lathing and extruding polygons, using the Follow Me and the Tape Measure tools, and understanding lines and faces.

Chapter 11

Designing with Google SketchUp

Google SketchUp — one of the greatest things about Google Earth — is a standalone companion program that lets you design 3-D models that you can then import into Google Earth and include as a part of the landscape. Like Google Earth itself, Google SketchUp comes in both free and paid versions ($249 for the Pro version); the paid version offers a few extras such as greater flexibility in exporting files, but the freebie is an almost unbelievably robust piece of 3-D software.

Even if you don't have a lot of artistic talent, you can use a whole slew of existing models as the basis for your own creations. 3D Warehouse (http://sketchup.google.com/3dwarehouse) is a collaboration between Google and SketchUp's original designers to provide a repository for various premade 3-D graphics and objects. It also provides a way for users to share their own 3-D designs. And the best news is that the models are free!

You can have it both ways with Google SketchUp — make your own dream house from scratch or pick one of the models and drop it into Google Earth. The flat image of the Statue of Liberty, for example, just doesn't have the zing you expect (see Figure 11-1). Add the model of that famous structure from 3D Warehouse, however, and the scene comes alive (see Figure 11-2).

Figure 11-1:
The normal
view of the
Statue of
Liberty.

Figure 11-2:
The scene is
better with
the 3-D
model in
place.

The Google SketchUp Interface

Google SketchUp is a powerful 3-D modeling program, and its controls reflect both its complexity and its versatility. Like with most graphics programs, the majority of the screen area is taken up by the drawing area, with menus and toolbars at the top and (in some cases) on the side.

Although the simple default version, as shown in Figure 11-3, will suffice for many of your design needs, sometimes you'll need more features, and Google SketchUp has plenty more, to put it mildly. Figure 11-4 shows the same program with all its toolbars active at once.

Touring the toolbars

Each of the toolbars in Google SketchUp supplies a set of tools for a specific type of task. For example, drawing tools are grouped together, as are the controls for setting different views.

To see each toolbar, choose View⇨Toolbars from the menu and then select any toolbar from the resulting popup menu (see Figure 11-5). Only the Google and Getting Started toolbars are active by default.

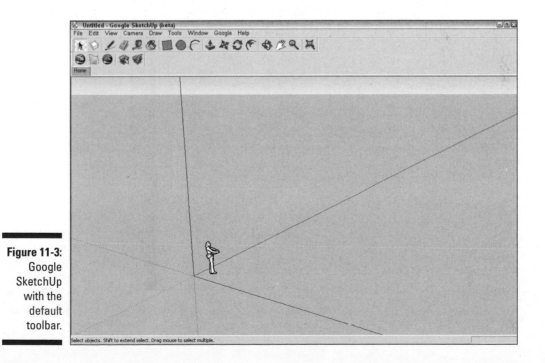

Figure 11-3:
Google
SketchUp
with the
default
toolbar.

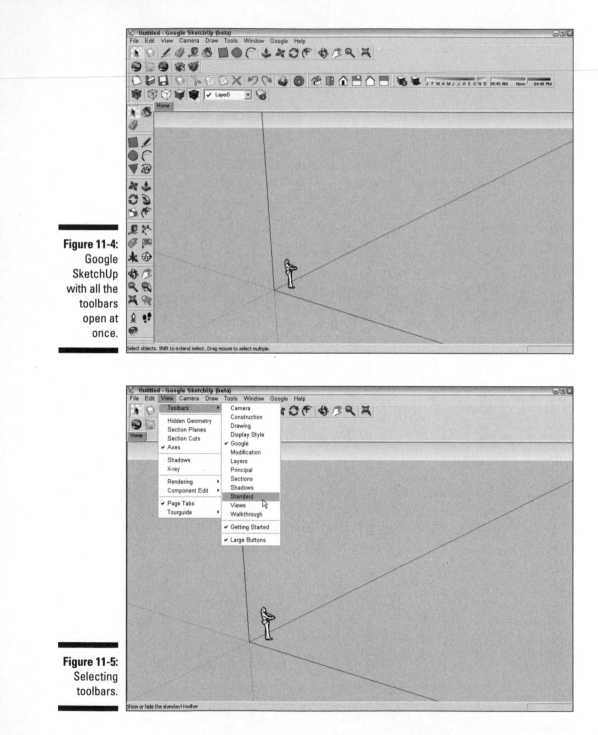

Figure 11-4:
Google
SketchUp
with all the
toolbars
open at
once.

Figure 11-5:
Selecting
toolbars.

The Camera toolbar

The Camera toolbar, as shown in Figure 11-6, includes several controls for altering the view onscreen.

Orbit   Pan

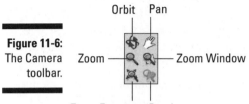

Figure 11-6:
The Camera
toolbar.

Zoom ——— ——— Zoom Window

Zoom Extents   Previous

The tools here are:

✔ **Orbit:** Lets you move the camera over, under, and around the 3-D object, viewing it from any angle.

✔ **Pan:** Used for moving the scene vertically, horizontally, or diagonally.

✔ **Zoom:** Used to zoom in, on, or out from the 3-D object. Move your mouse wheel away from you to zoom in and toward you to zoom out.

✔ **Zoom Window:** Used to zoom in or out from a part of the 3-D object.

✔ **Zoom Extents:** Lets you automatically zoom in or out so that the entire 3-D object is in view.

✔ **Previous:** Switches back and forth between the current view and the previous one.

The Construction toolbar

The Construction toolbar (see Figure 11-7) is more of a tool belt than a toolbar, with a trusty tape measure handy and several ways to work on your "blueprints."

Tape Measure   Dimension

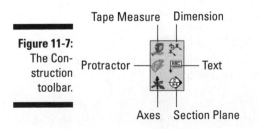

Figure 11-7:
The Con-
struction
toolbar.

Protractor ——— ——— Text

Axes   Section Plane

The tools here are:

- ✒ **Tape Measure:** Just like a tape measure in real life, you hook it at one end and drag it to the other to see how long something in the scene is.

- ✒ **Dimension:** Use this to add a line showing the measurement of an object.

- ✒ **Protractor:** Again, just like a real one; you lay the Protractor tool at a corner of an object, anchor it to another, and then move your cursor to interactively measure the angles from the base.

- ✒ **Text:** Use this to add *callouts* (text with a line pointing to a specific feature) to the scene.

- ✒ **Axes:** Use this to adjust the orientation of the three axes on the screen. Google SketchUp simply refers to them as the red, green, and blue axes, but these correspond to the normal X, Y, and Z axes familiar to all 3-D programs. When interfacing with Google Earth, the green (Y) axis points north, the red (X) axis points east, and the blue (Z) axis points straight up.

- ✒ **Section Plane:** This tool allows you to slice your 3-D models to show cutaway views of their interior construction.

The Drawing toolbar

The Drawing toolbar, as shown in Figure 11-8, provides the tools for adding basic shapes and lines as well as creating more complex variations on them.

Rectangle   Line

Figure 11-8:
The
Drawing
toolbar.   Circle ——— 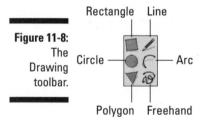 ——— Arc

Polygon   Freehand

The tools here are:

- ✒ **Rectangle:** Draws rectangles (including squares).

- ✒ **Line:** Draws straight lines. A series of straight lines can be interconnected end to end to form more complex designs.

- ✒ **Circle:** Draws circles.

- ✒ **Arc:** Draws *arcs* (partial circle segments). Like with the Line tool, you can use the end of one arc as the beginning point of another, chaining them together to design intricate patterns.

✔ **Polygon:** Draws *polygons* (multisided figures). The default polygon is hexagonal (six-sided). You can specify the number of sizes, but all polygons begin to approximate a circle when you add more than about a dozen sides.

✔ **Freehand:** For doodling. The Freehand tool works exactly as if you had a pencil in your hand with which you could draw onscreen. Use this tool to add hand drawings, signatures, and so on to your work.

The Display Style toolbar

The Display Style toolbar contains controls that determine how your work is rendered onscreen (see Figure 11-9). It is a common practice in 3-D design to use Wireframe during most of the design stages and Shaded with Textures only for fine-tuning or during the final stages of the project. Because Wireframe drawings have a lot less detail, they place fewer demands on a computer's resources than the more complex shaded renderings. This means that the program runs a lot faster, saving the memory- and processing-intensive fine touches for when everything else is just right.

Figure 11-9:
The Display
Style
toolbar.

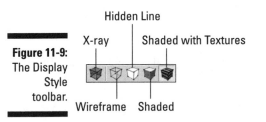

Hidden Line

X-ray   Shaded with Textures

Wireframe   Shaded

This grouping of five controls is really a 1/4 situation. The last four items all set various levels of rendering. The X-Ray control, however, has nothing to do with the kind of rendering that is used. Instead, it works with the other controls.

The controls here are:

✔ **X-Ray:** This control turns all *faces* (solid areas between lines) transparent in order to reveal the construction behind them. Using this doesn't affect rendering style.

✔ **Wireframe:** The least detailed (and least demanding) form of rendering, this control shows an object as a series of connected lines with no further detail. You can see through the whole object.

✔ **Hidden Line:** One step more detailed than Wireframe, this control adds faces between the lines. Anything that's behind a face is hidden by it. The effect is to create a more realistic image.

✔ **Shaded:** Moving into intensive computing demand, this option goes Hidden Line one better by adding color and shading to the object.

✔ **Shaded with Textures:** This control is by far the most computer-intensive setting but the one that produces the most detail in the image. Textures such as brick, wood grain, and so forth are now displayed in nearly photorealistic rendering.

The Google toolbar

The Google toolbar, as shown in Figure 11-10, is one of the default toolbars (along with Getting Started). It has five items that affect Google SketchUp's interaction with its companion program, Google Earth.

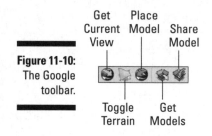

Get Current View Place Model Share Model

Figure 11-10: The Google toolbar.

Toggle Terrain Get Models

The tools here are:

✔ **Get Current View:** This transfers an image of whatever is in the Viewing area in Google Earth to Google SketchUp.

✔ **Toggle Terrain:** This turns the Terrain feature on and off, just like the Terrain layer in Google Earth.

✔ **Place Model:** This transfers the 3-D model you are working on from Google SketchUp into Google Earth.

✔ **Get Models:** This opens a 3D Warehouse Web page from which you can download 3-D models for use in SketchUp and Google Earth.

✔ **Share Model:** The flip side of Get Models, this lets you post your own 3-D models from SketchUp to 3D Warehouse.

The Modification toolbar

The Modification toolbar (see Figure 11-11) gives you various ways to either move or alter the shapes of the objects in Google SketchUp.

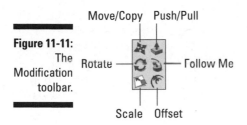

Move/Copy   Push/Pull

Rotate ——— Follow Me

Scale   Offset

The tools here are:

- **Move/Copy:** This tool is used to move a 3-D object or to reposition portions of an object. Pressing Ctrl changes the function to reposition a copy of an object while leaving the original where it was.

- **Push/Pull:** This tool is used to extrude *faces* (areas between connected lines). The extrusion can be either positive or negative. For example, a simple circle can become either a towering cylinder (positive) or a hole in the ground (negative).

- **Rotate:** This tool is used to turn an object or portion of an object in a circular motion, pivoting on a fixed point. Like with the Move/Copy control, you can press Ctrl to change this to "rotate a copy" mode.

- **Follow Me:** Similar to the Push/Pull control, this extrudes a face as well. However, the extrusion follows the path of your mouse pointer.

- **Scale:** This tool is used to interactively alter the measurements of some or all the dimensions of a 3-D object.

- **Offset:** This, too, creates a copy of a face, allowing you to enlarge or reduce the copy either inside or outside the original.

The Layers toolbar

The Layers toolbar, as shown in Figure 11-12, helps you manage — you guessed it — layers. Layers are like the canvas on which you create your 3-D artwork. In a simple model, everything will be done on one layer. When things get more complex, however, multiple layers are involved. When you load an image with terrain from Google Earth, for example, you end up with new layers.

Set Current Layer

Layer Manager

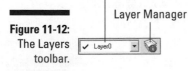

The tools here are:

- ✔ **Set Current Layer:** Selects the layer you want to work on. The number of layers available depends on how many you have created.

- ✔ **Layer Manager:** Opens the Layer Manager, from which you can add or delete layers, control which layers are visible as well as what their base colors are.

The Principal toolbar

The smallest toolbar in Google SketchUp (see Figure 11-13), the Principal toolbar, has only three basic controls, but they are ones you will use constantly.

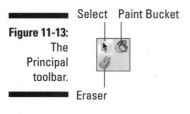

Figure 11-13:
The
Principal
toolbar.

Select   Paint Bucket

Eraser

The tools here are:

- ✔ **Select:** This is used to click objects or parts of objects to indicate which of them you want to work on.

- ✔ **Paint Bucket:** This "pours paint" onto your 3-D models to add color to them. It also adds textures such as wood or stone, which provide an extra touch of realism to your models.

- ✔ **Eraser:** This erases lines.

The Sections toolbar

If you've already used the Section Plane tool in the Construction toolbar to create cutaways, the Sections toolbar, as shown in Figure 11-14, controls how the results are displayed.

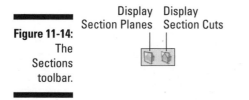

Figure 11-14:
The
Sections
toolbar.

Display   Display
Section Planes   Section Cuts

The tools here are:

- ✔ **Display Section Planes:** This shows the actual section plane itself — the "guillotine blade" that cuts the 3-D object.

- ✔ **Display Section Cuts:** This hides the section plane while showing the results of the cutaway.

The Shadows toolbar

Although this toolbar (see Figure 11-15) lets you quickly play with the date and time settings that affect which way the shadow goes and how long it is, the Shadow Settings dialog box gives you pinpoint control over the date and time.

Figure 11-15:
The Shadows toolbar.

Shadow Settings   Date

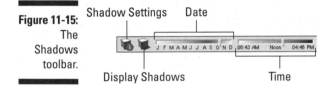

Display Shadows   Time

The tools here are:

- ✔ **Shadow Settings:** This opens the Shadow Settings dialog box, where you can set default date and time of day as well as adjust the darkness of the shadow.

- ✔ **Display Shadows:** This toggles the display of shadows on and off.

- ✔ **Date:** Click this control to choose which month it is in the scene.

- ✔ **Time:** Click this control to choose the time of day in the scene.

The Standard toolbar

This toolbar contains all the things you would expect in a typical toolbar in most programs (see Figure 11-16), yet it isn't one of the defaults. You'll probably want to activate this one first thing unless you like doing without Undo, Redo, Print, and the other usual functions available in the average program.

Figure 11-16:
The Standard toolbar.

New   Save   Cut   Paste   Undo   Print

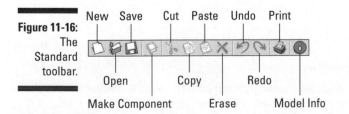

Open   Copy   Redo

Make Component   Erase   Model Info

The tools here are:

- **New:** Clears everything so you can start over
- **Open:** Opens a new file
- **Save:** Saves the current file
- **Make Component:** Creates a reusable copy of all selected elements by combining all into one object
- **Cut:** Simultaneously deletes and copies the selected item
- **Copy:** Copies the selected item
- **Paste:** Places a copy of a cut or copied item into the program
- **Erase:** Deletes the selected item without copying it
- **Undo:** Reverses the most current action
- **Redo:** Repeats an undone action
- **Print:** Sends a copy of the screen to the printer
- **Model Info:** Opens the Model Info dialog box, which presents you with many possibilities from setting the text size and background to viewing statistics on how many lines, materials, and so forth have been used in your model

The Views toolbar

The Views toolbar, as shown in Figure 11-17, presents five buttons, each of which automatically shifts the view to a different perspective. The first, Iso, gives the *isometric* view, which is the default in Google SketchUp. This means you are looking at the scene from a bit above and to the side. Which side depends upon what you were looking at before.

The five remaining perspective buttons are self explanatory: Top, Front, Right, Back, and Left.

Figure 11-17:
The Views
toolbar.

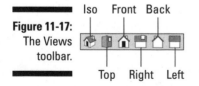

Iso   Front   Back

Top   Right   Left

The Walkthrough toolbar

The Walkthrough toolbar, as shown in Figure 11-18, is another tiny one. Its three occupants set the situation when you feel like you want to be a part of the scene on your screen.

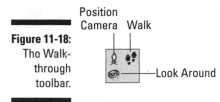

Figure 11-18:
Tho Walk-
through
toolbar.

The tools here are:

- ✔ **Position Camera:** This control allows you to specify the location of the walkthrough camera.
- ✔ **Walk:** This control shows an interactive view of the current scene as if you were walking within it.
- ✔ **Look Around:** Like Walk, this makes you feel like you are actually standing in the scene but instead of walking around, only your eyes move.

The Getting Started toolbar

This toolbar (see Figure 11-19) duplicates several tools found in different toolbars. The Paint Bucket, for instance, comes from the Principal toolbar, and the Rectangle tool comes from the Drawing toolbar. It is meant to be a hodgepodge of the controls you are most likely to use regularly. See those for the tools' descriptions.

The Getting Started toolbar is, along with the Google toolbar, one of the two defaults (active when you open the program).

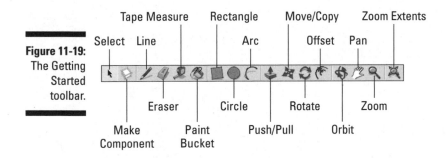

Figure 11-19:
The Getting
Started
toolbar.

The tools here are:

- ✔ **Select:** See the Principal toolbar.
- ✔ **Make Component:** See the Standard toolbar.
- ✔ **Line:** See the Drawing toolbar.
- ✔ **Eraser:** See the Principal toolbar.

- ✔ **Tape Measure:** See the Construction toolbar.

- ✔ **Paint Bucket:** See the Principal toolbar.

- ✔ **Rectangle:** See the Drawing toolbar.

- ✔ **Circle:** See the Drawing toolbar.

- ✔ **Arc:** See the Drawing toolbar.

- ✔ **Push/Pull:** See the Modification toolbar.

- ✔ **Move/Copy:** See the Modification toolbar.

- ✔ **Rotate:** See the Modification toolbar.

- ✔ **Offset:** See the Modification toolbar.

- ✔ **Orbit:** See the Camera toolbar.

- ✔ **Pan:** See the Camera toolbar.

- ✔ **Zoom:** See the Camera toolbar.

- ✔ **Zoom Extents:** See the Camera toolbar.

Large Buttons

The Large Buttons option isn't actually for a toolbar but is used to set the size of the icons and controls in the existing ones. Figure 11-20 shows the default large size, and Figure 11-21 shows the toolbars with the Large Buttons option deselected.

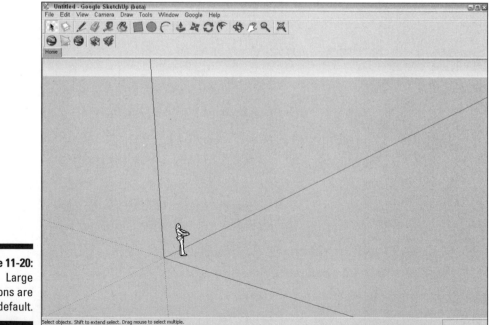

Figure 11-20:
Large
Buttons are
the default.

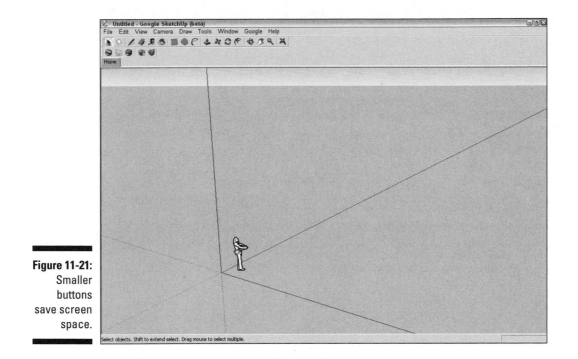

Figure 11-21:
Smaller
buttons
save screen
space.

Chapter 12

Designing with Google SketchUp, Part 2

*I*n this chapter, you can follow along as I work my way through a running example that shows you the basics of creating a 3-D model that you can use in Google Earth. Don't worry — it's nothing complicated, but you can walk away with a good grounding in how Google SketchUp works and what you can do with it. For the specifics of the various SketchUp tools, see Chapter 11.

The example demonstrates how you can "build" a house. Along the way, I show you how to spruce up the structure with details like windows and doors. Beyond the basics, the house will also have a swimming pool and a rooftop deck. I also explore using textures to create materials like wood, glass, and stone to enhance the realism of your creation.

Then, when the house is done, I show you how to move it into Google Earth and add it to the landscape.

After you understand how to do these things, you can either modify this model or create your own from scratch. Pop your model into Google Earth to test-fit it in various locations to see how it looks. Or, figure out how many homes like it could fit within a planned subdivision. Of course, you're not l imited to just making houses — the only limit is your own imagination.

Creating a 3-D Model

To avoid any confusion at a critical moment, make sure that the following toolbars are activated before you start:

- ✔ Views
- ✔ Getting Started
- ✔ Google

To activate a toolbar, choose View➪Toolbars from the menu and then choose the toolbar you want. If you need to review what's on which toolbar, read Chapter 11.

Creating a yard and a house

The two minimums when it comes to housing are some kind of building on some kind of lot. Start with the first things first and make a nice spot of land to build on — say 100' x 110'. Then you can lay down a nice green lawn.

Although you can certainly experiment if you want to, stay with me and use exactly the measurements I give you for this example because everything is designed to fit together.

To start with the yard:

1. **Click the Top icon on the Views toolbar.**

   This way, you're looking directly down.

2. **Select the Rectangle tool.**

3. **Click in the drawing area and without releasing the mouse button, drag the pointer to any other spot. Release the mouse button.**

   You see something like Figure 12-1.

4. **Type** 100,110.

   Do this before you do anything else. You don't have to click anywhere first — just type the numbers, including the comma — but no space.

   These numbers show up in the Dimensions text box in the lower-right corner (see Figure 12-2).

5. **Press Enter.**

   The rectangle is automatically sized to the dimensions of 100' x 110'.

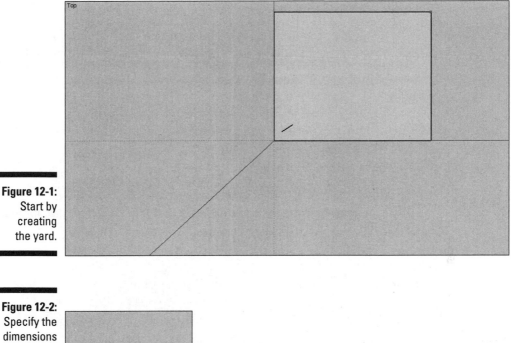

Figure 12-1:
Start by
creating
the yard.

Figure 12-2:
Specify the
dimensions
of your
lot first.

Now add some texturing to the rectangle so it looks like a real lawn. While the rectangle is still selected, follow these steps:

1. **Click the Paint Bucket icon.**

2. **In the Materials dialog box, as shown in Figure 12-3, choose Vegetation. Then choose the first item shown — Grass.**

3. **Click within the lawn rectangle.**

   It takes on the texture of a grass lawn.

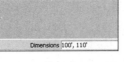

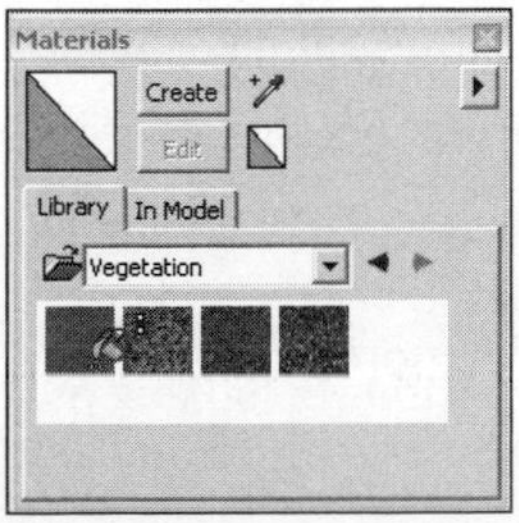

Figure 12-3:
Set a grass
texture for
your lawn.

With a little spot to call your own, put something — how about a house? — on it. Once again, start with a rectangle but do something special to it this time — extrude it upward so that it becomes a three-dimensional solid.

In order to fit neatly within the yard and still leave room for later development, the house will be 60' x 40'. Give it a height of 12'.

1. **Select the Rectangle tool.**

2. **Click within the lawn rectangle, drag the pointer to any other location and then release the mouse button.**

3. **Type** 60,40 **in the Dimensions text box and then press Enter.**

4. **Select the Move/Copy tool.**

5. **Click the house rectangle and drag it so that it is positioned as shown in Figure 12-4.**

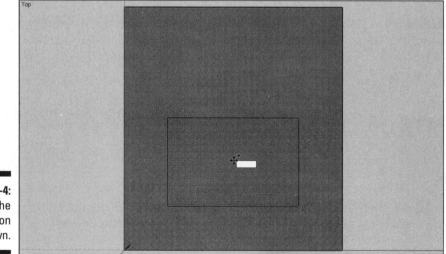

Figure 12-4:
Position the house on your lawn.

6. **Give the structure a texture:**

    a. *Click the Paint Bucket icon.*

    b. *In the Materials dialog box, as shown in Figure 12-5, choose Concrete and then choose Smooth Face Concrete Block.*

    c. *Click within the house rectangle to apply the concrete texture.*

7. **Click the Iso icon on the Views toolbar.**

    This changes the screen so that you're no longer looking at things from directly overhead but rather from above and a bit to one side, as shown in Figure 12-6 — an *isometric* view.

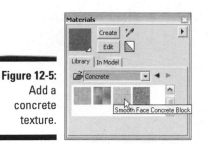

Figure 12-5:
Add a
concrete
texture.

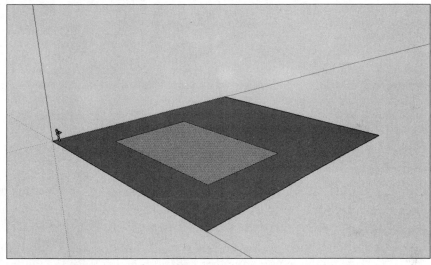

Figure 12-6:
View the
house in Iso.

8. **Click the Push/Pull tool.**

9. **Click the house rectangle; then, while holding down the mouse button, move the Push/Pull tool upward.**

   The rectangle follows the tool and extrudes upward from the ground (see Figure 12-7).

10. **Release the mouse button, type 12, and then press Enter.**

    The house is three-dimensional — measuring 60' x 40' x 12' — and all walls share the original concrete texture.

Adding the deck, porch, and patio

Your house can be way more than just a block of brick or cement sitting in the middle of a lawn. Spruce it up a bit by adding a deck to the top, a porch at the front, and a patio at the back. The porch will be the smaller of the group, measuring only 5' x 3', and the patio will be much larger at 60' x 30'.

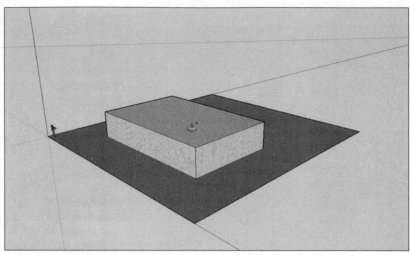

Figure 12-7:
Extrude the structure with the Push/Pull tool.

Building the deck

Tackle the deck first, which is sunken into the roof with dimensions of 58' x 38' x 3'.

1. **Click the Top icon on the Views toolbar so you are looking at the view from directly above.**

2. **Select the Rectangle tool.**

3. **Click within the rooftop area. While holding down the mouse button, move the tool to any other spot and then release the mouse button (see Figure 12-8).**

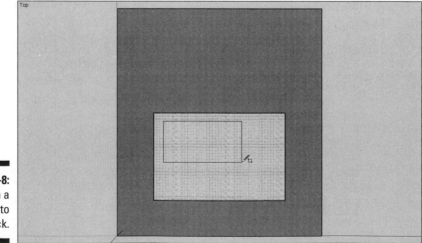

Figure 12-8:
Start with a rectangle to add a deck.

4. **Type** 54,34 **and then press Enter.**

5. **Select the Move/Copy tool, click within the deck rectangle, and position it so that it appears as shown in Figure 12-9.**

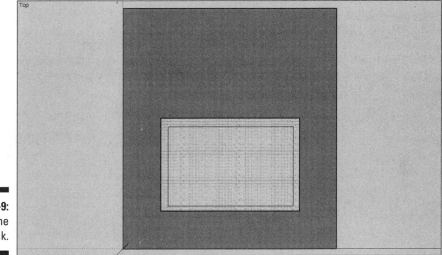

Figure 12-9:
Position the deck.

6. **Add a texture to the deck:**

   a. *Click the Paint Bucket icon.*

   b. *In the Materials dialog box, as shown in Figure 12-10, choose Wood and then choose Wood-floor-dark.*

   c. *Click within the deck rectangle to give it a wooden texture.*

7. **Click the Iso icon on the Views toolbar to get back to the isometric view.**

8. **Click the Push/Pull tool.**

9. **Position the tool within the deck rectangle; then, while holding down the mouse button, move it downward and release the mouse button.**

   The results look like Figure 12-11.

Figure 12-10:
Give your deck a wood texture.

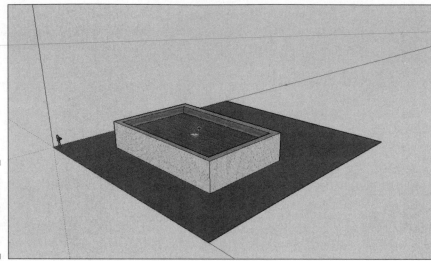

Figure 12-11:
The
completed
sunken
deck.

10. **Type** 4 **and then press Enter.**

This places the floor of the deck exactly four feet below the top of the surrounding wall.

The walls of the deck area share the sunken deck's wooden texture instead of the concrete texture of the outer walls.

Adding the porch and patio

The porch and patio are similar, but they are located at opposite ends and have different sizes. The porch will be larger than the front door (but not overwhelming), and the rear patio will be as wide as the house itself.

1. **Select the Rectangle tool.**

2. **Click the lawn behind the house, drag the pointer to any other location, and then release the mouse button.**

3. **Type** 60,30 **in the Dimensions text box and then press Enter.**

4. **Select the Move/Copy tool.**

5. **Click the patio rectangle and drag it so that it's positioned as shown in Figure 12-12.**

6. **Repeat Steps 1 through 5, this time creating the porch rectangle in front of the house. Also, for Step 3, enter** 3,5 **as the dimensions. For Step 5, drag the rectangle to a position like that shown in Figure 12-13.**

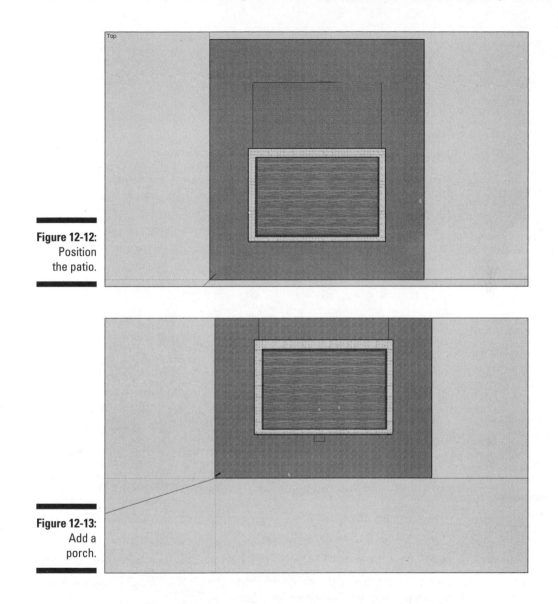

Figure 12-12:
Position
the patio.

Figure 12-13:
Add a
porch.

7. **Add their textures:**

   a. *Click the Paint Bucket icon.*

   b. *In the Materials dialog box, choose Concrete and then choose Concrete.*

   c. *Click within the patio rectangle and then click within the porch rectangle.*

   Both take on a concrete texture.

Adding a swimming pool

A few amenities never hurt anyone. I mean, a patio is nice, but a patio with a swimming pool is even nicer. In this part of your building saga, add a built-in pool at the back of your property and fill it with virtual water.

1. **Click the Top icon on the Views toolbar.**

2. **Select the Rectangle tool.**

3. **Click within the patio area. While holding down the mouse button, move the tool to any other spot and then release the mouse button (see Figure 12-14).**

Figure 12-14:
Add a pool while you're at it.

4. **Type** 40,20 **and then press Enter.**

   These dimensions make the pool fit neatly into the existing patio (60' x 30').

5. **Select the Move/Copy tool, click within the pool rectangle, and position it so that it appears as shown in Figure 12-15.**

6. **Select the Push/Pull tool.**

7. **Position the tool within the pool rectangle. While holding down the mouse button, move it downward and then release the mouse button.**

   The results look like Figure 12-16.

8. **Type** 6" **(that's inches, not feet) and then press Enter.**

   You have a sunken surface that will shortly become "water."

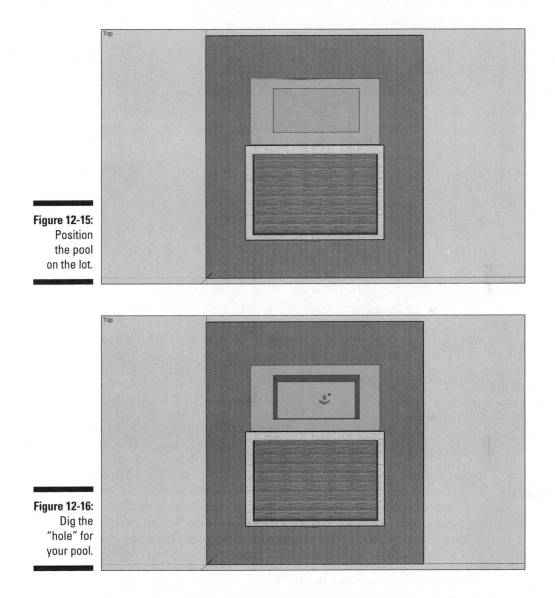

Figure 12-15:
Position
the pool
on the lot.

Figure 12-16:
Dig the
"hole" for
your pool.

Time to change the pool's texture. At this point, its texture is still concrete because it inherited the patio's texture, so I'll change it to one of the more liquid textures.

This process varies from the one used to create the wooden rooftop deck earlier because I want the pool walls to remain concrete and not to share in the water transformation. If you apply the water texture first, this isn't possible.

1. **Click the Paint Bucket icon.**

2. **In the Materials dialog box, choose Water and then choose either Water-pool or Pool Water.**

3. **Click within the pool rectangle.**

   The results look like Figure 12-17.

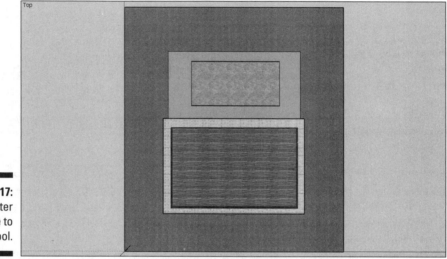

Figure 12-17:
Add a water texture to your pool.

Allowing entry and light: Adding doors and windows

The place is starting to look much more livable, but something significant is missing — namely, doors and windows. Read along to see how to add two different kinds of windows and two different kinds of doors to turn your plain old solid block into a normal house.

The standard windows will be 6' x 3', and the single picture window is 14' x 7'. Standard doors are 3' x 7', and the garage door is the same as the picture window: 14' x 7'.

1. **Click the Front icon on the Views toolbar so that you are looking at the front of the house.**

2. **Select the Rectangle tool and draw a rectangle on the front of the building, as shown in Figure 12-18.**

3. **Type 14,7' and then press Enter.**

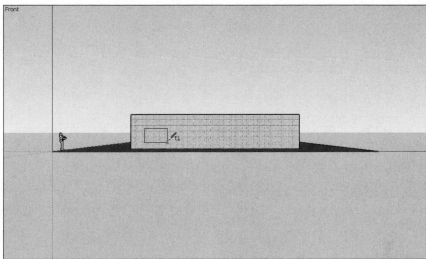

Figure 12-18:
Make a
window for
your house.

4. **Select the Move/Copy tool, click within the picture window rectangle, and position it so that it appears as shown in Figure 12-19.**

5. **After you have one window, you can work with copies of it instead of having to draw a new one every time. Press Ctrl; while holding it down, repeat Step 4.**

   The original picture window remains in place while a copy of it is moved.

6. **Position the copy as shown in Figure 12-20.**

   This copy becomes the garage door.

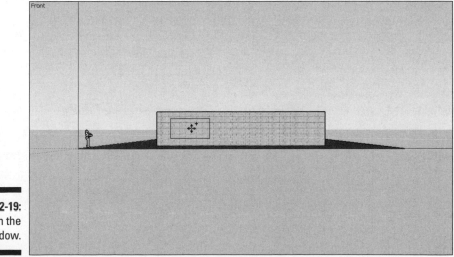

Figure 12-19:
Position the
window.

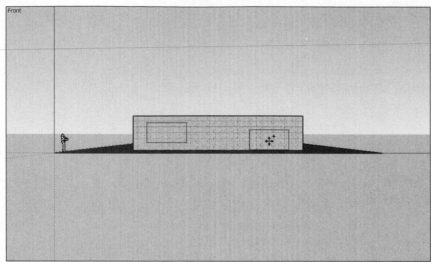

Figure 12-20:
Copy the
window to
make the
garage
door.

7. **Use the Paint Bucket, as in preceding portions of this chapter, to apply textures to the picture window first and then the garage door.**

- *For the picture window:* Choose Glass+Transparent⇨Glass Sky Reflection.

- *For the garage door:* Choose Metal⇨CorrogateShiny.

Your end results look like those shown in Figure 12-21.

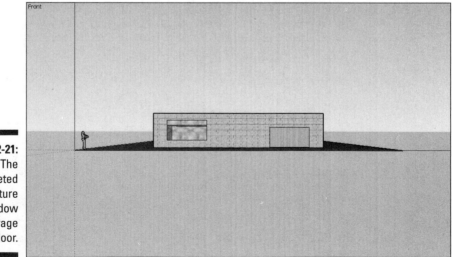

Figure 12-21:
The
completed
picture
window
and garage
door.

Notice that the glass window actually functions like a window: It's not just a pretty bit of reflection but allows you to see through the wall as if it were actually made of glass.

To add more, smaller windows, simply repeat Steps 1 through 4, using 6,3 as the measurements in Step 3.

Every home also needs some way to actually get inside, so toss in a front door as well, using the Push/Pull tool to inset it a few inches from the outer wall. Once again, you're dealing with a rectangular shape, so repeat Steps 1 through 4 of the preceding step list, with the exception that the measurements in Step 3 are 3,7 and that the door should finally be positioned as shown in Figure 12-22.

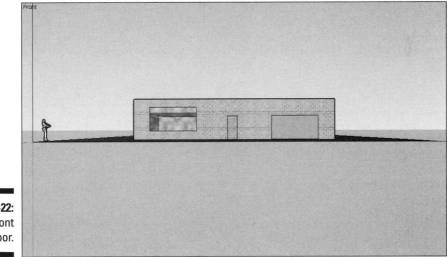

Figure 12-22:
Add a front
door.

Now you have a situation like with the pool. You want the door to be made of wood, but you want the surrounding doorway itself to be made of the same material as the walls. Thus, you need to do the "push" first.

1. **Select the Push/Pull tool.**

2. **Position the tool within the door rectangle; while holding down the mouse button, move it downward and then release the mouse button.**

   The results look like Figure 12-23.

3. **Type 4" (inches, not feet) and press Enter.**

4. **Use the Paint Bucket to add Wood,Wood-cherry texture to the front door (see Figure 12-24).**

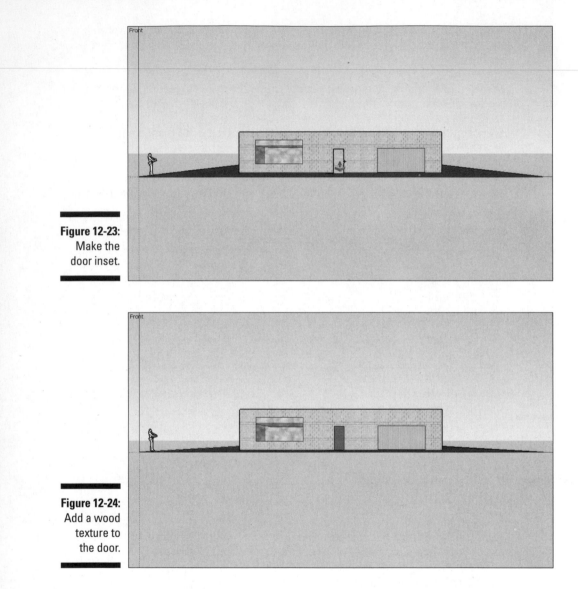

Figure 12-23:
Make the
door inset.

Figure 12-24:
Add a wood
texture to
the door.

To add windows and doors to the other sides, simply select the appropriate icon from the View toolbar (Left, Right, Back, and so on) and repeat the process. Don't forget to make it easier on yourself by using the Copy part of the Move/Copy tool!

Driveway

If you have a garage, it stands to reason that you have a driveway leading to it. The size of the driveway is pretty much constrained by all the other dimensions you've used to this point. It needs to be precisely as wide as that door — 14' — as well as reach from the edge of the lot to the garage door. In this part of your building endeavor, set the one figure as an absolute measurement while doing the other by eyeball.

1. **Select the Top icon on the Views toolbar.**

2. **Draw a rectangle approximately in front of the garage door, as shown in Figure 12-25.**

3. **Type 14 and press Enter.**

   This use of only the first measurement specifies the width of the driveway while leaving its length as you drew it. If you want to specify the opposite — the length — type something like **,20** instead. *Note:* Using the leading comma is important because that tells Google SketchUp that you're not supplying the first number.

4. **Switch to Iso view and then select the Move/Copy tool.**

5. **Position the driveway rectangle in front of the garage door.**

6. **Click the edge of the driveway that is farthest from the garage door. While holding down the mouse button, drag that edge until it reaches the edge of the lot.**

7. **Use the Paint Bucket tool to apply a texture of Colors⇨Black to the driveway rectangle.**

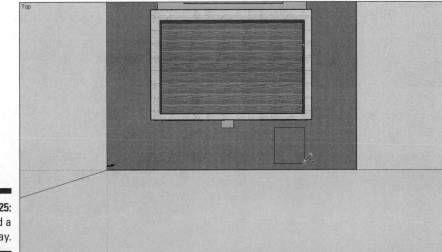

Figure 12-25:
Add a
driveway.

Stepping stones

One way people keep their lawns nice and neat is to provide a pathway from the street to the front door so that people don't wear their own path through the grass. Take a break from the rectangular world and put down a series of circular stepping stones.

In doing so, you create two pathways: one from the driveway to the porch, and one from the edge of the lot. Just to show that not everything runs in straight lines in the world of Google SketchUp, make the one from the driveway follow an arc:

1. **Select the Top icon on the Views toolbar.**

2. **Select the Line tool.**

3. **Click the edge of the porch at the center; while holding down the mouse button, draw a line to the edge of the lawn (see Figure 12-26).**

   This line won't be there long; it's only intended as a guideline for the placement of the stepping stones.

4. **Select the Circle tool.**

5. **Move the point of the pencil over the line you just drew.**

   A red dot shows at the tip when it's in the right spot.

6. **While holding down the mouse button, drag it outward a little bit, and then release the mouse button.**

7. **Type 1 in the Radius text box.**

   This creates a circle two feet in diameter, as shown in Figure 12-27.

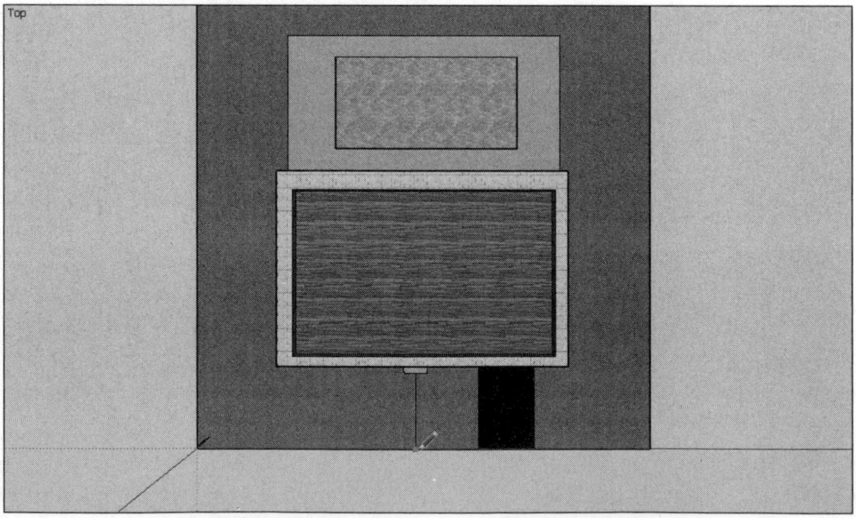

Figure 12-26: Set a temporary guideline for your stones.

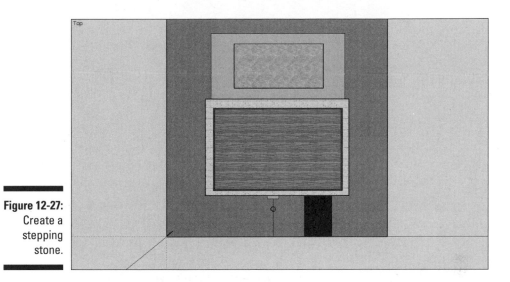

Figure 12-27:
Create a stepping stone.

8. **Select the Paint Bucket tool and use it to apply a texture of Stone⇨ Stone01 to the circle.**

9. **Select the Move/Copy tool and position the stepping stone near the porch.**

10. **Hold down Ctrl (to activate the Copy part of the Move/Copy tool) and then drag a copy of the original stepping stone to a position not far from it, along the same line.**

11. **Repeat Step 10 until the series of stepping stones stretches from the porch to near the edge of the lot (see Figure 12-28).**

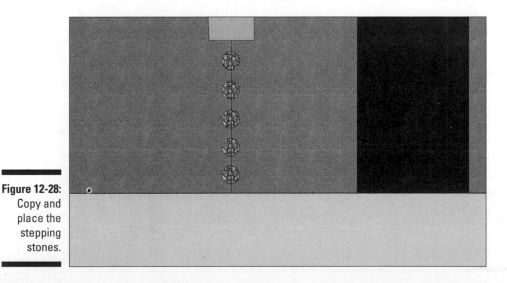

Figure 12-28:
Copy and place the stepping stones.

12. **Choose the Select tool.**

13. **Click the line that lies under the stepping stones to select it.**

14. **Press Delete to delete the line.**

Add the other portion leading to the driveway:

1. **Choose the Arc tool.**

2. **Move the point of the pencil over the stepping stone that is nearest to the porch.**

   When you see a green dot, you're right in the center of the stone.

3. **Click there and then move the pointer to the driveway, about halfway down (see Figure 12-29) and click again.**

   This sets the two outer limits of your arc, which are connected by a straight line.

4. **Move the pointer toward the edge of the lawn.**

   As you do so, the straight line becomes an arc.

5. **When it looks like the pathway you want to create (a gentle arc in this example), click again.**

6. **Repeat Steps 9 through 11 from the preceding step list to position copies of the stepping stones along the arc.**

   The end result looks like Figure 12-30.

7. **Choose the Select tool.**

8. **Click the arc that lies under the stepping stones so that it is selected.**

9. **Press Delete to delete the arc.**

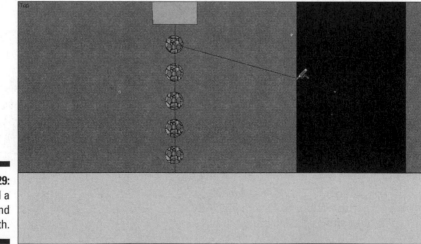

Figure 12-29:
Add a
second
path.

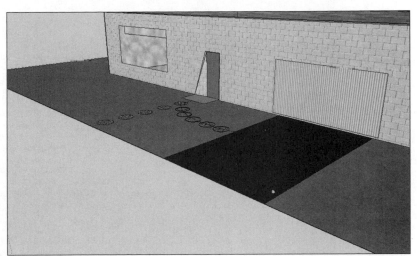

Figure 12-30:
The finished
stepping
stones.

Moving Your Creation to Google Earth

Monkeying around with 3-D models is fun, but the whole point of Google SketchUp is that you can use it with Google Earth. To do so, just follow these simple steps:

1. **Launch Google Earth.**

2. **Go to the location where you want to place your model.**

3. **Within Google SketchUp, click the Place Model icon on the Google toolbar (see Figure 12-31).**

   Your model appears shortly in Google Earth, listed at the bottom of the Places pane, under Temporary Places (see Figure 12-32).

After your creation is in Google Earth, you can change its properties just as with any other object except that you can't right-click it to do so. Instead, you have to right-click its name in the Places pane.

This is a fine approach if you want to try the model out in different locations. However, if you absolutely, definitely, positively, and without a doubt know where it's going to go before you start building it, here's an even better way: Just click the Get Current View button before you start. This automatically imports whatever is in the Viewing Area in Google Earth into Google SketchUp, where you can then go ahead and add your changes.

Use the Toggle Terrain button to switch between a flat view and one that shows the actual shape of the land (see Figure 12-33), so you know how the building sits.

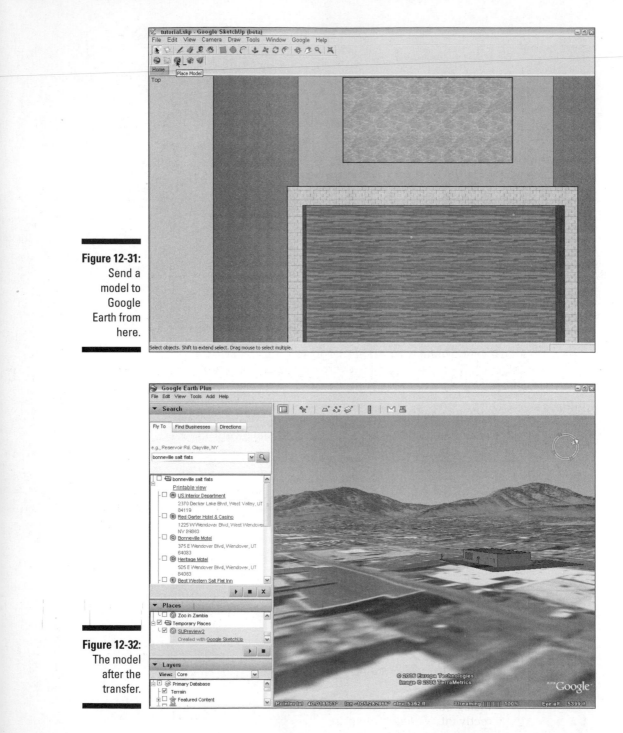

Figure 12-31:
Send a
model to
Google
Earth from
here.

Figure 12-32:
The model
after the
transfer.

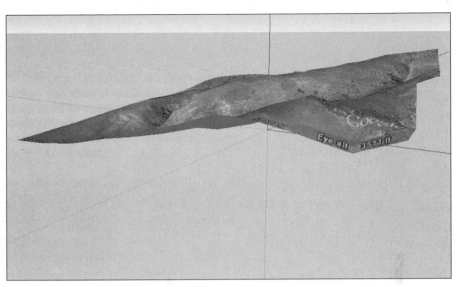

Figure 12-33:
You can turn Terrain on and off.

The Google SketchUp Community

Just like with Google Earth, a community of Google SketchUp users is active on the Web. It's not as large yet, of course, because SketchUp is a newcomer to the Google Earth toolbox, but it's well worth checking out. You can get there by choosing Help➪Google SketchUp Community from the menu. Or you can just use your Web browser to go directly to

```
http://groups.google.com/group/sketchup
```

In addition to exploring the forums, you should check out the existing 3-D models. These have been created both by Google and by Google SketchUp users, and many of them are very nice, indeed. Here's how:

1. **Click the Get Models button.**

   This brings up a Web page, as shown in Figure 12-34.

2. **To download one of the models on the main page, click it.**

3. **In the resulting description page (see Figure 12-35), click the Download Model button.**

   If you click the View in Google Earth button, the model is sent there instead. This is useful if you simply want to see the model but not modify it in any way.

   A dialog box appears, asking whether you want to download the model directly into Google SketchUp.

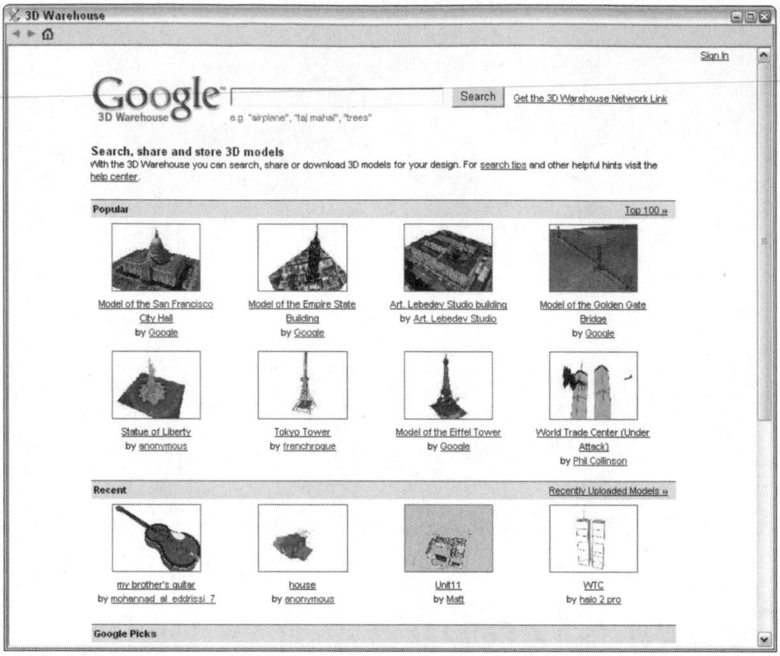

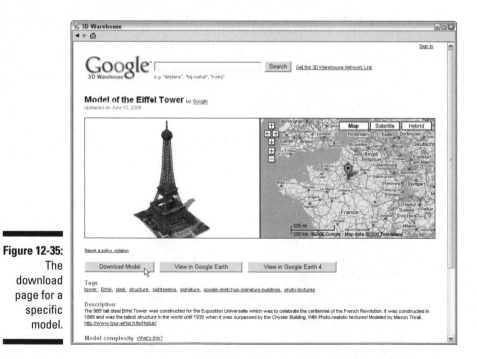

Figure 12-34:
Review
other 3-D
models from
the Get
Models
page.

Figure 12-35:
The
download
page for a
specific
model.

4. Click Yes.

The model appears in SketchUp (see Figure 12-36).

If you click the No button instead, you can save the model to your hard drive for later use.

Figure 12-36:
The model in Google SketchUp.

Chapter 13

Creating Polygons and Other Complex Structures

*W*orking with basic shapes in Google SketchUp is usually sufficient, as I show in the preceding chapter. After all, many things that surround us are made up of simple rectangles, circles, and the like, from our houses to our bookcases and tables, or even cereal boxes and cans of corn. However, Google SketchUp can do a whole lot more than that.

In this chapter and the following one, I wrap up the tour of Google SketchUp by showing you how you can use even more tools and techniques to create not only simple multisided figures like triangles and pentagons but truly complex structures like the ones in Figure 13-1. You can use these structures to create marvelous models to add to Google Earth, whether your intentions are to create industrial models, modify architectural structures, or to just plain get goofy and see what you can come up with.

Before starting these examples, make sure that you have the following toolbars activated:

✔ Views

✔ Modification

✔ Getting Started

✔ Drawing

To activate a toolbar, choose View➪Toolbars from the menu and then click the toolbar's name.

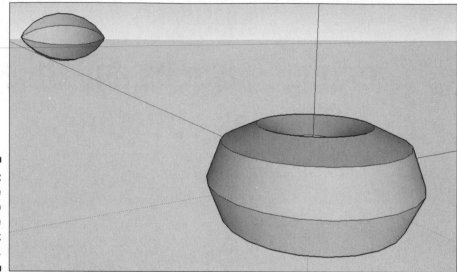

Figure 13-1:
Use Google
SketchUp
to create
complex
forms.

Joining Shapes

Even with the basic shapes, you can build more and more complex items by simply adding simpler ones to each other. Say, for example, that you want to create a World War I biplane model so that you can add a bunch of them to some former French field in Google Earth. Well, biplanes tended to be rather boxy and pretty simple in design, so they're not too much trouble to do — until you get to the most difficult part: the airplane's wings. You could just go with a simple balsa wood glider style and make a flat wing. If you want more realism, though, a true wing is a special shape called an *airfoil,* which is flat on the bottom but curved on the top. This shape is what causes the wing to provide lift; without that, a plane just doesn't get off the ground.

So, how do you create this more challenging shape? Follow along as I show you step by step:

1. **Click the Front icon on the Views toolbar.**

2. **Select the Line tool in the Drawing toolbar.**

3. **Draw a line to become the base of the wing, as shown in Figure 13-2.**

   The specific dimensions aren't important in this exercise.

4. **Select the Arc tool in the Drawing toolbar.**

5. **Click the left edge of the line to set the arc's first end point (see Figure 13-3).**

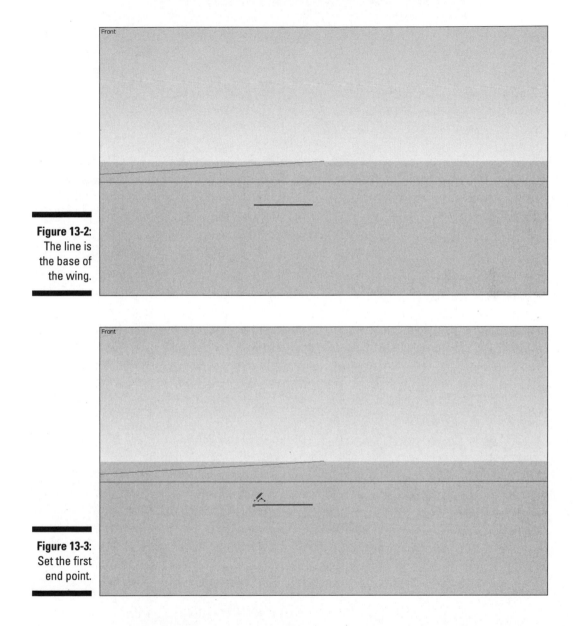

Figure 13-2:
The line is
the base of
the wing.

Figure 13-3:
Set the first
end point.

6. **Click the right edge of the line to set the arc's second end point (see Figure 13-4).**

7. **Move the mouse pointer upward.**

   As you do so, a curved line shows you the current shape of the arc you're creating (see Figure 13-5).

8. **When the arc's curvature is satisfactory to you, click to finish it.**

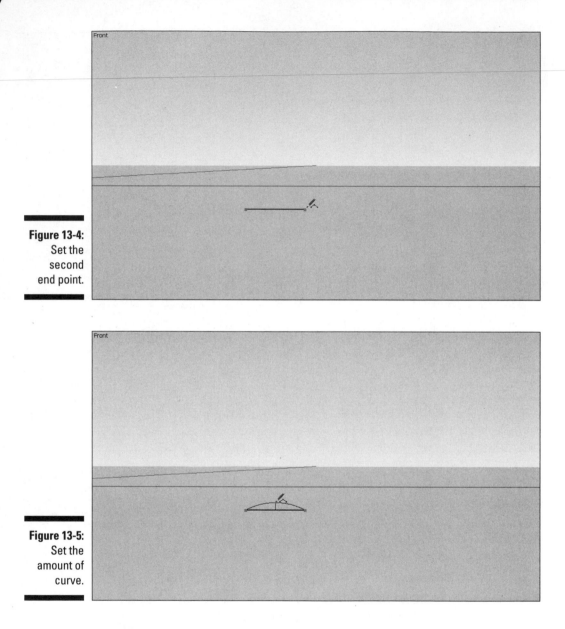

Figure 13-4:
Set the
second
end point.

Figure 13-5:
Set the
amount of
curve.

9. **Click the Iso icon on the Views toolbar.**

10. **Select the Push/Pull tool in the Getting Started toolbar.**

11. **Click in the center of the two-dimensional wing pattern. While holding down the mouse button, move the Push/Pull tool to the side (either side will do).**

    The shape follows the tool and extrudes from its flat state into a wing shape (see Figure 13-6).

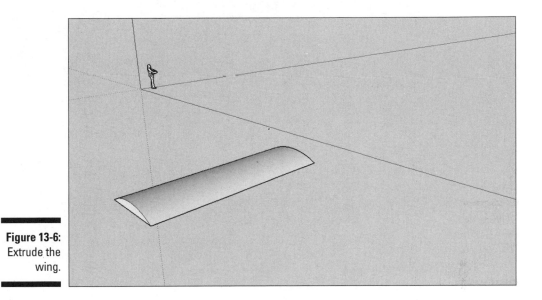

Figure 13-6:
Extrude the
wing.

Designing with the Offset Tool

The Offset tool is kind of specialized. It makes a copy of a shape and moves it either inward or outward from the original. This might not sound too exciting at first, but it saves you a lot of time and trouble when you need to replicate a pattern. This is a common technique in both art and architecture, from the frame around a painting to the eaves around a building's roof.

For this example, I show you how to use the Offset tool to help create a regulation archery target — without having to manually redraw an endless series of circles.

1. **Click the Top icon on the Views toolbar.**
2. **Select the Circle tool in the Drawing toolbar.**
3. **Click to set the center point of the circle.**
4. **While holding down the mouse button, drag it outward a little bit and then release the mouse button.**
5. **Type** 12" **as the radius. This value appears in the Value Control Box at the lower right side of the screen.**

   Because the radius is half of the diameter, this creates a regulation target size of 24", as shown in Figure 13-7.

   You don't have to click in the Value Control Box to activate it before you type values in Google SketchUp — whatever you type while creating an object automatically goes into the Value Control Box.

Figure 13-7:
Size the
original
circle.

6. **Select the Offset tool in the Modification toolbar.**

7. **Click the edge of the circle.**

   A copy of the circle appears. If you move your mouse pointer in or out, the copy follows your movements.

8. **Move the copy inside the original circle (see Figure 13-8).**

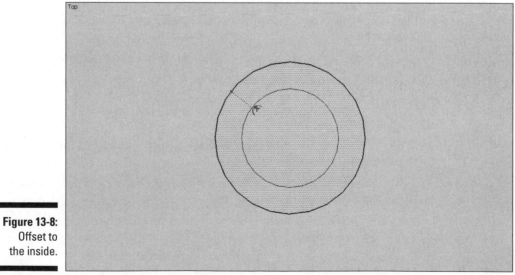

Figure 13-8:
Offset to
the inside.

9. **Type** 1.2".

   This sets the offset at the regulation size for the rings of a regulation archery target.

10. **Click the edge of the inner copy and repeat Steps 8 and 9 to make the second ring. Continue this process with each succeeding circle copy until you create ten rings in all (the bull's-eye being the last), as shown in Figure 13-9.**

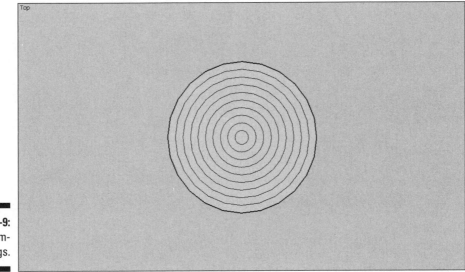

Figure 13-9:
The com-
pleted rings.

11. **Select the Paint Bucket icon.**

12. **Use the Paint Bucket tool on the Getting Started toolbar to apply a texture of Colors in the following manner:**

    - *White:* Outer two rings
    - *Black:* Third and fourth rings
    - *Blue:* Fifth and sixth rings
    - *Red:* Seventh and eighth rings
    - *Yellow:* Ninth and tenth rings

    Your target should look like the one in Figure 13-10.

White   Black   Blue   Red   Yellow

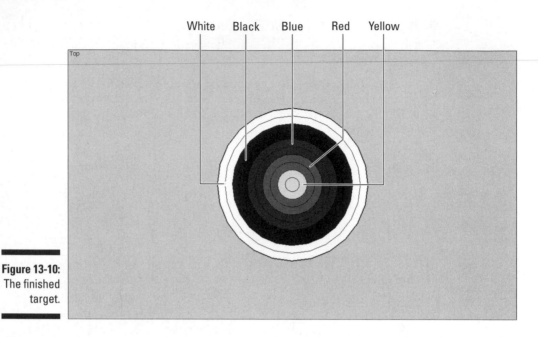

Figure 13-10:
The finished
target.

Creating Polygons

A *polygon* is a many-sided figure (see Figure 13-11). Any closed shape with
three or more sides (you can't possibly close a shape with fewer sides) can
be generated in Google SketchUp.

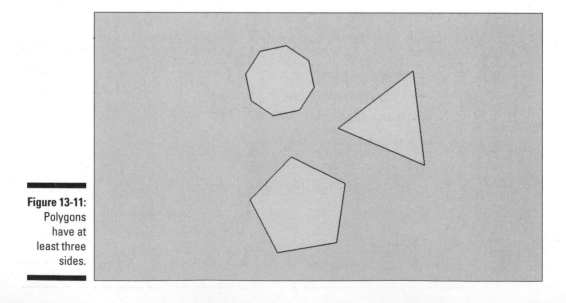

Figure 13-11:
Polygons
have at
least three
sides.

There is a practical limitation, however. Simpler shapes, such as triangles or pentagons, are very distinctive. As you add more sides, though, all polygons tend to look like circles. Figure 13-12 shows a circle next to a polygon with 100 sides.

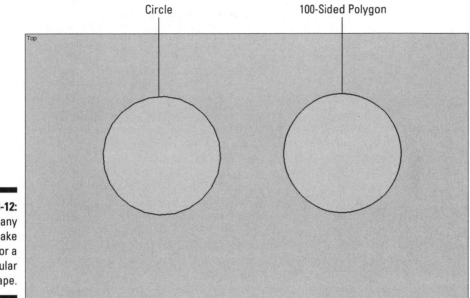

Figure 13-12:
Too many sides make for a circular shape.

This circularizing effect begins to become apparent after a polygon has approximately ten sides (a *decagon*). Table 13-1 shows the names for several of the common polygons.

Table 13-1	Common Names for Polygons
Number of Sides	*Proper Term*
3	Triangle
4	Rectangle
5	Pentagon
6	Hexagon
7	Heptagon
8	Octagon
9	Nonagon
10	Decagon

Making a simple polygon

Take a look at how to make a polygon in Google SketchUp:

1. **Click the Top icon on the Views toolbar.**

2. **Select the Polygon tool in the Drawing toolbar.**

3. **Click to set the center point of the polygon.**

4. **Move your mouse pointer outward.**

   As you do so, the size of the polygon changes in response to your action (see Figure 13-13).

   It doesn't matter at this point how many sides the polygon has; I show you how to set that next.

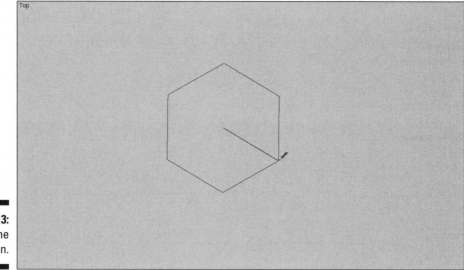

Figure 13-13:
Size the
polygon.

5. **When you're satisfied with the size, click to set it.**

6. **(Optional) If you want a different number of sides, enter the number of sides you want, followed by an *s* (with no space between the number and the *s*), and then press Enter.**

   For instance, say that you just drew an octagon but really want a triangle. Just type **3s** and then press Enter.

   The figure instantly changes to a three-sided one, as shown in Figure 13-14.

Of course, if you want a pentagon, type **5s** instead, **6s** for a hexagon, and so forth.

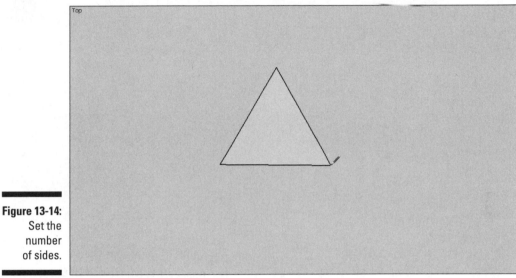

Figure 13-14:
Set the
number
of sides.

Making an arrowhead

I'll wrap this chapter up with a more complex example before moving on to the really fancy stuff in the next one. As long as I'm on an archery theme, why not make a four-pointed arrowhead? It's easy to do in Google SketchUp — just a couple of triangles, after all — but, in the process, I'll fill you in on a few more tips and tricks that'll stand you in good stead on your later projects.

This example starts with the triangle that I created in the preceding exercise. (If you didn't do it, just back up a page or so — you can catch up in a minute.)

1. **Select the Push/Pull tool in the Getting Started toolbar.**

   You can find this tool in the Modification toolbar as well.

2. **Click the triangle and move your mouse pointer upward a little bit.**

3. **Type** 0.1mm **and then press Enter.**

   This makes the triangle three-dimensional although it is now a blade of razor sharpness (see Figure 13-15).

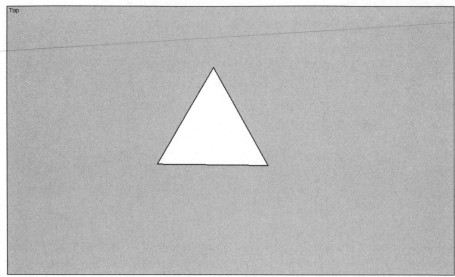

Figure 13-15:
Make a thin
3-D object.

Before moving on to the next steps, you need to select the blade. However, what you and I think of as one three-dimensional figure is actually composed of several elements (every line and the space between lines are individual parts of the whole — see the next chapter for details), and you need to select them all at once. There are two ways to do this, depending upon what you have on your screen (assuming that you have followed these steps religiously, there should be nothing else there but, if you're the sort of person who likes to experiment, you may have several items on screen right now).

- *If that blade is the only thing there,* all you have to do is press Ctrl+A. This automatically selects everything in Google SketchUp.

- *If you have other objects besides the blade,* click the Selection icon. If you press Ctrl+A, the other objects would be selected as well, which is probably not desirable.

4. **Click above and to the side of the blade. Hold down the mouse button and drag your pointer all the way across and down so that you draw a box around it, as shown in Figure 13-16.**

5. **Release the mouse button.**

   The entire range of elements that was within the box is now selected, but nothing else is. Here's how to solve that problem once and for all.

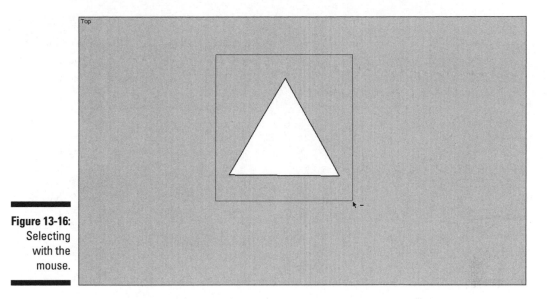

Figure 13-16:
Selecting
with the
mouse.

6. **Take all these disparate parts (the lines and faces that make up the developing arrowhead) and make them into one unit by choosing Edit➪Make Group from the menu.**

   Now — and from now on — all the parts will move together. In the next step, we will use this feature to make an exact copy.

7. **Select the Move/Copy tool in the Getting Started toolbar.**

8. **Hold down the Ctrl key to turn on the Copy function and then click the blade.**

9. **While holding down the mouse button, drag a copy of the blade to the side, far enough away that the original and the copy are not in contact (see Figure 13-17).**

   In the next steps, I show you how to rotate one so that they are at right angles to one another.

10. **Switch to Front view by clicking the Front icon.**

11. **Select the Rotate tool in the Modification toolbar and move it over one of the blades.**

    A protractor appears, as shown in Figure 13-18. As you move the mouse pointer over different parts of the blade, various names appear, such as Endpoint in Group or Midpoint of Group.

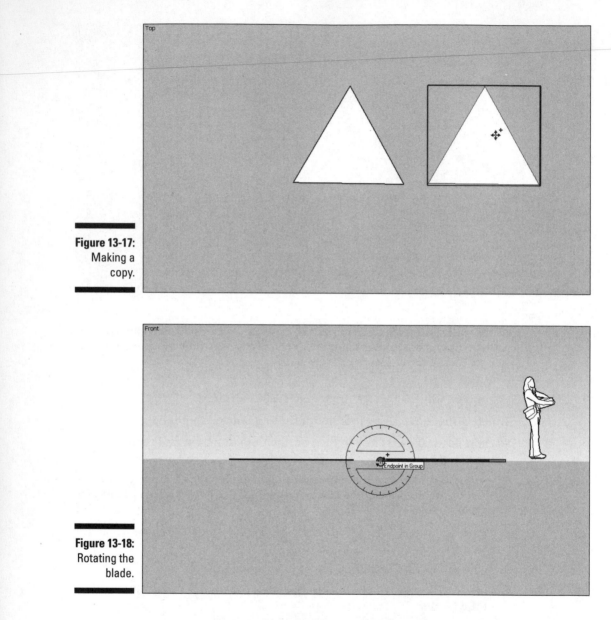

Figure 13-17:
Making a
copy.

Figure 13-18:
Rotating the
blade.

12. **Click the two rear endpoints of the blade.**

13. **Type** 90 **and then press Enter.**

    The blade rotates a quarter turn (90 degrees), as shown in Figure 13-19. Now it's time to bring the two blades together.

14. **Select the Move/Copy tool in the Getting Started toolbar.**

Figure 13-19:
Set the
blade at 90
degrees.

15. Click the rotated blade and, while holding down the mouse button, drag it until it bisects the other blade (see Figure 13-20).

16. Repeat Steps 4 through 6 to make the finished arrowhead a unit.

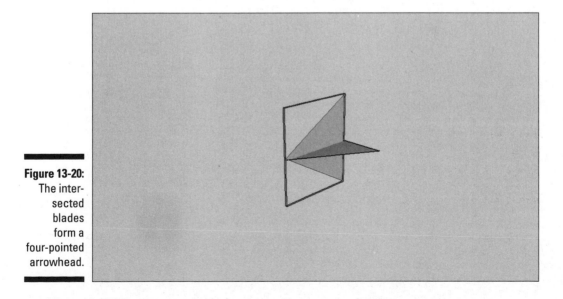

Figure 13-20:
The inter-
sected
blades
form a
four-pointed
arrowhead.

Chapter 14

Digging Deeper with Google SketchUp

In this final chapter on Google SketchUp, I dig into some of the more fascinating things you can do when creating three-dimensional models. Despite the fact that the program mainly works with flat surfaces, I can show you a few tricks — such as text callouts and dimensional markings — to bring to the party that will allow you to go way beyond using simple right angles in your work. Before starting these tutorials, make sure that you have the following toolbars activated:

✔ Views

✔ Drawing

✔ Getting Started

✔ Modification

✔ Construction

To activate a toolbar, choose View➪Toolbars from the menu and then choose the toolbar name.

Slicing and Extruding a Stairway

Assuming that you use Google SketchUp (at least occasionally) to make house models, you might want to include a stairway. As with most actions in this program, you'll be working with rectangular shapes to do so. (See later sections for creating fancier shapes.)

To make a stairway with the Push/Pull tool, follow these steps:

1. **Select the Iso view on the Views toolbar.**

2. **Select the Rectangle tool on the Drawing toolbar.**

3. **Click to set the first corner of the rectangle and then drag the pointer until the rectangle is of sufficient size, as shown in Figure 14-1. Then release the mouse button.**

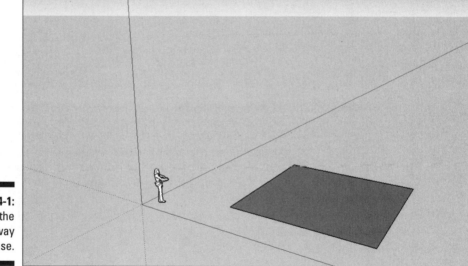

Figure 14-1:
Create the stairway base.

4. **Click the Push/Pull tool in the Getting Started toolbar.**

5. **Click the rectangle and move the mouse pointer upward to extrude it (see Figure 14-2).**

6. **Click the Line tool in the Drawing toolbar.**

7. **Click the left side of the extruded rectangle to set the start point for the line.**

8. **Click the right side to set the end point.**

The result looks like Figure 14-3.

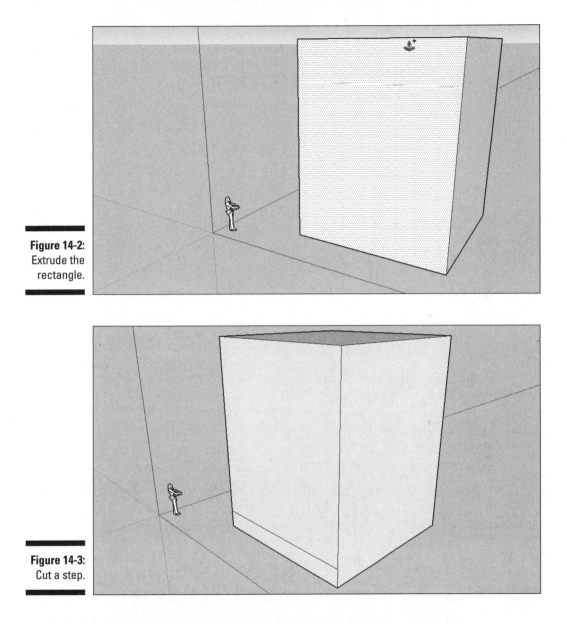

Figure 14-2:
Extrude the
rectangle.

Figure 14-3:
Cut a step.

9. Repeat Step 8, drawing more lines (see Figure 14-4).

10. Click the Push/Pull tool in the Getting Started toolbar.

11. Click between the two bottom lines and pull the area outward to form the lower step (see Figure 14-5).

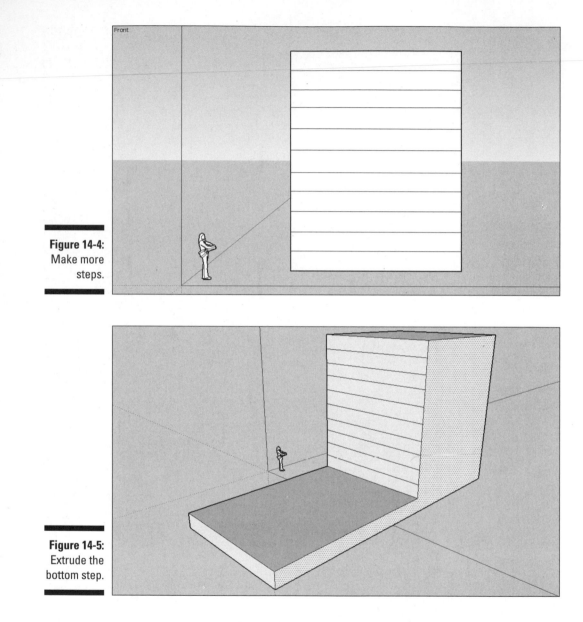

Figure 14-4:
Make more steps.

Figure 14-5:
Extrude the bottom step.

12. **Click between the next set of lines and repeat Step 11, pulling the step out a little bit less than the lower one, as shown in Figure 14-6. Continue to do so until all the steps have been extruded, as shown in Figure 14-7.**

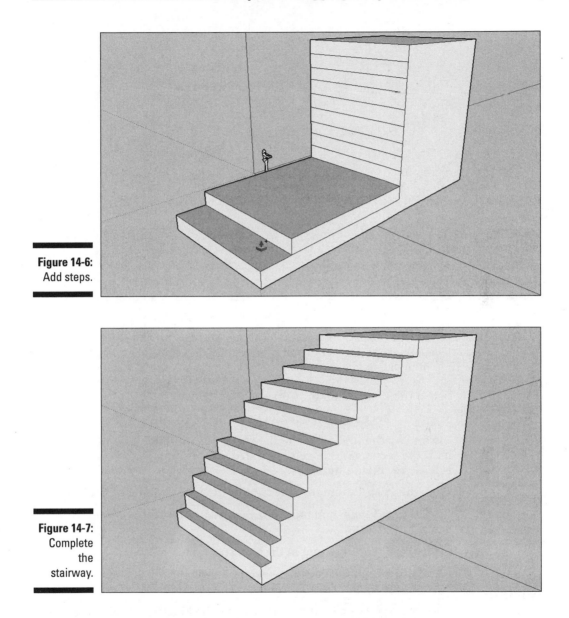

Figure 14-6:
Add steps.

Figure 14-7:
Complete
the
stairway.

Understanding Lines and Faces

It's time for some technical stuff about these figures I've been showing you. Everything you've been doing in the earlier chapters on Google SketchUp is composed of two basic elements: lines and faces. A *line* is, well, a line, plain and simple. When you work with figures like a rectangle, however, the area between those four lines isn't empty. Rather, it's filled by the *face,* just like how glass in a picture frame fills the area inside it (see Figure 14-8).

Figure 14-8:
Lines
surround
faces.

Lines and faces behave very differently from one another, and altering them can have a powerful impact on your modeling. You can gain an intuitive feel for the difference between the ways they act by doing the following exercise:

1. **Select the Iso view on the Views toolbar.**

2. **Select the Rectangle tool on the Drawing toolbar.**

3. **Click to set the first corner of the rectangle and then drag the pointer until the rectangle is of sufficient size, as shown in Figure 14-9. Finally, release the mouse button.**

4. **Click the Push/Pull tool in the Getting Started toolbar.**

5. **Click the rectangle and move the mouse pointer upward to extrude it (see Figure 14-10).**

6. **Click the Move/Copy tool in the Getting Started toolbar.**

7. **Click any face in the rectangle; while holding down the mouse button, move the pointer.**

   The results are exactly the same as using the Push/Pull tool — the face extrudes in the direction in which it is moved.

The Move/Copy tool works this way only with three-dimensional shapes. If you try this with a two-dimensional rectangle, you simply move the whole thing — not extrude the face.

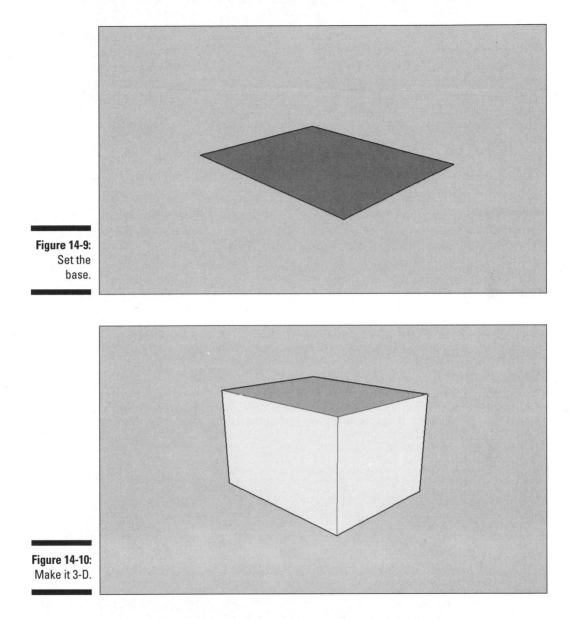

Figure 14-9:
Set the
base.

Figure 14-10:
Make it 3-D.

8. **Now comes the fun part. Click any line and repeat the moves you used in Step 7 for faces.**

   The exact shape you create varies, depending upon which line you pick and in what direction you move it. Figure 14-11 shows one possible result.

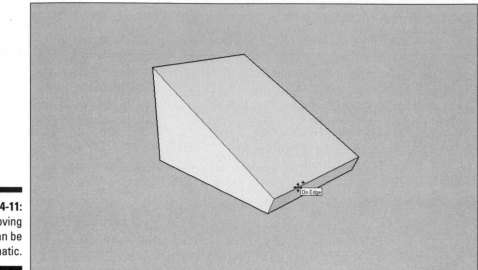

Figure 14-11:
Moving lines can be dramatic.

9. **Click the Undo icon (or press Ctrl+Z) as many times as necessary to return to the basic solid rectangle. Then try moving different faces and different lines in different ways.**

Figure 14-12 shows several possible results that all started as simple extruded rectangles.

Repeat this step until you feel comfortable modifying your models this way.

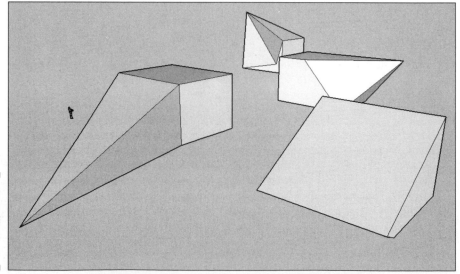

Figure 14-12:
Some examples of distorted rectangles.

Think of it this way: When you extrude or move a face, the attached lines follow along. When you move a line, however, it is the faces that follow along. The first method allows for nothing more dramatic than extending things at right angles to one another. The second, however, lets you create any kind of angle you want, helping you to create sharp corners, sloping ramps, or even twisted creations that would confuse M.C. Escher himself.

The Follow Me Tool

The Follow Me tool might seem oddly named at first, but you'll soon see just exactly how apt it is. When you want to add something like a projecting eave to an existing figure, the Follow Me tool allows you to drag it along the edge of that figure — the new element follows your mouse cursor as you do so.

1. **Select the Iso view on the Views toolbar.**

2. **Select the Rectangle tool on the Drawing toolbar.**

3. **Click to set the first corner of the rectangle, drag the pointer until the rectangle is of sufficient size (as shown in Figure 14-13), and then release the mouse button.**

4. **Click the Push/Pull tool on the Getting Started toolbar.**

5. **Click the rectangle and move the mouse pointer upward to extrude it. (You know the drill by now.)**

6. **Click one of the upper corners of the extruded rectangle and then draw a small rectangle, as shown in Figure 14-14.**

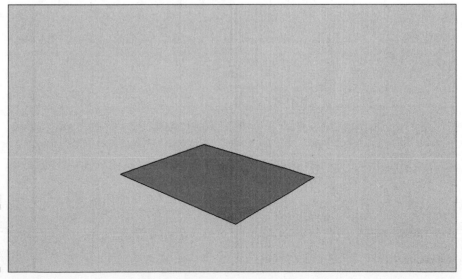

Figure 14-13:
Create the
base.

Figure 14-14:
Add the item
to follow.

7. **Click the Follow Me tool on the Modification toolbar.**

8. **Click the edge of the 3-D rectangle and drag the mouse pointer around the first two sides.**

   The line you are following turns red as you do so, and the smaller rectangle is subtracted from the larger one, as shown in Figure 14-15.

Figure 14-15:
The fol-
lowing in
progress.

9. When you reach the endpoint of the second side, click.

The completed figure is shown in Figure 14-16.

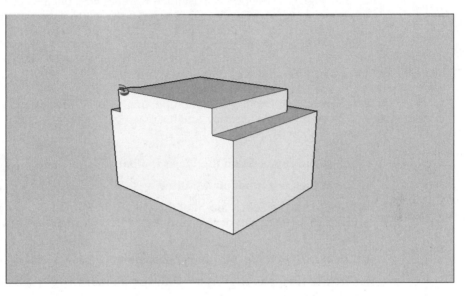

Figure 14-16:
The original shape with the other shape subtracted from it.

Note that this example used a shape that was *within* the boundaries of the extruded rectangle, which is why it was subtracted from the shape. If you use the Follow Me tool with an intersecting shape that starts outside the boundaries instead, the resulting shape is *added* to the original one (see Figure 14-17).

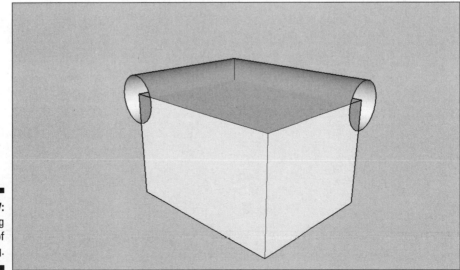

Figure 14-17:
Adding instead of subtracting.

Lathing a Polygon

The Follow Me tool can be very useful in working with flat surfaces, but it has a very special feature as well — unlike the Push/Pull tool, you can use it to create some very complex curved surfaces. The method for doing so involves creating a flat base shape and then sweeping it around in a circle, resulting in a three-dimensional version. This technique is also called *lathing* because it produces results similar to those of a wood lathe.

If it sounds like a complicated operation, don't worry. The user interface in Google SketchUp makes it easy, and it's reasonably similar to the normal way to use the Follow Me tool:

1. **Select the Top view on the Views toolbar.**

2. **Select the Circle tool on the Drawing toolbar.**

3. **Click to set the center point of the circle, drag the pointer until the circle is the size you desire, and then release the mouse button. (See Figure 14-18.)**

4. **Click the Front icon on the Views toolbar.**

5. **Click the Polygon tool on the Drawing toolbar.**

6. **Click the left edge of the circle to set the center point of the polygon, as shown in Figure 14-19.**

7. **Move your mouse pointer outward until it looks like the one in Figure 14-20; then click to set the size.**

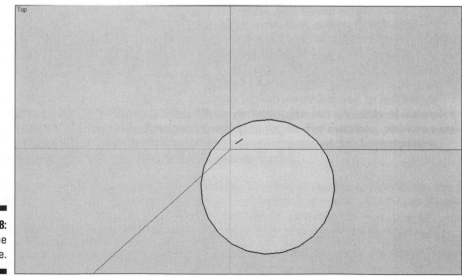

Figure 14-18:
Setting the
circle.

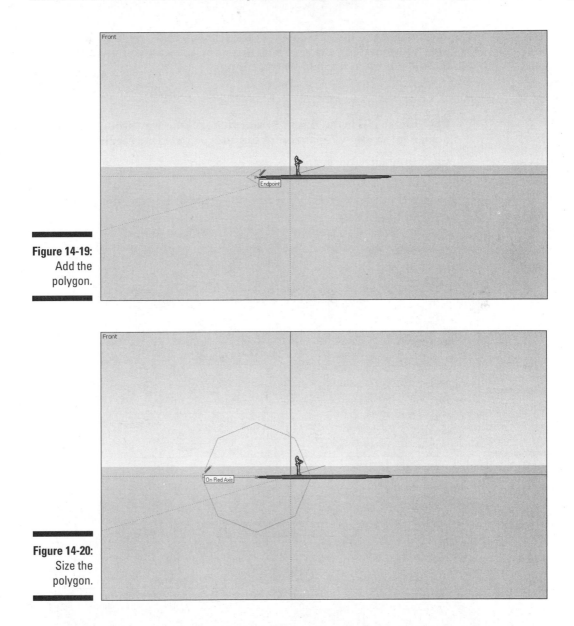

Figure 14-19:
Add the
polygon.

Figure 14-20:
Size the
polygon.

8. **If the figure is not already an octagon, type** 8s **and then press Enter to make it into one.**

   Read more about creating polygons in Chapter 13.

9. **Select the Follow Me tool on the Modification toolbar.**

10. **Select Iso from the Views toolbar.**

11. **Click the octagon.**

12. **Click the rim of the circle next to the octagon and drag the mouse pointer around the circle (which turns red to assist you — you can even see it when it's behind something).**

   As you do so, the octagon follows the pointer around the circle, as shown in Figure 14-21.

13. **Continue to circle the rim until you come all the way around and the octagonal shape sweeps around the entire circle (see Figure 14-22).**

14. **Click to finalize the shape.**

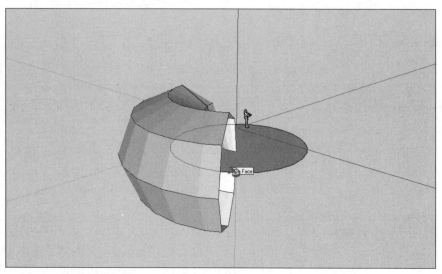

Figure 14-21: The sweep in process.

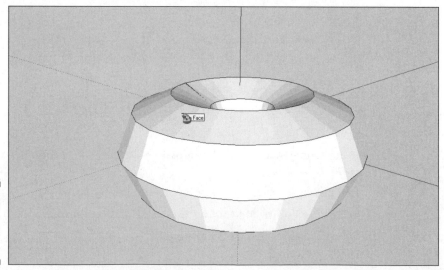

Figure 14-22: The completed lathing.

As you can see, the shape is vastly more complex than the run-of-the-mill rectangular or cylindrical solids. The exact nature of the resulting three-dimensional shape, of course, depends upon several factors:

- ✔ The shape of the original two-dimensional figure
- ✔ The size of the circle about which it is swept
- ✔ Its exact placement on that circle

Varying any of these points creates a different shape.

Setting Leader Text

You've probably noticed that some of the figures in this book include *text callouts* — brief descriptions of things like toolbar icons with a line indicating where the named item is found. They can be very helpful in communicating exactly what is where. Google SketchUp lets you add callouts, also called *leader text*, to your own creations as well.

Here's how it's done:

1. **Click the Text icon in the Construction toolbar.**

2. **Click the point you want the text to refer to.**

3. **Move the mouse pointer to where you want to place the text.**

   As you do so, the leader line extends from the point you choose in Step 2 and follows the movement of the pointer (see Figure 14-23).

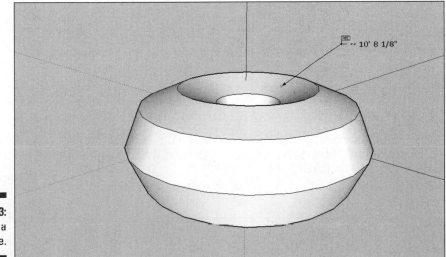

Figure 14-23: Extending a leader line.

4. Click to set the text location.

An editable text box appears at that location, as shown in Figure 14-24.

By default, some text is already in the text box, depending upon the object you clicked in Step 2. Usually, this is one of the measurements of some element of the object. Simply ignore it.

Figure 14-24:
Add leader text.

‹~ 10' 8 1/8"

5. Type your text into the text box; then click outside the text box (or press Enter twice).

The results should look something like Figure 14-25.

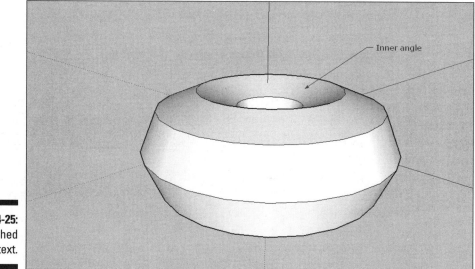

Figure 14-25:
The finished leader text.

To edit existing text, click the Select icon and then double-click the text on screen. The text box opens, and the text within can be edited just like when you first created it.

Understanding the Tape Measure and Dimension Tools

Two tools measure dimensions in Google SketchUp. The Tape Measure and Dimension tools are very similar, but they have slightly different purposes:

- **Tape Measure:** The Tape Measure tool is used just like you use a physical tape measure from your toolbox — to get a momentary idea of exactly how long an object on your screen is.

- **Dimension:** The Dimension tool is kind of a blend of the Tape Measure and Text tools. Like the Tape Measure tool, it gets the length of an object; like the Text tool, it lets you mark that measurement much as leader text is used.

Follow along and you'll quickly get the hang of it. Tackle the Tape Measure tool first:

1. **Select the Iso view on the Views toolbar.**

2. **Select the Rectangle tool on the Drawing toolbar.**

3. **Click to set the first corner of the rectangle, drag the pointer to set the opposite corner, and then release the mouse button.**

4. **After you have something to measure, select the Tape Measure tool on the Construction toolbar.**

5. **Click at the point where you want to begin the measurement.**

6. **Move the Tape Measure to the end point of your measurement.**

   The metaphor for Steps 5 and 6 is precisely as if you were actually using a tape measure in real life. As you move the pointer, a line extends from the starting point. When you pause in your movement, the current length of that line is shown (see Figure 14-26).

7. **When you're done measuring, click.**

   The "tape" automatically "rewinds."

8. **Click the Dimensions tool on the Construction toolbar.**

9. **Click one corner of the rectangle to set the start point for the measurement.**

10. **Move the pointer and click another corner to set the end point (see Figure 14-27).**

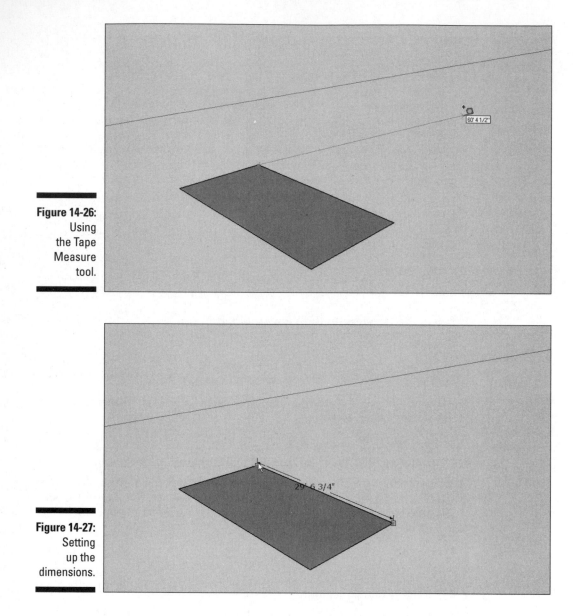

60' 4 1/2"

Figure 14-26:
Using
the Tape
Measure
tool.

29' 6 3/4"

Figure 14-27:
Setting
up the
dimensions.

11. Move the pointer away from the rectangle.

As you do so, a set of dimensioning lines with the length displayed in the middle follows the pointer (see Figure 14-28).

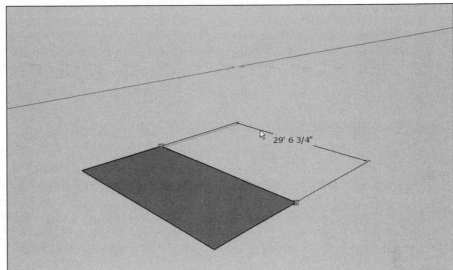

Figure 14-28:
Moving the
dimension
info
outward.

12. **When the dimension display is positioned as you wish, click to set it in place.**

You can also use the Move/Copy tool to reposition the dimension display on the screen later.

Part V
The Part of Tens

The 5th Wave   By Rich Tennant

SOMEWHERE IN THE CITY, SASQUATCH, BIGFOOT AND ELVIS SPEND ANOTHER WARY NIGHT.

"Look – all I'm saying is that every time they come out with a new version of Google Earth with an improved search function, it's just a matter of time."

In this part . . .

Chapter 15 shows you where to go when you need to find out where something is. These ten sites will give you the latitudes and longitudes of just about any place you can imagine.

Chapter 16 tells you where to find those external data files you need. These ten sites have everything from Neolithic map images to ecological data that you can add to Google Earth.

Chapter 17 turns you on to some things you'll want to add to your toolbox — things like data converters that let you adapt the output from other popular GIS programs to Google Earth or image-manipulation tools that help you explore what you've already found.

Chapter 15

Ten Great Places to Get Coordinates

•••

*I*n this chapter, I take a look at ten Web sites that are useful for finding locations of both famed and obscure places around the world. Each site has its own purpose and method of searching. One, for example, might be geared toward pilots and another toward astronomers, but all provide you with the information you need to track down locations for use in Google Earth.

As great as Google Earth is, it can't anticipate what's important to everyone on Earth, so here I give you a hodgepodge of Web sites that are dedicated to helping you find anything, even if it's not already in the Google Earth database. Each of these ten sites provides differing ways of showing where something exists on the Earth, without you needing to already know what the latitude/longitude of the objects in question are. Each site has its own distinct user base. For example, Google Earth Community core members tend to be older and professional users (pilots, geographers, teachers, and so on), but something like Google Earth Hacks (GEH) has a younger user base that isn't as focused on forums and discussion. Aliensview is similar in its user base to GEH.

You'll find, somewhere among these dozen-minus-two sites, not only one that you'll want to use every day but the backups that you'll need when your favorite site just doesn't have the info you need. Somewhere, though, among the Web sites in this chapter, you can find the exact location of nearly every place on Earth.

You can find a ready-made list of interesting locations to look for in Appendix C.

Aliensview Sightseeing

Aliensview Sightseeing is literally made for Google Earth users. Although its database is not as comprehensive as some, it meshes nicely with Google Earth because it is designed to. The locales revealed in its searches can be opened automatically in Google Earth.

Here's how to get your bearings:

1. **Go to www.aliensview.com.**

2. **In the menu on the left side of the page (see Figure 15-1), click the Search option (located between Donate and New Entries).**

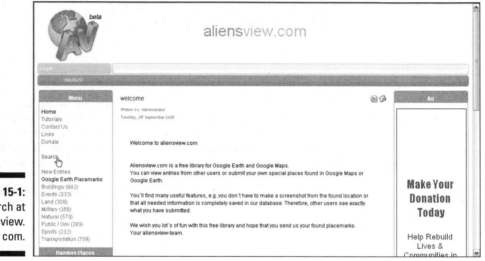

Figure 15-1: Search at Aliensview. com.

3. **In the resulting Search Engine page, as shown in Figure 15-2, enter the name of the location you're looking for in the Keywords text box.**

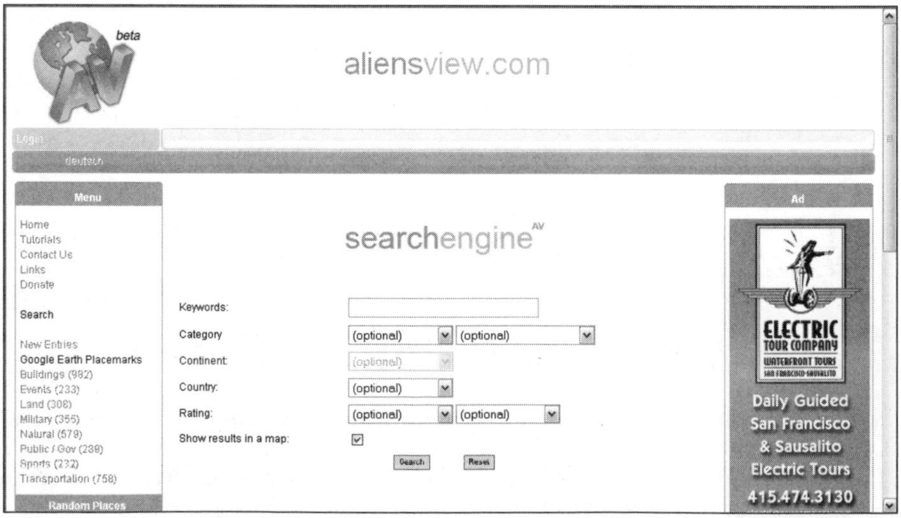

Figure 15-2: Enter data on the Search Engine page.

4. (Optional) Click the Category drop-down lists to specify the type of thing you're hunting.

Categories include Buildings, Military, Sports, and so on. After you choose a category, the Options drop-down list becomes active as well. For example, if you choose Buildings, you also gain options such as Castles, Factories, and Skyscrapers to help you limit your search still further.

5. You can do the same thing with the Continent and Country options to further narrow your search.

For instance, if you're looking for Paris, Texas (not Paris, France), you can use these options to skip past the better-known city in Europe.

6. (Optional) Limit the search by checking the user rating of the locale (popularity ratings by the registered users of Aliensview). To do this:

a. Click the first Rating drop-down list and choose either At Least or At Most

b. Click the second Rating drop-down list and choose a rating from 1 to 5, 1 being the lowest.

7. If you want to see a map of the search result, select the Show Results in a Map check box.

8. Click the Search button.

The instructions on the resulting page are in German (see Figure 15-3), but the links are usually in English.

9. Click the desired link. (In this example, I chose Notre Dame de Paris.)

1. **Paris** Sign
Ugly one.

2. Disneyland **Paris** Resort

3. Notre Dame de **Paris**

4. Eiffel tower in **Paris** France
Eiffel Tower (Tour Eiffel) in **Paris**, France

5. Locomotive Turntable - **Paris**

6. Pont Neuf
This is the oldest bridge in **Paris**; work started on it in 1578 under Henry III, and it was finished in 1606 under Henry IV. For the way it was conceived, however, it is extremely modern, ...

7. La Grande Arche de la D?fense
"The Other Arch" just outside **Paris**.

8. Pantheon of **Paris**
A monument to skip when visiting **paris**. No longer a church. Now a memorial to France's greats. Also site of the famous Foucault's Pendulum experiment. The area behind the Pantheon is ...

9. **Paris** Opera House
Mainly used for Ballet nowadays. This is the location of the musical Phantom of the Opera.

10. Circus in **Paris** 06

11. Circus in **Paris** 03
Le cirque du Grand C?leste.

Figure 15-3:
The results page shows all matching locations.

10. **When the link opens, scroll down beneath the image to where it reads** `Eintrag downloaden und in Google Earth öffnen` **(which means** *Download this entry and open it in Google Earth*) **and click that.**

    If you click the Open button in the resulting dialog box, Google Earth opens at that location (as in Figure 15-4). If you choose Save, you can store the KML file for later viewing.

You can find this file in the Temporary Places folder in your Places pane. When you exit Google Earth, you are asked whether you want the file moved to My Places. Clicking Yes will mean the location is permanently added; clicking No deletes it.

Figure 15-4:
The location opened in Google Earth.

After you find what you're looking for, take the time to click the other links to explore the other locations offered here.

Lat-Long.com

The site at Lat-Long.com has information for U.S. locations only, but if that's what you're looking for, it's one of the best. It offers a fast search function if you're in a hurry as well as the capability to click your way through the browse option if you feel like exploring.

To use the search function, follow these steps:

1. **Take your Web browser to www.lat-long.com.**

2. **In the Location Name text box, type the name of the place you're looking for (see Figure 15-5).**

3. **Choose which state to look in from the State drop-down list.**

4. **(Optional) Enter a name in the County text box.**

5. **If you wish to limit the search by the kind of place you're hunting, choose one of the options in the Feature Type drop-down list (Airport, Church, Geyser, School, Stream, and so on).**

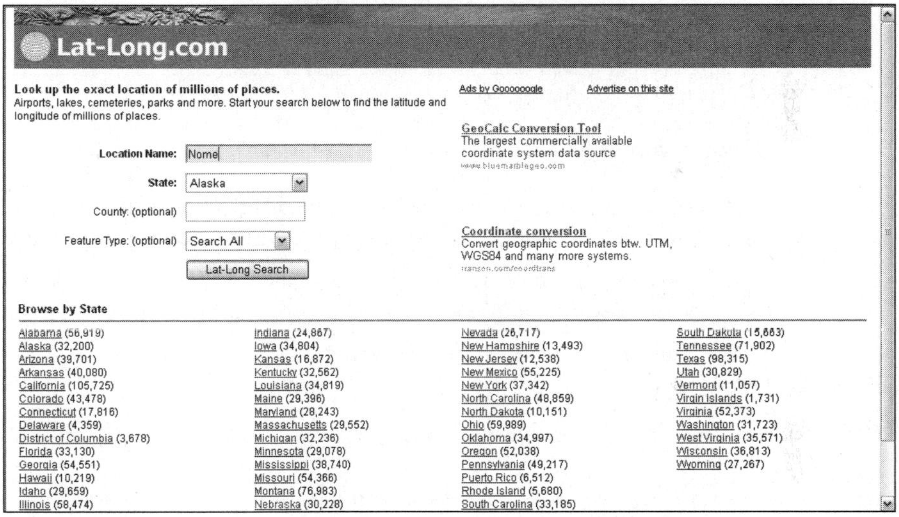

Figure 15-5:
Search the
U.S. at Lat-
Long.com.

6. **Click the Lat-Long Search button.**

7. **On the resulting Web page, click the desired link.**

   This opens a final results page (see Figure 15-6) on which the latitude and longitude are listed in both minutes and decimal forms.

REMEMBER

At Lat-Long.com, as with all databases, you can find some surprising gaps. For example, if you search for Cape Hatteras in North Carolina and you specify the Feature Type as Cape, you get nothing. However, if you search for it with the Feature Type set to Search All, you will find it.

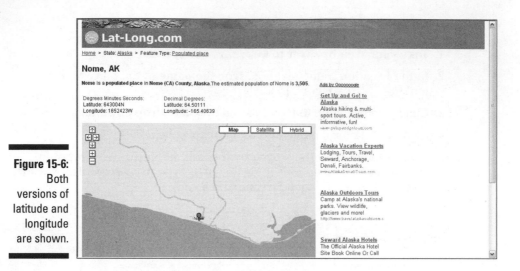

Figure 15-6: Both versions of latitude and longitude are shown.

If you'd rather browse features by state, here's how:

1. **On the main Lat-Long.com page, scroll down beneath the search form and click the name of the state you want to browse through.**

   The resulting page (see Figure 15-7) lists features by Location Type, such as Airport, Bay, and so on.

2. **Click the location type you want.**

3. **Click the one you want.**

   You get the same kind of results page shown earlier in Figure 15-6.

   This brings up a page listing all locations of that sort in that state.

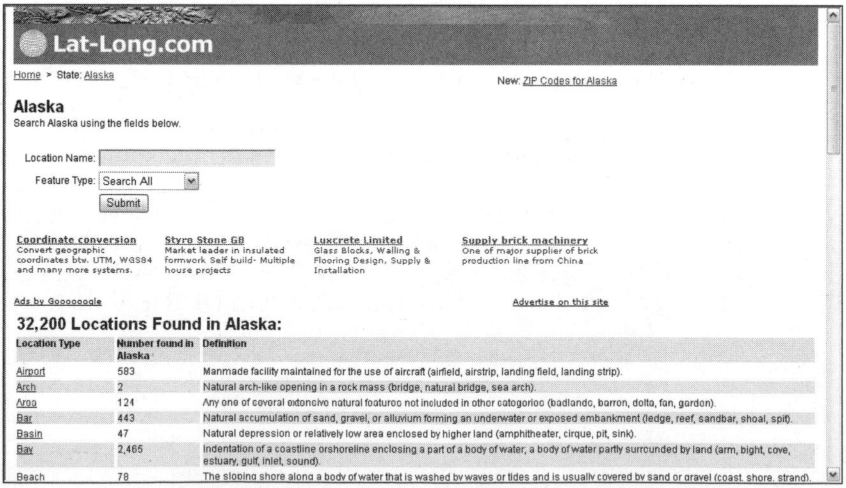

Figure 15-7: Choose the type of location.

fallingrain.com

This excellent Web site is aimed at a target market of pilots. Therefore, it includes a lot more information than just locations — average cloud cover, nearest alternative airports where you can land in an emergency — that sort of thing. It lacks a search feature, so you must browse manually. However, its database of longitude and latitude information is the tops, and it includes maps as well, so you can be absolutely sure that you're not getting some other place that just has the same name as the one you're looking for.

To find out what's where, follow these steps:

1. **Point your browser to www.fallingrain.com/world.**

2. **Click the name of the country you want to look in.**

   This takes you to a Regions list (essentially, states, provinces, and so on).

3. **Click the region. Depending upon the number of entries in that region, you might need to choose the beginning letters from one further page as well.**

   Nota bene (note well, as they used to say back in Rome) that the location names are the native ones — not *your* native language, but that of the people who live there. If you're looking for a place in a Spanish-speaking country, you'd better know how they say it there, and if you're looking for a city in Russia, you'd better know the word *gorod* for city.

   The resulting Web page (see Figure 15-8) lists all the cities in the region, along with their latitude and longitude in decimal format. You can simply copy the info from here and paste it into Google Earth's search box.

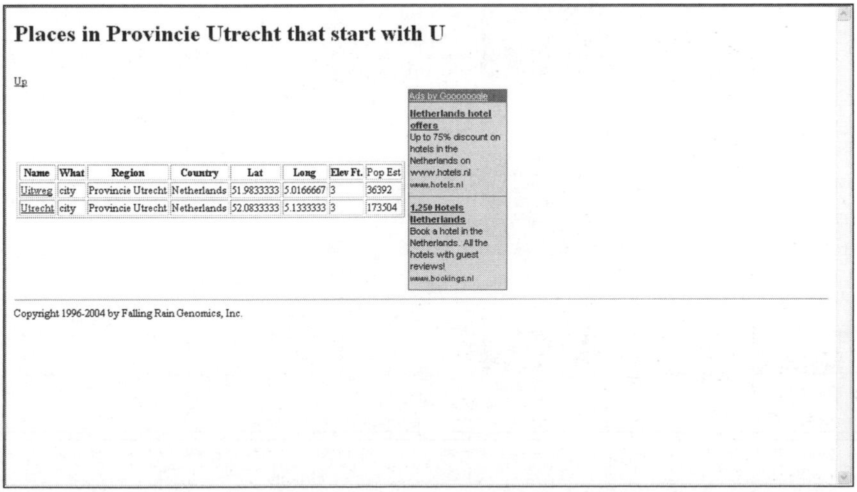

Places in Provincie Utrecht that start with U

Up

Name	What	Region	Country	Lat	Long	Elev Ft.	Pop Est
Uitweg	city	Provincie Utrecht	Netherlands	51.9833333	5.0166667	3	36392
Utrecht	city	Provincie Utrecht	Netherlands	52.0833333	5.1333333	3	173504

Ads by Gooooooogle

Netherlands hotel offers
Up to 75% discount on hotels in the Netherlands on www.hotels.nl

1,250 Hotels Netherlands
Book a hotel in the Netherlands. All the hotels with guest reviews!
www.bookings.nl

Copyright 1996-2004 by Falling Rain Genomics, Inc.

Figure 15-8:
Get data from Falling Rain.

Clicking one of the city links provides you with a much more detailed page, including weather info and maps of the area. On this page, latitude and longitude are given in decimal form in the first line, and the same values on the second line are given in degrees, minutes, and seconds. Either can be used in Google Earth.

NASA WorldWind

NASA WorldWind is a program similar to Google Earth although in my opinion, it's destined to be less popular. Face it: Google understands the popular psyche a lot better than some government agency does. Regardless, its users, like those of Google Earth, do their fair share of exploring the planet and sharing their findings with others.

To dig into the NASA WorldWind database of interesting locales, do this:

1. **Go to www.worldwindcentral.com/hotspots.**

2. **To search for a location, enter its name in the Search text box on the left side of the Web page (see Figure 15-9) and then click Search.**

3. **On the resulting page, click the link for any item of interest.**

   This takes you to a detail page with an image of the location.

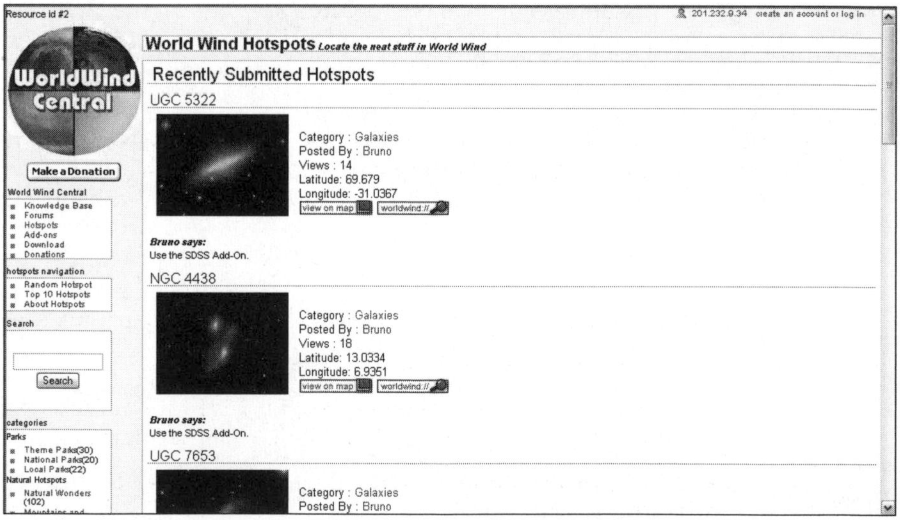

Figure 15-9:
Search the NASA WorldWind database.

4. **Scroll down below the image to see the latitude and longitude information.**

   If you'd rather browse the categories on the left, just scroll down to view them all. (You can do this from any page, not just the home page.) Click anything you like to get a nice set of thumbnail images complete with latitude and longitude (see Figure 15-10).

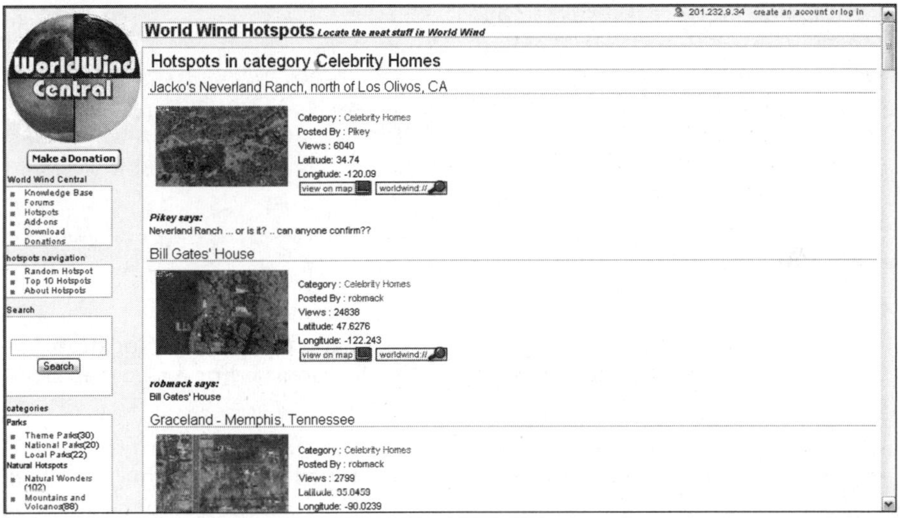

Figure 15-10: Browse NASA WorldWind categories.

World Gazetteer

The World Gazetteer site is geared toward population figures and can be a bit confusing at first, but it's well worth it when you need to track down the coordinates for a place. Just follow the steps carefully, and you'll be happy you did.

To find something:

1. **Fire up your Web browser and go to www.world-gazetteer.com.**

2. **Click the Search Tools link at the top of the page.**

   This takes you to a new page where you have the option of either using a search engine or browsing alphabetically (see Figure 15-11).

3. **To use the search engine, click the small Search link near the upper-left corner.**

population of cities news countries/cities summary statistics search tools info/help options
search contents place index
sponsor:
Get the next generation of Smileys!
((Now with Sound!))
Click here!
Free
Play
Free
World Gazetteer
Alphabetic index of all geographical entities
For name sorting these alphabets are applied,
especially for the additional characters of the Cyrillic and the Arabic alphabet.
The characters are sorted according to the UTF-8 character set.
Latin alphabet
a b c d e f g h i j k l m n o p q r s t u v w x y z
Cyrillic alphabet
а б в г д е ж з и й к л м н о п р с т у ф х ц ч ш щ ъ ы ь э ю я ё ђ ѓ є і ї ј љ њ ћ ќ ў џ ґ

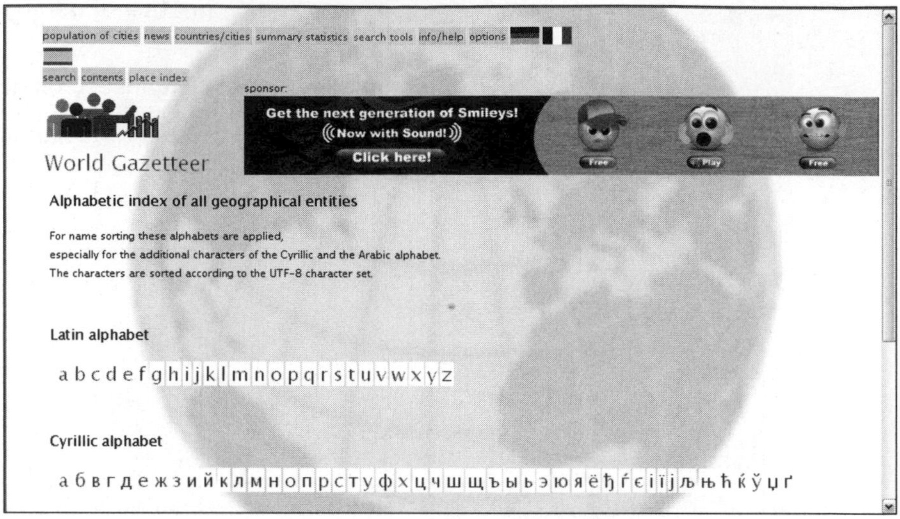

Figure 15-11: The World Gazetteer search page.

4. **In the resulting text box, enter the name of the location you are searching for and then click the Search For a Geographical Entity button.**

   TIP: To browse the alphabetical listings instead, return to the search tools page and click the first letter of the location's name. This takes you to a new list like the one in Figure 15-12, and you do the same thing here, gradually narrowing down the list until you find what you want.

5. **When the final results page is displayed, copy the coordinates shown and paste them into Google Earth.**

population of cities news countries/cities summary statistics search tools info/help options
search contents place index
sponsor:
See The Real Lithuania
Affordable small group trips. Get off the bus & see what others miss.
Ads by Goooooogle
World Gazetteer
Alphabetic index of all geographical entities
geographical object (bold) or sorted string
information on geographical object (administrative divisions in brackets) or number of different names matching the sorted string
jaa 11
jab 62
jac 52
jad 9
jae 7
jaf 11
jag 56
jah 31
jai 31
jaj 13
jak 44
jal 141
jam 143

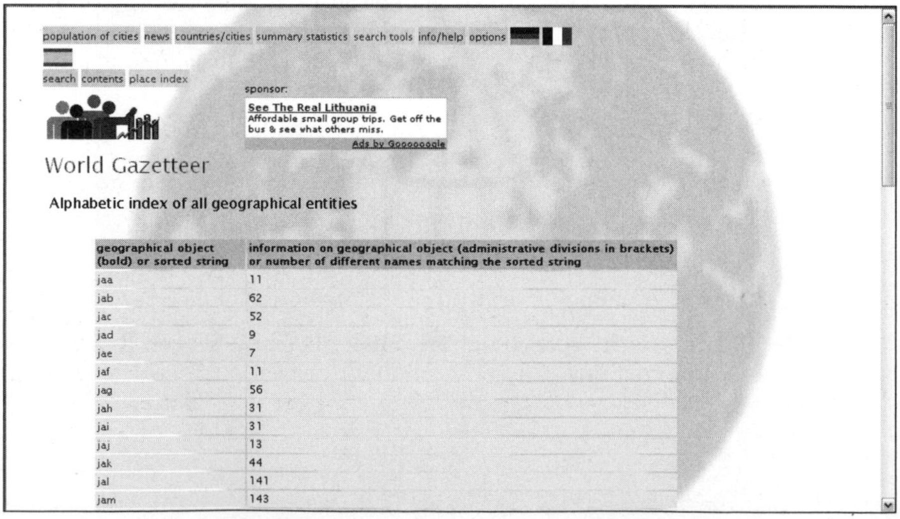

Figure 15-12: Browsing the World Gazetteer.

How Far Is It?

Strictly speaking, How Far Is It? is just another longitude/latitude lookup tool. Its primary purpose is to provide the distance between two points on the surface of the Earth. You enter the names of both places, and it gives you not only the distance between them but also the latitude and longitude of each. However, entering the second location is optional. If you enter only one place name, — you guessed it — you get the latitude and longitude for just that one, so you can use this tool to find a location's coordinates even if you don't care how far it is from anything.

To go locating:

1. **Head to www.indo.com/cgi-bin/dist.**

2. **Scroll down until you see the form shown in Figure 15-13.**

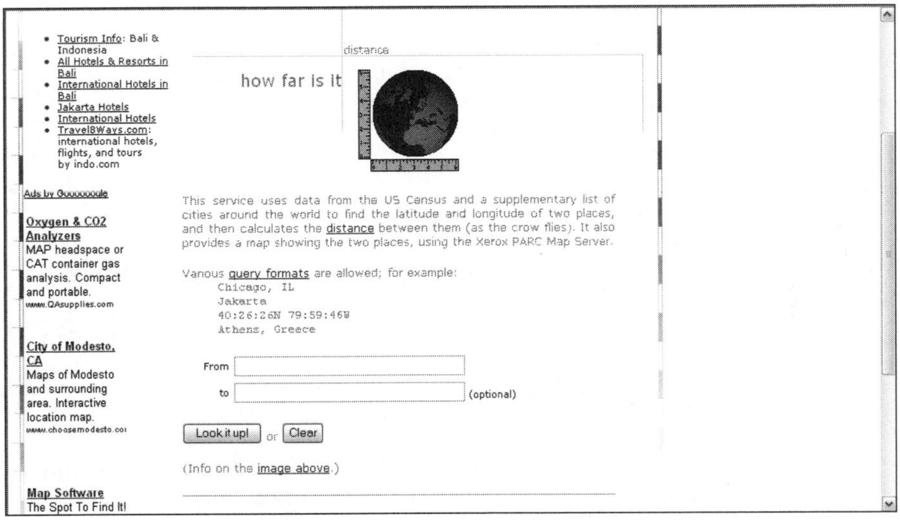

Figure 15-13: Use the search form.

3. **Enter the location's name in the From text box and then click the Look It Up! button.**

   If there is only one possible answer — say, Russiaville, Indiana — it shows up on the result page. If the name wasn't specific enough — say, Paris — you get a Please Clarify result page, which lists the various possibilities. Simply scroll down the list until you find the right one; the latitude and longitude information are right there.

Heavens Above

Heavens Above specializes in astronomy, but it's one of those places that Google Earth-ers will want to drop in on for its database of terrestrial locations. It's a bit of an odd combination of browsing and searching, with the search being limited to one country at a time.

Jump right in:

1. **Surf to `www.heavens-above.com/countries.asp`.**

2. **Click the name of the country you're interested in (see Figure 15-14).**

Figure 15-14: Start by choosing a country.

3. **In the Search String text box on the next page, enter the name of the place you're looking for and then click the Submit button.**

You can use *wild cards* with the Heavens Above search engine. For example, you can use a question mark (?) to take the place of any one letter or an asterisk (*) for any amount of letters. Thus, if you look for ay??s in France, you would find Aymas, Aynes, and Ayros. Comparatively, if you use ay*s, you would get nearly a dozen responses.

The results page shows all matching locations along with their latitude and longitude.

U.S. Gazetteer

If you ever wondered where your tax dollars go to, this is one of the few delightful answers. The United States Census Bureau has a gazetteer (geographic index) online that you can use for free. Of course, it's limited to locations in the U.S. and its territories, but within those limits, it's about as concise and comprehensive as gazetteers get.

Here's what you need to do:

1. **Go to `www.census.gov/cgi-bin/gazetteer`.**

2. **Enter the location's name in — you guessed it — the Name text box (see Figure 15-15).**

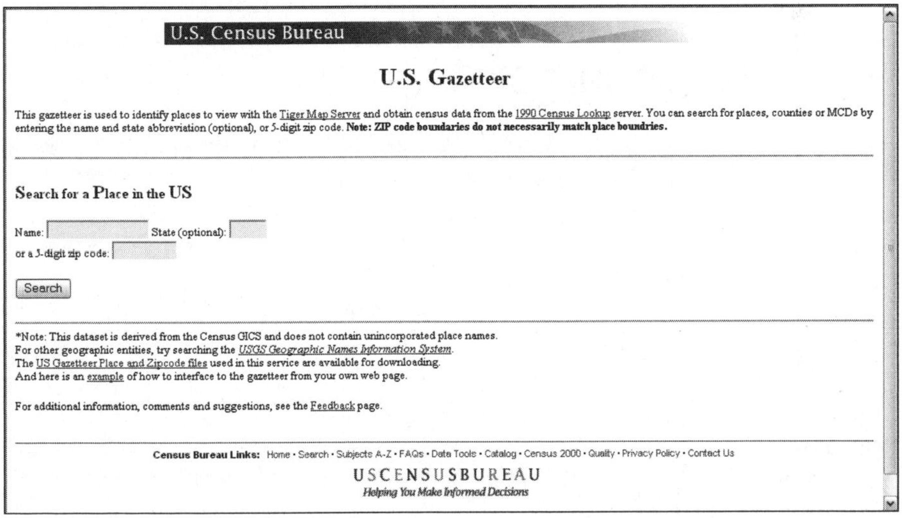

Figure 15-15: Check out the Census Bureau gazetteer.

U.S. Census Bureau

U.S. Gazetteer

This gazetteer is used to identify places to view with the Tiger Map Server and obtain census data from the 1990 Census Lookup server. You can search for places, counties or MCDs by entering the name and state abbreviation (optional), or 5-digit zip code. **Note: ZIP code boundaries do not necessarily match place boundries.**

Search for a Place in the US

Name: [   ]   State (optional): [   ]
or a 5-digit zip code: [   ]

[Search]

*Note: This dataset is derived from the Census GICS and does not contain unincorporated place names. For other geographic entities, try searching the USGS Geographic Names Information System. The US Gazetteer Place and Zipcode files used in this service are available for downloading. And here is an example of how to interface to the gazetteer from your own web page.

For additional information, comments and suggestions, see the Feedback page.

Census Bureau Links: Home · Search · Subjects A-Z · FAQs · Data Tools · Catalog · Census 2000 · Quality · Privacy Policy · Contact Us

U S C E N S U S B U R E A U
Helping You Make Informed Decisions

If you want to do a nationwide search, don't enter anything else. If you want to limit the search to a particular state, enter its two-letter postal code in the State text box. To further narrow things down, you can also specify a ZIP code.

3. **Click the Search button.**

The results page lists all matching answers.

USGS Geographic Names Information System

The United States Geological Survey (USGS) is the premier government mapping agency, and its gazetteer is so detailed that it tops even the Census Bureau's. It includes some features for serious geography buffs, like the ability to specify the altitude of a location.

To see what it can do, follow these steps:

1. Go to `http://geonames.usgs.gov/pls/gnispublic`.

2. Enter the location's name in the Feature Name text box (see Figure 15-16).

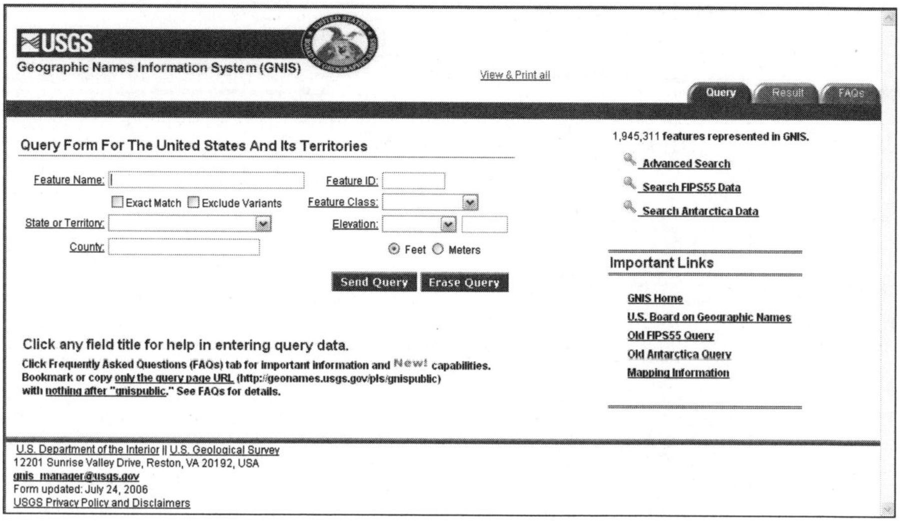

Figure 15-16:
The USGS options.

3. To limit your search to one state, choose one from the State or Territory drop-down list. You can also enter the name of the county in the County text box.

4. To look for a specific type of geographic feature (such as an airport, a geyser, and so on), choose one from the Feature Class drop-down list.

5. To specify the altitude of the location, click the Elevation drop-down list and choose from these relationships: Between, Equals, Higher Than, or Lower Than. Next, enter a value in the Elevation text box and then select either the Feet or the Meters radio button.

If you choose the Between option, the page reloads with an extra text box so that you can enter both the low and high altitude values to search between.

6. Click the Send Query button.

The results page displays all responses that match the name, along with a variety of information, including latitude and longitude.

Maps of World

As you might guess, this site mainly offers maps themselves, but a very good selection of latitude and longitude figures is provided as well, divided by countries. Note that although the list is in alphabetical order, USA is an exception, being the first link.

To find the location of a site, follow these steps:

1. Surf to www.mapsofworld.com/lat_long.

2. Scroll down the page until you find the name of the country you want; then click its link (see Figure 15-17).

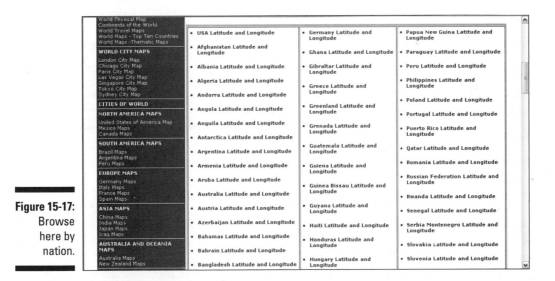

Figure 15-17: Browse here by nation.

The page for that country lists the cities in alphabetical order along with their coordinates.

3. Simply scroll down or use your Web browser's page search function to find the one you want.

Chapter 16

Ten Reliable Sources for Data Files

. . . .

*W*hen it comes to getting your hands on digital data, you often find that you have to go to a lot of trouble, and the expense can be a bit much for a noncommercial budget. Fortunately, more and more Geographical Information System (GIS) information is becoming available online — and a lot of it is available for free!

WebGIS

The folks at WebGIS offer three types of digital data for free download: terrain, land use/land cover, and digital line. The first is in the form of standard Digital Elevation Model (DEM), and the latter two categories contain ArcView shapefiles (.shp format).

Here's how to download the files:

1. **Go to www.webgis.com.**

2. **Click one of the links on the left side (see Figure 16-1) to choose the type of digital file you wish to download.**

   For this example, follow the U.S. terrain data.

3. **When a map of the United States appears, click the state you want.**

   The map changes to the selected state.

4. **Click the desired county.**

   A list of available map data appears, showing both the name of the area covered and the latitudes and longitudes involved (see Figure 16-2).

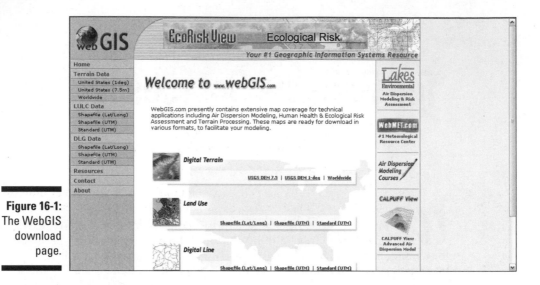

Figure 16-1:
The WebGIS download page.

5. **Click the link for the data you wish to get.**

   You are asked whether you want to open or save the file.

6. **Click Save and save the file to your computer.**

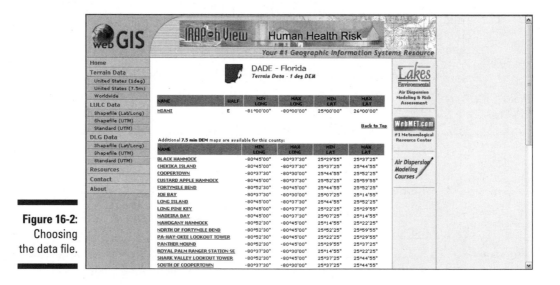

Figure 16-2:
Choosing the data file.

USGS Geographic Data Download

The United States Geological Survey (USGS) is one of the primo suppliers of free digital GIS data. This site offers a wide variety of products ranging from elevation to hydrography data. Here's how it works:

1. **Go to `http://eros.usgs.gov/geodata`.**

2. **Scroll down and click the type of data you want.**

   An information box appears (see Figure 16-3).

   This site violates Web norms in that the links on the page aren't blue underlined text but rather appear as normal text. Just go ahead and click them anyway — they still work just fine. The links in the information box, however, follow the norm.

3. **Click the Alphabetical List link.**

   This takes you to exactly that — a Web page that lists links from A to Z.

4. **Click the starting letter of the location you want.**

   Once again, you get another Web page: this one listing a variety of places that start with that letter (see Figure 16-4).

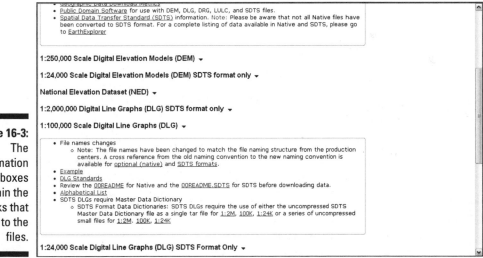

Figure 16-3: The information boxes contain the links that lead to the files.

Index of /pub//data/DLG/100K/B

Name	Last modified	Size	Description
Parent Directory	26-Apr-2005 13:00	-	
baffin_bay-e_TX/	26-Apr-2005 10:58	-	
baffin_bay-w_TX/	26-Apr-2005 10:58	-	
bagdad-e_AZ/	26-Apr-2005 10:57	-	
bagdad-w_AZ/	26-Apr-2005 10:57	-	
baggs-e_WY/	26-Apr-2005 11:01	-	
baggs-w_WY/	26-Apr-2005 11:01	-	
bailey-e_CO/	26-Apr-2005 10:56	-	
bailey-w_CO/	26-Apr-2005 10:56	-	
bainbridge-e_GA/	26-Apr-2005 11:01	-	
bainbridge-w_GA/	26-Apr-2005 11:00	-	
bairoil-e_WY/	26-Apr-2005 10:55	-	
bairoil-w_WY/	26-Apr-2005 10:55	-	
baker-e_MT/	26-Apr-2005 11:01	-	
baker-w_MT/	26-Apr-2005 11:01	-	
baker_city-e_OR/	26-Apr-2005 10:56	-	
baker_city-w_OR/	26-Apr-2005 10:56	-	
baltimore-e_MD/	26-Apr-2005 10:55	-	

Figure 16-4:
Narrow
your list.

5. **Once more, click the desired link.**

   This leads you to (you guessed it) another Web page: this one listing the kinds of data that are available for this location.

6. **Click the link you want to follow.**

   Now you go to — really — the final Web page, where the file you've been seeking is found.

7. **Click the filename and save it to your computer.**

DIVA-GIS

DIVA-GIS provides several kinds of free data from many different sources. Thus, I cannot specify a uniform series of steps to retrieve it. In essence, however, you simply click the links that lead in the direction you want to go (see Figure 16-5). In some cases, this results in an immediate request to save the file; in others, you'll have to click a few more links to get where you're going.

The URL to get started is www.diva-gis.org/data.htm.

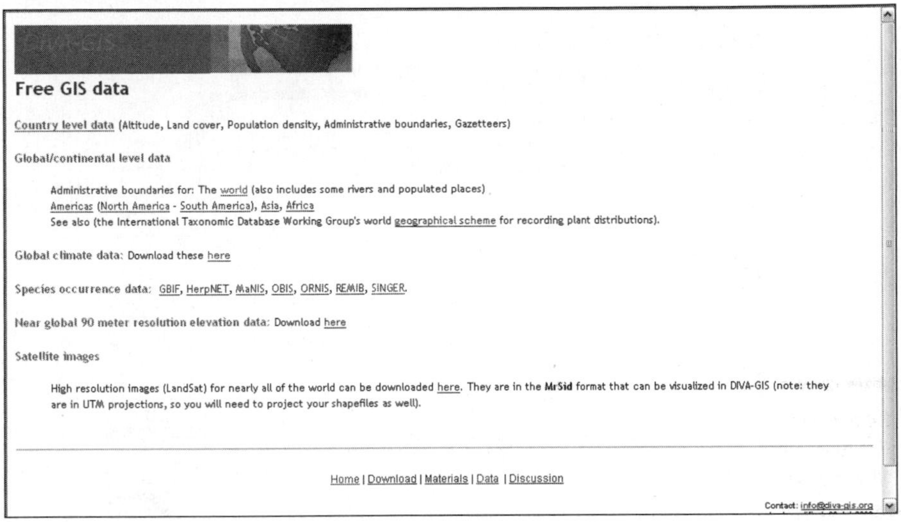

Free GIS data

Country level data (Altitude, Land cover, Population density, Administrative boundaries, Gazetteers)

Global/continental level data

Administrative boundaries for: The world (also includes some rivers and populated places)
Americas (North America - South America), Asia, Africa
See also (the International Taxonomic Database Working Group's world geographical scheme for recording plant distributions).

Global climate data: Download these here

Species occurrence data: GBIF, HerpNET, MaNIS, OBIS, ORNIS, REMIB, SINGER.

Near global 90 meter resolution elevation data: Download here

Satellite images

High resolution images (LandSat) for nearly all of the world can be downloaded here. They are in the **MrSid** format that can be visualized in DIVA-GIS (note: they are in UTM projections, so you will need to project your shapefiles as well).

Home | Download | Materials | Data | Discussion

Contact: info@diva-gis.org

Figure 16-5:
DIVA-GIS
links to
several data
sources.

Clary-Meuser Research Network

The Clary-Meuser people have lots of material for no cost and some items for a reasonable fee. Some of the links lead outside the site (for instance, to the Census Bureau's site).

Here are the steps to follow:

1. **Head over to www.mapcruzin.com/download_mapcruz.htm.**

2. **Scroll down until you see the Categories part, as shown in Figure 16-6.**

3. **Click Categories if you want to choose a specific kind from a drop-down list. Otherwise, just leave it at All Layers.**

4. **Click the View List of Maps button.**

   This takes you to a new Web page that displays the data in the chosen category.

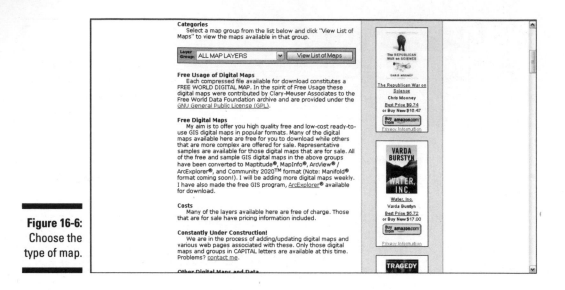

Figure 16-6:
Choose the
type of map.

5. Click the specific data you want (for instance, National Parks or Superfund sites).

This takes you to the file download page, where you can choose the format in which you want the data (see Figure 16-7).

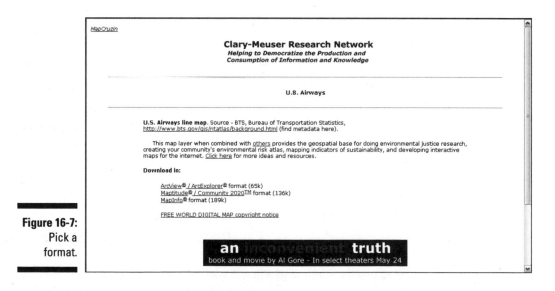

Figure 16-7:
Pick a
format.

6. Save the file to your computer.

GIS Data Depot

Like the preceding site, the GIS Data Depot has a mix of free and paid digital data for you. You have to be a member in order to download data — even the free data — but membership costs you nothing, so it's no problem.

Here's the procedure:

1. **Go to** `http://data.geocomm.com/catalog`.

2. **Scroll down until you see the part of the page shown in Figure 16-8.**

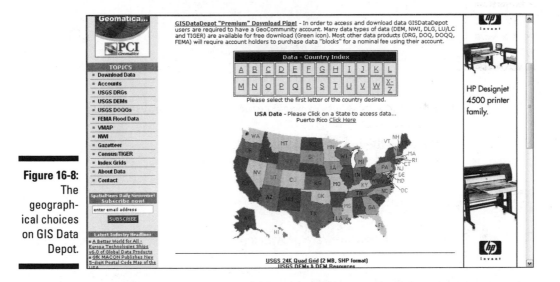

Figure 16-8:
The geographical choices on GIS Data Depot.

3. **To get data on a state of the United States, you simply click the state in the image map. To get data on another nation, click the first letter of its name in the box above the image map.**

   This takes you to another Web page with further subdivisions. Depending upon which link you click, this might be a list of states or counties.

4. **Click the desired link to further narrow the search.**

5. **On the succeeding Web page, click the link for the type of data you want (boundaries, transportation, and so on).**

   This leads you to the final page such as the one in Figure 16-9, which presents you with various options for obtaining the data. In many cases, you can simply download it immediately at no cost. In some others, you have to pay.

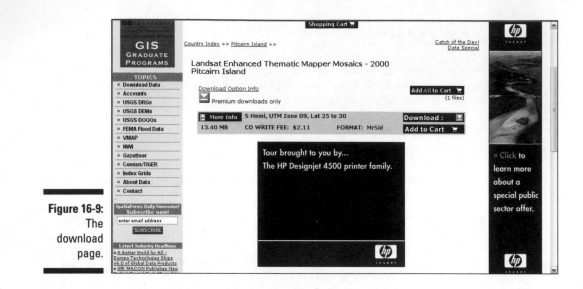

Figure 16-9:
The
download
page.

6. **Click the arrow (green for freebies, brown for pay) to initiate the download.**

7. **Save the file to your computer.**

Free GIS Data by Region

This site by Collins Software provides links to other sites that have regional GIS data:

```
www.collinssoftware.com/freegis_by_region.htm
```

Just click the links and follow them to the other places. The listing of links, however, isn't just for heading offsite. As shown in Figure 16-10, each one also specifies the type of file you're going after (shapefile, CSV, and so on.).

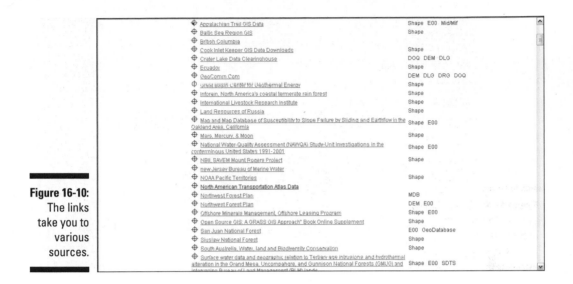

✛ Appalachian Trail GIS Data	Shape	E00 Mid/Mif
✛ Baltic Sea Region GIS	Shape	
✛ British Columbia		
✛ Cook Inlet Keeper GIS Data Downloads	Shape	
✛ Crater Lake Data Clearinghouse	DOQ DEM DLG	
✛ Ecuador	Shape	
✛ GeoComn.Com	DEM DLG DRG DOQ	
✛ Great Basin Center for Geothermal Energy	Shape	
✛ Inforain, North America's coastal temerate rain forest	Shape	
✛ International Livestock Research Institute	Shape	
✛ Land Resources of Russia	Shape	
✛ Map and Map Database of Susceptibility to Slope Failure by Sliding and Earthflow in the Oakland Area, California	Shape E00	
✛ Mars, Mercury, & Moon	Shape	
✛ National Water-Quality Assessment (NAWQA) Study-Unit Investigations in the conterrninous United States 1991-2001	Shape E00	
✛ NBII, SAVEM Mount Rogers Project	Shape	
✛ new Jersey Bureau of Marine Water		
✛ NOAA Pacific Territories	Shape	
✛ North American Transportation Atlas Data		
✛ Northwest Forest Plan	MDB	
✛ Northwest Forest Plan	DEM E00	
✛ Offshore Minerals Management, Offshore Leasing Program	Shape E00	
✛ Open Source GIS: A GRASS GIS Approach" Book Online Supplement	Shape	
✛ San Juan National Forest	E00 GeoDatabase	
✛ Siuslaw National Forest	Shape	
✛ South Australia, Water, land and Biodiversity Conservation	Shape	
✛ Surface water data and geographic relation to Tertiary age intrusions and hydrothermal alteration in the Grand Mesa, Uncompahgre, and Gunnison National Forests (GMUG) and intervening Bureau of Land Management (BLM) lands	Shape E00 SDTS	

Figure 16-10:
The links take you to various sources.

Happy hunting!

FreeGIS.org

FreeGIS.org is dedicated to helping you find anything and everything that's both free and related to GIS (no kidding). In addition to the digital data that I discuss here, FreeGIS.org has items to help everyone from software developers to those of us who, from time to time, need to convert one file format to another.

It's worth taking a bit of time to explore the site, but for now, time to get back to why you're here:

1. **Go to `http://freegis.org/database`.**

2. **Click the Geodata link (see Figure 16-11).**

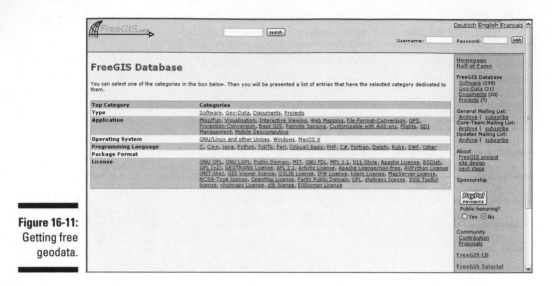

Figure 16-11:
Getting free
geodata.

3. **Scroll down to view each type of file currently available and click anything that interests you.**

   The links lead offsite to a variety of sources, so you're on your own after you get there.

Global Elevation Data

One of the things the Space Shuttle did while floating around "up there" was to use radar to check out the elevations of every part of Earth. This was the famed Shuttle Radar Topography Mission, which you can read about at `http://srtm.usgs.gov`. The data from that mission is freely available, and here's how to get it for yourself:

1. **To download US data, go to**

   ```
   ftp://e0srp01u.ecs.nasa.gov/srtm/version2/SRTM1
   ```

   To download data for the rest of the world, go to

   ```
   ftp://e0srp01u.ecs.nasa.gov/srtm/version2/SRTM3
   ```

2. **For the U.S. version, click the number of the region you want (see Figure 16-12).**

Look at `Region_definition.jpg` in that folder to see which numbers cover which states.

For the world version, click the name of the continent.

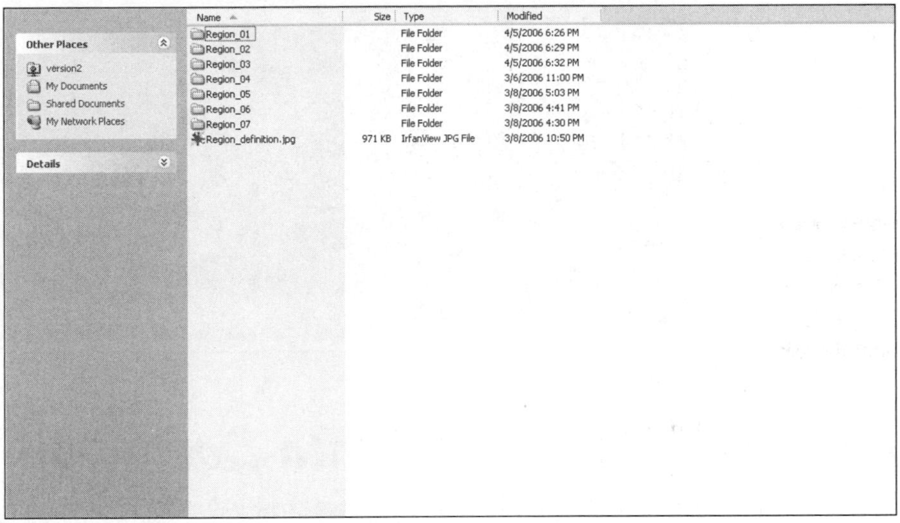

Name ▲	Size	Type	Modified
Region_01		File Folder	4/5/2006 6:26 PM
Region_02		File Folder	4/5/2006 6:29 PM
Region_03		File Folder	4/5/2006 6:32 PM
Region_04		File Folder	3/6/2006 11:00 PM
Region_05		File Folder	3/8/2006 5:03 PM
Region_06		File Folder	3/8/2006 4:41 PM
Region_07		File Folder	3/8/2006 4:30 PM
Region_definition.jpg	971 KB	IrfanView JPG File	3/8/2006 10:50 PM

Other Places

- version2
- My Documents
- Shared Documents
- My Network Places

Details

Figure 16-12:
Choosing a region.

3. **Double-click the name of the file you want to download (the file names specify the latitude and longitude of the bottom-left corner of the area) and save it to your computer.**

NGDC

The National Geophysical Data Center (NGDC) has a nice, easy interface for downloading digital data. To get your free data files right away, follow these easy steps:

1. **Surf to www.ngdc.noaa.gov/mgg/topo/gltiles.html.**

2. **Click one of the tiles in the world map shown in Figure 16-13.**

3. **Save the file to your computer.**

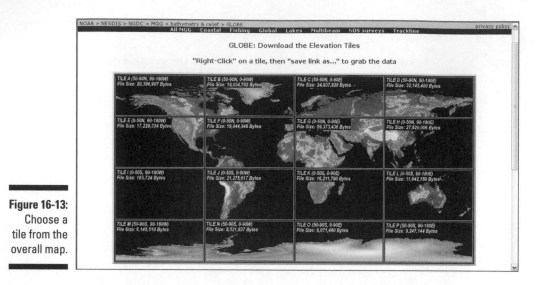

Figure 16-13:
Choose a tile from the overall map.

National Atlas Raw Data Download

I'm betting you probably didn't know the federal government has an online national atlas. Well, it does, and it's not just a pretty set of maps on the Web. It's also a site where you can download the data they used to make those maps. Here's how to go about doing that:

1. **Go to `http://nationalatlas.gov/atlasftp.html`.**

2. **Click the category you're interested in (see Figure 16-14).**

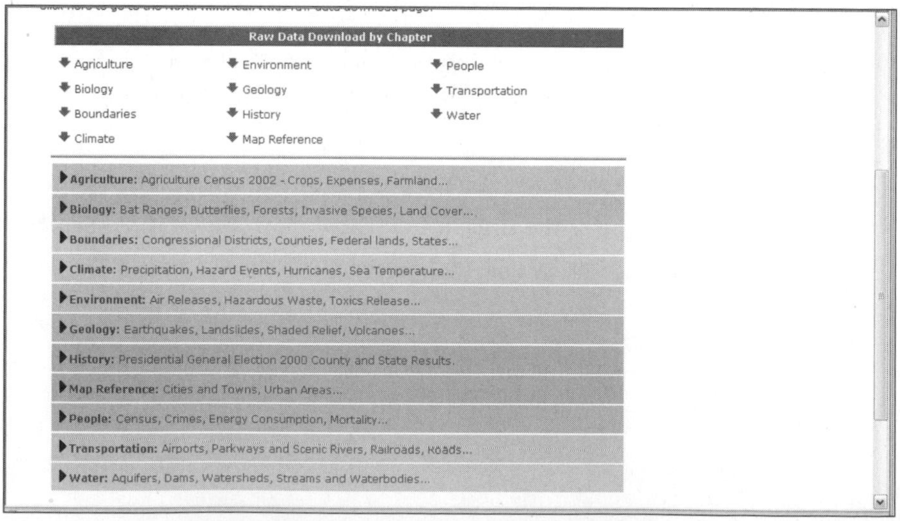

Figure 16-14:
Choose a category.

3. **When the category expands (see Figure 16-15), click the link for the data file you want to download.**

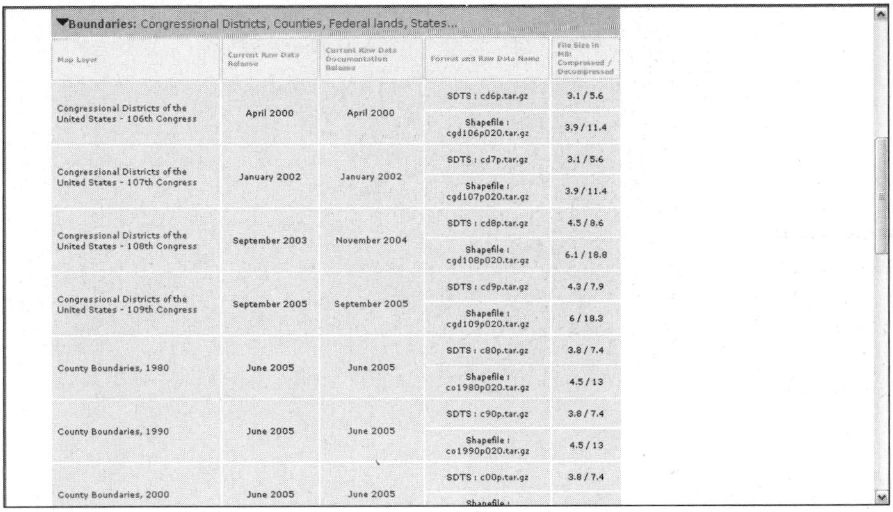

Boundaries: Congressional Districts, Counties, Federal lands, States...

Map Layer	Current Raw Data Release	Current Raw Data Documentation Release	Format and Raw Data Name	File Size in MB: Compressed / Decompressed
Congressional Districts of the United States - 106th Congress	April 2000	April 2000	SDTS : cd6p.tar.gz	3.1 / 5.6
			Shapefile : cgd106p020.tar.gz	3.9 / 11.4
Congressional Districts of the United States - 107th Congress	January 2002	January 2002	SDTS : cd7p.tar.gz	3.1 / 5.6
			Shapefile : cgd107p020.tar.gz	3.9 / 11.4
Congressional Districts of the United States - 108th Congress	September 2003	November 2004	SDTS : cd8p.tar.gz	4.5 / 8.6
			Shapefile : cgd108p020.tar.gz	6.1 / 18.8
Congressional Districts of the United States - 109th Congress	September 2005	September 2005	SDTS : cd9p.tar.gz	4.3 / 7.9
			Shapefile : cgd109p020.tar.gz	6 / 18.3
County Boundaries, 1980	June 2005	June 2005	SDTS : c80p.tar.gz	3.8 / 7.4
			Shapefile : co1980p020.tar.gz	4.5 / 13
County Boundaries, 1990	June 2005	June 2005	SDTS : c90p.tar.gz	3.8 / 7.4
			Shapefile : co1990p020.tar.gz	4.5 / 13
County Boundaries, 2000	June 2005	June 2005	SDTS : c00p.tar.gz	3.8 / 7.4
			Shapefile :	

Figure 16-15: Picking the exact file.

4. **Save the file to your computer.**

Chapter 17

Ten Cool Tools

As great as Google Earth is, it can't do everything. Plenty of tools are available to round out your Google Earth experience, however, from image enhancement and file format converters to utilities that link Google Earth to other servers.

IrfanView

This handy little graphics utility offers a slough of features in a simple, easy to use package. Although it's no competitor for high-powered paint programs like Photoshop or Fireworks, it has all the essentials for rapidly manipulating or enhancing the images you save from Google Earth:

- Gamma correction
- Rotate or flip image
- Crop image
- Resize/resample
- Increase/decrease color depth
- Contrast and brightness
- File format conversion (a particularly important feature because Google Earth only saves images in JPEG format)

In addition to all this, IrfanView (as shown in Figure 17-1) has multi-language support, a built-in set of filters, and the ability to utilize Photoshop-compliant filters as well.

Get your copy at www.irfanview.com. It's free for noncommercial users and costs only $12 for commercial purposes.

Figure 17-1:
IrfanView
crams a lot
of power
into a simple
package.

Arc2Earth

An awful lot of geographical data is available in ESRI's popular ArcGIS format. If you want to use it in Google Earth, of course, you have to convert it to KML. A number of utilities are available for doing so, but Arc2Earth is the one generating all the excitement.

Arc2Earth doesn't just move a map from one program to another: It has a wonderful selection of options that can enhance your presentations. Its 3-D extrusion function, for example, enables you to make parts of the map jut out from the ground, thus turning a plain map with some linked non-geographical data (such as population figures, poll results, and so on) into a three-dimensional display like the one shown in Figure 17-2.

This program also has good support for label creation, marker symbols, and polygons. It can also create and link Google Earth pop-up information balloons. You can download it at

www.spatialdatalogic.com/cs/blogs/brian_flood/archive/2005/09/12/98.aspx

The trial version has a 30-day limit, and the license beyond that ranges from $99–$299.

Figure 17-2:
Arc2Earth
generates
great maps.

Juice Analytics Census Files

The Census layer in Google Earth has a minimum of information about each county: population, median income, and per capita income. The U.S. Census Bureau, however, has a lot more than that to share. The folks at Juice Analytics are developing `.kmz` files that contain some of this information.

The Census layer is under US Government in the Layers pane, which does not show up if you have only the Core Layers selected. You have to choose All Layers view to see it.

The data, which is available for both counties and block groups, is currently limited to

- ✔ Population density
- ✔ Median age
- ✔ Male/female ratio

Just point your Web browser to

```
www.juiceanalytics.com/weblog/?p=119
```

Scroll down to the links (see Figure 17-3) and start downloading. It's free!

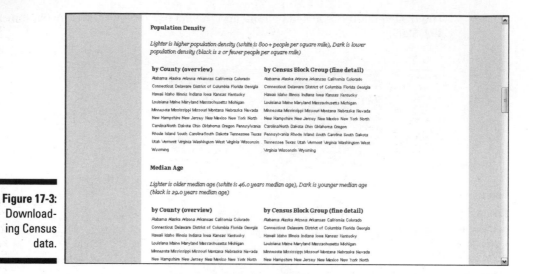

Figure 17-3: Downloading Census data.

Juice Analytics Geocoding Tool

While I'm on the subject of the nice folks at Juice Analytics, they also have a geocoding tool. (See Chapter 2 for more information on geocoding.)

This utilizes Microsoft Excel (see Figure 17-4) to convert a list of addresses into latitude and longitude values and then export them as maps for Google Earth. It performs this task by querying either Yahoo! or `geocode.us` for the location data, which it then converts to a `.kml` file and exports to the Google Earth Temporary Places folder.

To get your copy, head on over to

```
www.juiceanalytics.com/weblog/?p=158
```

Just like the Census data files, this is a freebie.

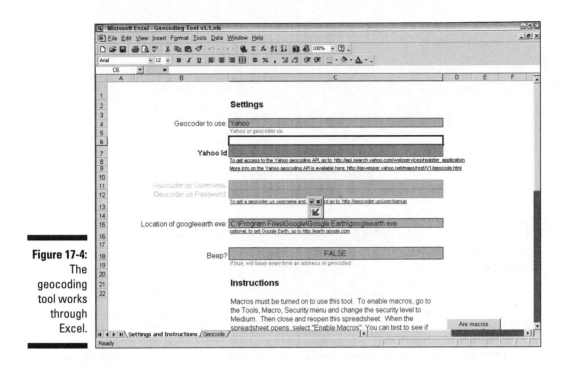

Figure 17-4:
The geocoding tool works through Excel.

MyFsGoogleEarth - Link Google Earth with Flight Simulator (FS2004, FS9)

I suppose this was kind of inevitable — that someone would think of a way to link up Google Earth and Microsoft's Flight Simulator. MyFsGoogleEarth is a Web server that does just that. This clever little application allows you to see the plane in flight in real time, along with its expected location in one minute as well as the AI (artificial intelligence) traffic flying near it (see Figure 17-5).

Although it requires a bit of bother to get it all set up and running, you can't beat the price, which is nothing, so pop in and try it out:

www.elbiah.de/flusi/MyFsGoogleEarth/MyFsGoogleEarth.htm

Figure 17-5:
Merging the functions of Flight Simulator and Google Earth.

KML2X3D - Google Earth to Web 3D Converter

X3D used to be called VRML, and it's a standard for displaying three-dimensional objects on Web pages. Whereas Arc2Earth converts ArcGIS files into Google Earth formats, KML2X3D changes Google Earth files into X3D.

This allows Webmasters to utilize the ever-growing number of 3-D models designed for Google Earth on their own Web pages. (See Chapter 12 for more information on Google Earth models.) This is yet another free program for Google Earth users, and this one even has the source code available under the Lesser GNU Public License (LGPL).

Take your Web browser to www.mediamachines.com/KML2X3D (see Figure 17-6) and check out this program.

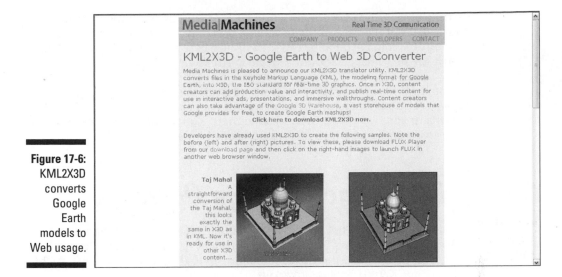

Figure 17-6:
KML2X3D
converts
Google
Earth
models to
Web usage.

EarthPlot and EarthPaint

EarthPlot (see Figure 17-7) is a honey of a program. It can import ASCII data and read Excel files. It generates several kinds of maps including post and raster image. Perhaps most impressive, however, is EarthPlot's ability to snag input from the Microsoft TerraServer and import it into Google Earth.

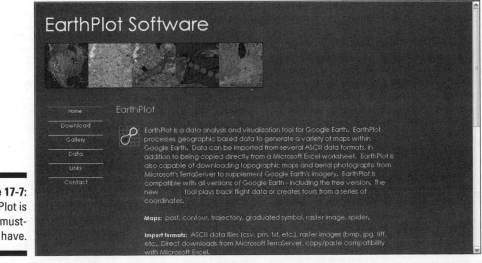

Figure 17-7:
EarthPlot is
a must-
have.

EarthPaint is, as you might have guessed, a paint program. Unlike others, however, it interfaces with Google Earth, bringing the current image in the viewing area into EarthPaint. You then draw whatever you have in mind and export the new image back into Google Earth as an overlay.

The limited-feature trial versions can be downloaded at `www.earthplot software.com`. The fully functional version of EarthPlot costs $29.95, and EarthPaint goes for $14.95. While you're there, you might as well grab the free program *EarthShape,* which creates polygons for use in Google Earth.

Google Earth Hacks Image Overlays

Your average overlay isn't particularly exciting, but these people have come up with some real stunners. The maps of the ancient Earth alone (see Figure 17-8) are worth the visit, and there is a lot of more up-to-date material as well, such as Hurricane Katrina and Iraq overlays.

You can browse their image overlays by category, such as Real-time Traffic and Weather: Forecasts, or by country. The URL is

`www.googleearthhacks.com/dlcat44/Image-Overlays.htm`

And it's all free!

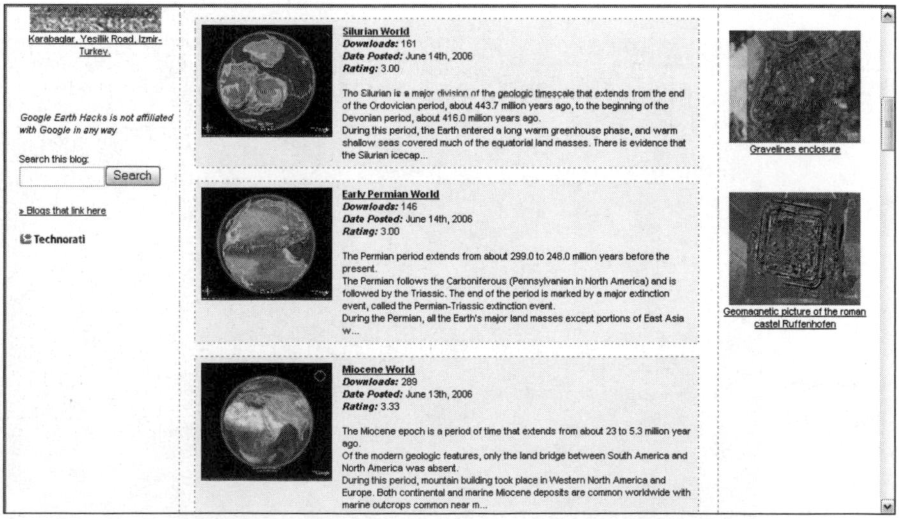

Figure 17-8: These image overlays are unique.

GPS Utility

If you use Google Earth with a GPS (Global Positioning System) device, you'll probably want to check out this nice add-on (see Chapter 9 for more on working with GPS devices). It can import and export in Google Earth's native file format. Although Google Earth cannot currently export to GPS devices, this utility can provide a bridge between them.

The GPS Utility Web page is located at www.gpsu.co.uk. The free trial version is limited in the number of waypoints and such that it can process, but the full version's top end is 65,000. The registration fee is $55.

GE-Path and GE-Graph

GE-Path, as shown in Figure 17-9, puts Google Earth paths on steroids (see Chapter 3 for more on paths). You can import Google Earth files into it and then monkey with the paths in many ways. You can, for example, add the latitude and longitude coordinates to each point in the path, find the distance between each point and the bearing from one to the other, and link the end point to the starting point.

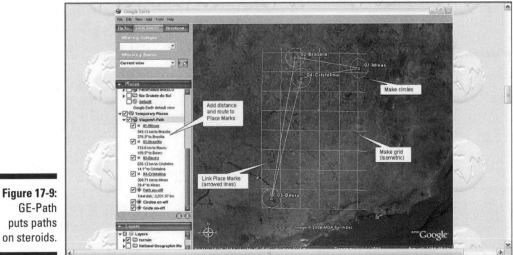

Figure 17-9: GE-Path puts paths on steroids.

The whole shebang can then be exported back into Google Earth, or you can choose from a variety of other file formats.

GE-Graph (see Figure 17-10) creates graphs from Google Earth data, allowing you to set different options based on the data appended to a placemark, such as a different color or a larger size than the other placemarks. It can also import and export data with other programs like Microsoft Excel.

You can find them both at www.sgrillo.net/googleearth. The two programs are free of charge.

Figure 17-10:
GE-Graph creates graphs from Google Earth.

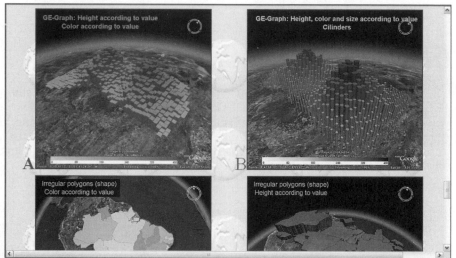

Part VI
Appendixes

In this part . . .

Here's a collection of odds and ends that you'll want to dig into. Appendix A is a glossary of the book's technical terms as well as explanations of the various file formats that you can either import into or export from the program. Appendix B is a reference that shows you all the default layers in Google Earth. Appendix C gives your Earth exploration a kickstart by guiding you to some of the more interesting places on the planet.

Appendix A

Glossary

● ●

3D Buildings layer: A layer within Google Earth that supplies a more realistic view of cities by adding models of major buildings. This is currently available for only the largest and most populous locations.

anisotropic filtering: A technique for softening the harsh edges along the horizon when you tilt the image onscreen. It's very memory intensive, so go for this only if you have 32MB of video RAM or better.

ASCII (American Standard Code for Information Interchange): A standard for encoding text. ASCII files are the simplest kind of plain text files and can be imported and exported by virtually any program.

AVI: Microsoft Audio/Video Interleave movie format. Makes very large movie files.

bandwidth: The total amount of information that a network connection can transmit. The higher the bandwidth, the more data that can be sent over the connection in the same amount of time. A dialup modem, for example, has a much lower bandwidth than a DSL line.

base map: The simplest part of Google Earth. This is nothing more than the most basic imagery and spatial coordinate information: in other words, just the map with no frills. Layers, overlays, and such are placed upon the base map to generate more complex and informative displays.

bearing: The direction from a specific location to another destination or object, generally expressed in terms of compass points. (That is, "North" is zero degrees.)

BMP: The older Windows bitmap format. Although it is *lossless* — that is, the file that it saves is identical to the current image, down to the last pixel, when it's redisplayed — it lacks any form of compression and therefore creates extremely large files.

border: The dividing line between political entities on a map. Also sometimes referred to as *boundary* or *limit*.

cache: An area for temporary data storage. Caching data saves time and bandwidth because the client doesn't have to ask the server for the same information over and over again but can access it locally instead.

camera: Your viewpoint when you look at a scene. The metaphor results from thinking of the image onscreen as being taken by a camera that is at a particular altitude and location, aimed in a certain direction.

check box: A method of setting optional values, represented by a small, hollow square. A check box that is blank is not selected. When it is selected, it has a check mark inside. Check boxes are used for nonconflicting options.

client/server: Two computers in a relationship in which one makes a request of the other and the second fulfills the request. When using Google Earth, your computer is the client, and Google is the server.

compass: The circular ring in the upper-right corner that indicates which direction is north.

CSV: Comma-Separated Value. These files are perhaps the most commonly used method of moving tabular database information from one program to another. Such a list consists of values that are separated by a *delimiter,* which is a character that isn't used in any of the values themselves so that it's obvious where one value ends and another begins. Despite the name of the format, that character isn't always a comma, and Google Earth can import both comma-delimited and tab-delimited versions.

default settings: The settings that Google Earth comes with. In most cases, you can alter the default values in order to customize the program.

detail area: The amount of space in the center of the viewing area where maximum screen resolution is applied. The smaller the detail area, the lower the demands on your system but the less appealing the overall image.

DGN: MicroStation Geographical Information System (GIS) format.

Digital Elevation Model (DEM): A type of file containing geographical data with three points: one for latitude, one for longitude, and one for elevation. GIS programs are able to construct 3-D maps using these figures. *See also* Geographical Information System.

distortion: The amount of error found in a map. All maps are approximations, and all have to accept some compromises. The classic example is simply trying to show a round globe on a flat screen. *See also* projection.

docking: Locking a screen element into a particular location. The only dockable element in Google Earth is the built-in Web browser, which can be docked either at the bottom or on the right side of the viewing area.

elevation: The height of a point above sea level. Elevation is not visible in Google Earth unless the Terrain layer is turned on. *See also* sea level, terrain level.

equator: The imaginary dividing line between the northern and southern halves of the Earth. *See also* latitude, longitude, prime meridian.

full-screen mode: An option in which all unnecessary screen elements are temporarily hidden in order to make more of the screen available for the expansion of the viewing area.

geocoding: The matching of a street address with a physical location, typically expressed in terms of latitude and longitude. Because of the irregular manner in which addresses are usually assigned and the absolute regularity of latitude and longitude, the two do not always mesh perfectly. *See also* latitude, longitude.

Geographical Information System (GIS): Any of the vast array of computerized systems for displaying and working with maps and related data.

GIF: Graphics Interchange Format. The venerable old workhorse of the early days, the CompuServe GIF format fell from favor as it became entangled in a seemingly unsolvable legal wrangle about patents and licensing. Although the patents have now expired and the points are all moot, other formats like PNG and JPEG have taken the lead. Every graphics program still supports GIFs, however, because uncountable images already exist in this format. Images are limited to 256 colors.

Global Positioning System (GPS): A high-tech way of finding the latitude and longitude of where you are at any given moment and recording the location of places as you travel. GPS devices use information from orbiting satellites to pinpoint locations with much greater accuracy than earlier methods. Information from most GPS devices by either Garmin or Magellan can be imported into Google Earth.

GPX: TopoGrafix GPS eXchange format. This format for GPS data is pretty much the standard today.

History drop-down list: A record of earlier operations within a program, generally displayed in the form of a drop-down list. This history is accessible by clicking on the arrow on its right side. The history is then shown onscreen. Clicking any item in the list repeats the action. Your Web browser, for example, keeps a history of sites you have visited, and Google Earth keeps track of searches that you've performed.

icon: A small image used to represent a variety of items in a program. In Google Earth, both the toolbar buttons and elements such as placemarks are icons. *See also* placemark, toolbar.

image: Any graphical representation. In Google Earth, the scene in the viewing area can be saved as an image in the form of a JPEG file.

image overlay: An imported graphics file that is placed over the scene in Google Earth. Typical overlays include current weather information or forecasts, traffic data, and so on.

JPG or **JPEG:** Joint Photographic Experts Group graphics format; used by Google Earth to save screen images. JPEGs store image data as a bitmap, using a sophisticated compression scheme. This has the benefit of creating smaller files but has an inevitable loss of information compared with other bitmap formats. However, the amount of detail that is lost is minimal and is usually not visible to the human eye.

key combination: Pressing more than one key at a time. Key combinations are typically used when issuing a command, to save time compared with using the mouse to access a menu option. If you want to display the Latitude/Longitude Grid, for example, it is faster for most people to press the Ctrl and L keys at the same time than to click View in the menu and then choose Lat/Long Grid from the resulting submenu. Key combinations are represented by the names of the keys connected by plus signs, such as Ctrl+L or Ctrl+Alt+B.

Keyhole Markup Language (KML): The native language of Google Earth. KML is similar to HTML but is geared toward GIS systems instead of Web pages. Compressed KML files are KMZ files. *See also* markup language.

KML: Keyhole Markup Language; the native format of Google Earth. This is used to represent geological information and to process how it is shown onscreen.

KMZ: A compressed KML file.

label: The textual information that accompanies an icon. For instance, a label is the name given to a placemark, which appears next to the icon in the viewing area.

lat/long grid: A series of lines that show the latitude and longitude of the scene in the viewing area. When you zoom in more and more, the figures become more detailed.

latitude: A method of determining the relationship of a particular location with the equator. Latitude increases as you move away from the equator. *See also* equator, longitude.

layer: Any kind of information that is in addition to the basic satellite images shown in Google Earth. Everything from National Geographic Webcams to the location of restaurants is a different layer.

LOC: EasyGPS storage method for waypoints.

longitude: A method of determining the relationship of a particular location with the prime meridian. Longitude increases as you move away from the prime meridian. *See also* latitude, prime meridian.

loop: The number of times a tour repeats when it is played back. *See also* tour.

markup language: Any of several computer languages that are meant to define the appearance of things on a computer screen. The best known of the markup languages is HTML, the heart of the World Wide Web, but several other specialized markup languages also exist. *See also* Keyhole Markup Language.

model: A representation of something by an image. A wide variety of three-dimensional models is available for use in Google Earth, ranging from the Eiffel Tower to whimsical pieces of art.

MOV: Apple QuickTime movie format.

MPS: Garmin MapSource Global Positioning System (GPS) waypoint data.

navigator: The navigation controls located in the upper-right corner of the viewing area. By default, they're not visible unless the mouse pointer is over them, thus making the screen a bit less cluttered.

opacity: *See* transparency.

overlay: *See* image overlay.

Overview Map: A small screen insert that shows where the displayed scene is on the Earth's surface.

pane: Any of the smaller areas on the computer screen that contain a subset of controls or other features. In Google Earth, the sidebar contains the Search pane, the Places pane, and the Layers pane.

pause: The amount of time to wait at a point when playing back a tour. The default value is 1.7 seconds.

PIX: PCIDSK database file.

placemark: Marks a particular location so that you can easily return to it. A placemark is to Google Earth what a bookmark is to a Web browser.

PNG: Portable Network Graphics format. This format was developed in response to legal problems entangling the older GIF format. It shares many of the same features with GIF files, but it includes a compression scheme that works sort of like a JPEG.

polygon: A two-dimensional object composed of connected, closed lines. A square, for example, is a polygon. When the third dimension of altitude is applied to a polygon, it becomes 3-D, or an *extruded polygon,* which is the basis of all 3-D models in Google SketchUp.

prime meridian: An imaginary north-south line drawn through Greenwich, England. This is the partner of the equator, dividing the world into two halves. *See also* equator, latitude, longitude.

projection: A method of showing a representation of the more-or-less spherical Earth on a flat surface. Google Earth uses Simple Cylindrical projection, also known as *Platte Carree* or *Equidistant Cylindrical projection.*

public domain: The body of works that are not covered by copyright law and are therefore nobody's intellectual property. There is a large variety of public domain data available for GIS purposes.

radio button: Similar to a check box but round instead. Unlike check boxes, radio buttons are used for mutually exclusive options. *See also* check box.

rotation: The pivoting movement of the currently displayed scene around a central axis. Rotating the view 180 degrees results in north being at the bottom of the screen.

Ruler: The tool in Google Earth for measuring distances. The ruler is sort of like a digital measuring tape.

Scale Legend: Like the scale on a printed map that shows the ratio of map distance to real distance (for example, one inch to the mile). In Google Earth, the Scale Legend's ratio varies as you zoom in and out.

scroll wheel: The wheel in the center of most computer mice, used in Google Earth for navigation control. Many mouse wheels can also be pressed as well as rolled, thus adding a third button to the mouse.

sea level: The value between high tide and low tide. Sea level is used as a basis for defining altitude (or depth).

server: *See* client/server.

SHP: ESRI ArcView's shapefile format. This format is another popular method for storing GIS information.

sidebar: The area in Google Earth on the left side that contains the Search, Places, and Layers panes.

SketchUp: A companion program to Google Earth that allows the user to create three-dimensional models that can then be added to the view in Google Earth. SketchUp is surprisingly sophisticated for a free program.

SKP: SketchUp 3-D model format (extruded polygons).

slider: A method of setting values for options or for controlling navigation (tilt, zoom). Sliders are used by dragging the center element within them with your mouse.

status bar: The place at the bottom of the viewing area that displays information, such as the latitude and longitude of your mouse pointer.

TAB: The format for the program MapInfo.

Terrain layer: The display of land elevations instead of just a flat image onscreen. With the Terrain layer turned on, Google Earth shows the three-dimensional aspects of the scene.

terrain quality: The amount of detail used when displaying terrain onscreen. The higher the quality, the more demand on your system. The lower the quality, the faster Google Earth will work.

text box: A blank rectangle in which to enter textual information. The Search pane, for example, uses text boxes for entering locations, business types, and so on. Text boxes are also often used in setting option values.

texture colors: The degree of precision with which *textures* (the fine details of terrain) are displayed, depending upon the capabilities of your video card.

TGA: Targa image file format. This was created by Truevision to support its line of true-color graphics cards.

TIF or **TIFF, GeoTiff,** and **compressed TIFF:** Tagged Image File format. This format is very flexible. It has both compressed and uncompressed versions as well as the ability to store geographic information in the GeoTiff version.

tilt: The angle at which the view onscreen is presented. By using the Terrain layer in combination with tilting, views can be obtained that are both more realistic and more appealing to the average viewer.

toolbar: The set of icons or buttons at the top of the viewing area, providing quick access to some functions.

ToolTip: A rectangular pop-up that contains information about the object beneath your mouse pointer.

topography: The representation of the surface of the Earth in three dimensions, including elevations.

tour: An automated, virtual journey in Google Earth, composed of a series of placemarks that are displayed one after another.

trackpoint: A series of location data which is automatically logged by a GPS device as it moves. *See also* waypoint.

transparency: The degree to which the background behind an image overlay can show through it.

TXT: Plain text files using the ASCII code, which uses the numbers 0–127 to represent the most commonly used letters, numbers and symbols in the English system.

United States Geological Survey (USGS): The U.S. government agency that is the primary source for digital map information.

vector data: A method of storing image data as a series of points, lines, and polygons rather than as a standard image file. Software like Google Earth reconstructs the image from vector data.

waypoint: A GPS device's version of a placemark, created by the device's user. *See also* trackpoint.

WMV: Microsoft Windows Media Video movie format.

zoom: The act of changing the scale of the map in the viewing area. The visual effect of zooming is as if you are coming closer to the surface of the Earth or moving higher above it.

Appendix B

Default Content of the All Layers Pane

. . . .

*T*he All Layers view setting in the Layers pane shows every one of the available layers. This Appendix gives you a comprehensive listing of the whole shebang as of the time of writing. ***Note:*** Bear in mind that Google is always looking for new layers to add, so this list might vary somewhat from what you find on your computer when you read this. The majority of the content is self explanatory. Germany Roads, for example, shows roads in Germany, and Island Names shows the names of (you guessed it) islands. If you're not looking for these particular things, you probably won't want to turn on those layers.

The three settings for the Layers pane are

- ✔ **Core:** Includes all the layers except for US Government
- ✔ **All Layers:** Shows just that
- ✔ **Now Enabled:** Shows only those layers that have either some or all of their elements selected

A few of the layers, however, require a bit of explanation:

- ✔ **The Google Earth Community Showcase:** The Showcase hosts some personal input on various specialized topics. Thus, when you see something like *US Lighthouses - Phred,* you know that Phred is hard at work keeping you up to date on these structures.
- ✔ **Airports:** Similarly, under Airports, you'll find two listings:
    - *Airports:* This simply shows an image of an airplane at the appropriate location.
    - *Airport Maps:* This shows you an outline of the runways themselves in addition to the location (see Figure B-1).
- ✔ **DG Coverage:** This is the layer for images from Digital Globe, which is a major supplier of data to Google Earth.

Figure B-1:
The Airports
and Airport
Maps layers
together.

Table B-1	Default Content of All Layers	
Layer	*Sublayers*	*Sub-sublayers*
Terrain	None	
Featured Content	Tracks4Africa	T4A Roads
		T4A Points of Interest
		T4A Community Photos
	Spotlight on Africa	
	European Space Agency	Earth beauty seen from space
		Phenomena seen from space
	National Geographic Magazine	Feature Articles and Photographs
		Sights and Sounds
		Africa Megaflyover

Layer	Sublayers	Sub-sublayers
		Multimedia
		ZipUSA
		Live WildCams
	Discovery Networks	Atlas Tour: China, Italy, Brazil, Australia
		World Tour
	US National Parks	Park Descriptions
		Park Boundaries
		Visitor Facilities
		Trails
	Jane Goodall's Gombe Chimpanzee Blog	Gombe Chimpanzee Blog
		Chimp Bios
	UNEP: Atlas of our Changing Environment	
	Turn Here: City Video Guides	
Roads	US Roads	
	Japan Roads	
	Canada Roads	
	Andorra Roads	
	North American Car Ferries	
	Austria Roads	
	Belgium Roads	
	Switzerland Roads	
	Czech Republic Roads	
	Germany Roads	
	Denmark Roads	

(continued)

Table B-1 *(continued)*

Layer	Sublayers	Sub-sublayers
	Spain Roads	
	Finland Roads	
	France Roads	
	UK Roads	
	Greece Roads	
	Ireland Roads	
	Italy Roads	
	Luxembourg Roads	
	Netherlands Roads	
	Norway Roads	
	Poland Roads	
	Portugal Roads	
	San Marino Roads	
	Sweden Roads	
	Other Roads	
Borders	International Borders	
	Country Names	
	Island Names	
	Coastlines	
	1st Level Admin Borders (States/Provinces)	
	1st Level Admin Names (States/Provinces)	
	2nd Level Admin Regions (Counties)	
Populated Places	Capitals	
	Major Cities	
	Cities	

Layer	Sublayers	Sub-sublayers
	Cities/Towns	
	Towns	
	Villages	
Alternative Place Names	English	
	French	
	Italian	
	German	
	Spanish	
	Dutch	
	Portuguese	
	Japanese	
	Other	
3D Buildings	None	
Dining	Dining	Dining - Barbecue
		Dining - Asian
		Dining - Fast Food
		Dining - Indian
		Dining - Italian
		Dining - Japanese
		Dining - Mexican
		Dining - Pizza
		Dining - Seafood
		Dining - Steakhouses
		Dining - Other
		Dining - Family
	Coffee Shops	
	Bars/Clubs	

(continued)

Table B-1 *(continued)*

Layer	Sublayers	Sub-sublayers
Lodging	None	
Google Earth Community	Google Earth Community Forums	Earth Browsing
		Travel Information
		Transportation
		Military
		People and Cultures
		Nature and Geography
		History Illustrated
		Huge and Unique
		Sports and Hobbies
		The Seer's Best*
		Phil Verney's Discoveries**
		Where Eagles Soar**
		Housing Projects**
		Education
		Environment and Conservation
	Community Showcase	UNESCO World Heritage Sites - Herminator
		Worldwide Panoramas - wuz
		Webcams - BenSisko & Telescope
		Webcams - St_Louis_Hawk
		US Lighthouses - Phred
		Ants - AntWeb

Layer	Sublayers	Sub-sublayers
		Confluence Placemarks – greenwood***
	Shopping and Services	Grocery Stores
		Convenience Stores
		Movie/DVD Rental
		Pharmacy
		Banks/ATMs
		Shopping Malls
		Major Retail
	Google Earth Community (Unranked)	
Transportation	Airports	Airports
		Airport Maps
	Railroads	
	Transit	
	Gas Stations	
	Ferries	
Geographic Features	Volcanoes	
	Mountains	
	USA Features	
	Water Bodies	
	Earthquakes	
Travel and Tourism	Tourist Spots	
Parks and Recreation Areas	Parks/Recreation Areas	Parks
		Recreation Areas
	Sports Venues	
	Golf	

(continued)

Table B-1 *(continued)*

Layer	Sublayers	Sub-sublayers
Community Services	Schools	
	School Districts	Unified School Districts
		Elementary School Districts
		Secondary School Districts
	Places of Worship	
	Fire	
	Hospitals	
US Government	US Senators	
	US Congressional Districts	
	Census	
	Postal Code Boundaries	
	City Boundaries	
	Crime Stats	
Digital Globe Coverage	DG Coverage 2006	2006 - Cloud Cover (0–10%)****
		2006 - Cloud Cover (11–50%)
		2006 - Cloud Cover (51+%)
	DG Coverage 2005	2005 - Cloud Cover (0–10%)
		2005 - Cloud Cover (11–50%)
		2005 - Cloud Cover (51+%)
	DG Coverage 2004	2004 - Cloud Cover (0–10%)
		2004 - Cloud Cover (11–50%)
		2004 - Cloud Cover (51+%)

Layer	Sublayers	Sub-sublayers
	DG Coverage 2003	2003 - Cloud Cover (0–10%)
		2003 - Cloud Cover (11–50%)
		2003 - Cloud Cover (51+%)
	DG Coverage 2002	2002 - Cloud Cover (0–10%)
		2002 - Cloud Cover (11–50%)
		2002 - Cloud Cover (51+%)

Appendix C

Latitudes and Longitudes of Major Landmarks

• •

*N*o matter how much you might come to rely upon the search features of Google Earth, lots of places still haven't made it into the database of eventful places, no matter how much they might deserve to be there.

This Appendix is an attempt to fill in the blanks — to give you an advantage over other Google Earth users when it comes to locating historical places on the map.

Current Events

Table C-1 shows a variety of locales that keep cropping up in news events year after year. Figure C-1, for instance, shows the border between the warring states of Israel and Lebanon.

Figure C-1:
The border
between
Israel and
Lebanon.

Table C-1	Locations in the News	
Name	*Latitude*	*Longitude*
Baghdad, Iraq	33.330001	44.439998
Beirut, Lebanon	33.887189	35.513404
Gaza	31.524250	34.445808
Israel/Lebanon border	33.088396	35.166503
Java, Indonesia	−7.328940	109.590795
Jerusalem	31.773594	35.225441
New Orleans	29.954444	−90.075000
Pyongyang, North Korea	39.031632	125.753743
Seoul, South Korea	37.531986	126.957450
Tehran, Iran	35.696157	51.422971

Historical Conflicts

There is not one inch of ground on the surface of the earth that is not soaked with the blood of its former inhabitants.

—Anonymous

Setting this simple truth aside, there are certain spots where the more important conflicts between nations have taken place, locales like Waterloo or Saratoga or Pusan (see Figure C-2), where the course of history was changed and a study of the landscape can help you to understand the event. Table C-2 details scenes of historical conflicts.

Table C-2	Scenes of Historical Conflicts	
Name	*Latitude*	*Longitude*
Alamo	29.425686	−98.486032
Boyacá	5.449999	−73.349998
Bull Run	38.783609	−77.520818
Fort Sumter	32.75222	−79.87472
Gettysburg	39.842199	−77.244674
Ground Zero	40.7117	−74.0124
Guadalcanal	−9.596350	160.141858
Hiroshima	34.377552	132.444831
Inchon	37.474616	126.634970
Nagasaki	32.765315	129.866385
Nanjing (Nanking)	32.048275	118.769080
Pearl Harbor	21.355000	−157.971944
Pusan	35.157743	129.054574
Saratoga	42.997693	−73.633681
Tiananmen Square	39.902845	116.391752
Vicksburg	32.362974	−90.850057
Waterloo	50.715433	4.396227
Yorktown	37.22524	−76.523556

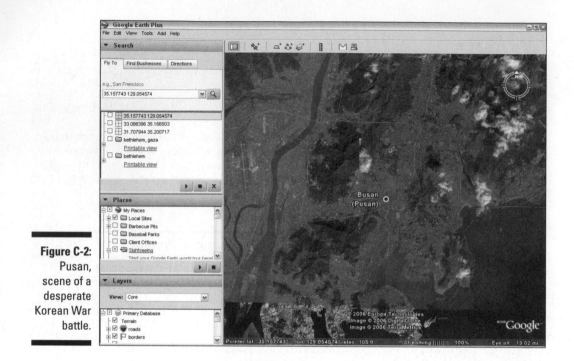

Figure C-2:
Pusan,
scene of a
desperate
Korean War
battle.

Monuments, Statues, and Historical Addresses

We like to commemorate our past, which helps preserve some elements from bygone days. Sometimes this is in the form of a monument, like the Statue of Liberty shown in Figure C-3. Other times, it's a traditional old building kept in use. Table C-3 shows latitude and longitude of monuments, statues, and historical addresses.

Figure C-3:
The world's
most
famous
statue.

Table C-3	Monuments, Statues, and Historical Addresses	
Name	**Latitude**	**Longitude**
10 Downing Street	51.503167	−0.126134
Cleopatra's Needle	40.779630	73.965404
Eiffel Tower	48.858205	2.294359
Kremlin	55.751748	37.615536
Lincoln Memorial	38.889340	−77.050085
London Bridge	34.471408	−114.347573
Potala Palace	29.657893	91.117162
Statue of Liberty	40.689400	−74.044700
Washington Monument	38.889429	−77.035212
White House	38.897490	−77.036562

Items of Geographic Importance

From the mightiest rivers to the highest mountains, nature never loses its capacity to inspire awe, as in this shot of Mount Everest (see Figure C-4). Table C-4 shows items of geographic importance.

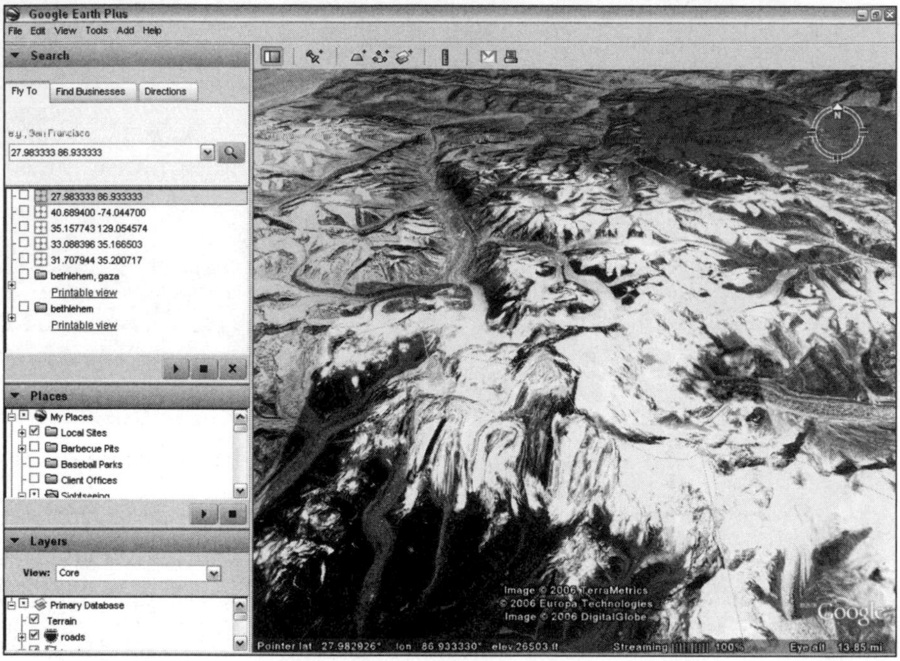

Figure C-4: Mount Everest stretches toward the sky.

Table C-4	Items of Geographical Importance	
Name	*Latitude*	*Longitude*
Amazon River delta	0.132958	−50.231584
Angel Falls	5.582853	−62.313426
Gulf of Venezuela	11.664937	−70.946371
Lake Tana	11.986375	37.336613
Lake Victoria	−1.000000	33.000000
Meteor Crater, Arizona	35.028266	−111.022274
Mississippi River delta	29.769145	−89.925615

Name	Latitude	Longitude
Mount Everest	27.983333	86.933333
Nile River delta	31.462147	30.369293
Rio Grande	25.862533	−97.441991
Rock of Gibraltar	36.129318	−5.352001
Victoria Falls	−17.925017	25.856412

Religious Sites

Around the world, the human need for spiritual experience has resulted in various spots being thought of as holier than the norm. From the city of Jerusalem, sacred to three world religions, to Bethlehem (as seen in Figure C-5) to the popular New Age ruins of Stonehenge, here's a quick overview of sacred ground. Table C-5 shows the locations of religious sites.

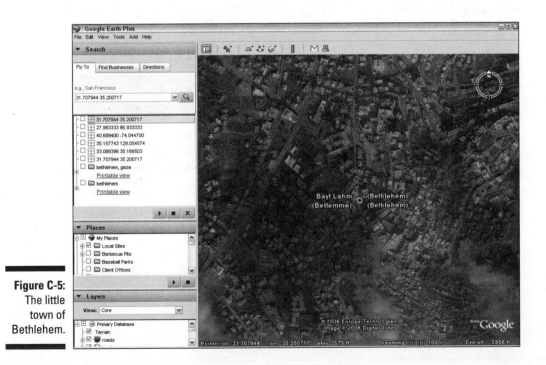

Figure C-5:
The little
town of
Bethlehem.

Table C-5	Religious Sites	
Name	*Latitude*	*Longitude*
Bethlehem	31.707944	35.200717
Ganges River	23.113179	90.591358
Jerusalem	31.773594	35.225441
Lourdes	43.094287	−0.046471
Mecca	21.427419	39.814796
Medina	24.460899	39.620190
Mount Sinai	28.516700	33.950000
Notre Dame Cathedral	48.853056	2.349722
Rosslyn Chapel	55.854100	−3.158100
Salt Lake City	40.760833	−111.890278
Stonehenge	51.178866	−1.826407
Vatican City	41.902743	12.456050

Major Cities

For the first time in history, half the world's population can be found within city limits, and many cities now have populations over or at least approaching 10 million, such as Mexico City, as shown in Figure C-6. Here's a listing of some of the world's largest cities. Table C-6 shows the location of major cities.

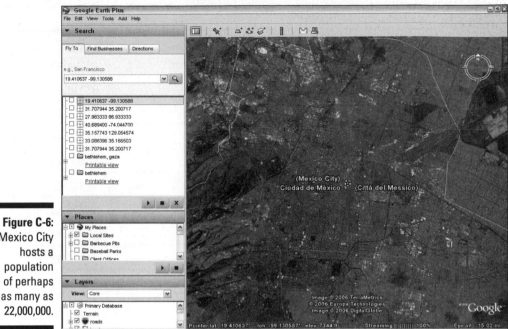

Figure C-6:
Mexico City
hosts a
population
of perhaps
as many as
22,000,000.

Table C-6	Major Cities	
Name	*Latitude*	*Longitude*
Beijing (Peking), China	39.908620	116.391220
Buenos Aries, Argentina	−34.612101	−58.417324
Calicut (Calcutta), India	11.255400	75.781212
Delhi, India	28.637603	77.206239
Istanbul, Turkey	41.065950	29.006107
Jakarta, Indonesia	−6.211634	106.845124
Karachi, Pakistan	24.893309	67.028053
Lagos, Nigeria	6.441159	3.418016
London, England	51.508957	−0.126143
Los Angeles, California	34.052222	−118.242778

(continued)

Table C-6 *(continued)*

Name	Latitude	Longitude
Madrid, Spain	40.422299	−3.704249
Mexico City, Mexico	19.410637	−99.130588
Moscow, Russia	55.748374	37.624140
Mumbai (Bombay), India	19.030866	72.849076
New York City, New York	40.714167	−74.006389
Paris, France	48.855727	2.349532
São Paulo, Brazil	−23.581634	−46.623118
Seoul, South Korea	37.531986	126.957450
Shanghai, China	31.247890	121.472742
Tokyo, Japan	35.668558	139.824379

Engineering and Architectural Achievements

The world contains many more than seven Wonders these days. From the ancient ruins of Egypt (see Figure C-7) to the soaring Sydney Opera House, the hand of humanity has left its mark on the landscape. Table C-7 takes you to some of the best.

Table C-7 **Engineering and Architectural Achievements**

Name	Latitude	Longitude
Acropolis	37.995000	23.751000
Coliseum	41.890185	12.492376
Erie Canal	43.138019	−78.722637
Golden Gate Bridge	37.818774	−122.478415

Name	Latitude	Longitude
Great Pyramid	29.979033	31.134009
Machu Picchu	−13.156389	−72.542778
Nazca Lines	−14.710049	−75.166760
Panama Canal	8.968089	−79.573603
Sphinx	29.975254	31.137633
Suez Canal	31.249440	32.334426
Sydney Opera House	−33.857053	151.214677
Taj Mahal	27.173129	78.042200
Teotihuacan	19.690082	−98.846810
Tiahuanaco	−16.551993	−68.678813

Figure C-7:
The Sphinx is as enigmatic as ever.

Index

• *M* •